Monitoring National Standards of Attainment in Schools

Papers given at the first European Contact Workshop held at Windsor in June, 1976, under the auspices of the Council of Europe Committee for Educational Research.

Edited by R. Sumner

CONTRIBUTORS (in order)

B.W. Kay	A.N. James
C. Burstall	I. Wedman
T. Kellaghan	A.S. Wilmott
R. Sumner	H. Scheiblechner
G. Pollock	B. Choppin
J. Cardinet	M. Seibel
L.K. Allal	B. Rodmell

NATIONAL FOUNDATION FOR EDUCATIONAL RESEARCH IN ENGLAND AND WALES

SLOUGH, ENGLAND

Published by the NFER Publishing Company Ltd.,
Darville House, 2 Oxford Road East,
Windsor SL4 IDF

Printed in Great Britain

ISBN O 85633 I44 9

CONTENTS

ACKNOWLEDGEMENTS

On behalf of those who took part, I should like to thank the Council of Europe and
the National Foundation for Educational Research for initiating the workshop on
this theme and for providing the necessary finance and organisational support.
Member governments of the Council of Europe also contributed by assisting with
the attendance their nominees or the invited speakers.

The workshop proceedings were greatly facilitated by the excellent services of the
translators, Mr. N. Edwards and Mrs. F. Forster. Members of the N.F.E.R. Administration and Information Services assisted in receiving conference members and
research teams generously made time available to discuss their projects with the
visitors.

For their contributions towards planning the programme and in approaching speakers,
I wish to thank the Steering Group members, Dr. J. Cardinet, Dr. T. Kellaghan,
Mr. G. Pollock, Dr. G. Stark and Dr. A.S. Wilmott. Miss J. Hazell gave invaluable
help with administrative details and with documentation. The preparations for the
workshop and the proceedings benefited enormously from the energy and wit of
Dr. M. Tyerman.

Finally, my thanks to Gill Nyfield for her detailed checking of the pre-production
typescript.

Dr. R. Sumner

PARTICIPANTS

Those who took part in the workshop, either as authors of invited papers or as national representatives, were :-

Dr. L.K. Allal, Assistant Professor, University of Geneva, Switzerland.

Mr. Bittlinger, Studiendirektor, Staatsuniversitat fur Schulpadagogik, Munich, Germany.

Dr. C. Burstall, Deputy Director, N.F.E.R. England & Wales.

Professor J. Cardinet, Head of the Research Department, Institut romand de recherches et de documentation pedagogiques, Neuchatel, Switzerland.

Dr. B. Choppin, Principal Research Officer, N.F.E.R. England & Wales.

Prof. Dr. H. Giesen, Professor, Deutsches Institut fur International Padagogische Forschung, Frankfurt, Germany.

Prof. J. Gregerson, Associate Professor, Royal Danish School of Educational Studies, Copenhagen, Denmark.

Dr. W. Harlen, Director of Schools Council project on progress of learning science, University of Reading, England.

Prof. Henrysson, Professor, The University of Umea, Sweden.

Mr. A.N. James, Head of Statistical Services, N.F.E.R. England & Wales.

Mr. B.W. Kay, H.M. Staff Inspector, Department of Education & Science, London, England.

Dr. T. Kellaghan, Director of Educational Research, St. Patrick's College, Dublin, Ireland.

Mr. B. Lebrun, Research Officer, University of Brussels, Belgium.

Mlle J. Levasseur, Service des Etudes Informatiques et Statistiques, Ministere de l'Education, France.

Mr. A. Papjoannou, Educational Psychologist, Ministry of Education, Nicosia, Cyprus.

Mr. G.J. Pollock, Deputy Director, Scottish Council for Research in Education.

Mr. B. Rodmell, Senior Economics Adviser, Department of Education & Science, U.K.

Prof. H. Schieblechner, Professor, Philips Universitat, Marburg, Germany.

Prof. R. Skemp, Professor of Education & Chairman of Education Department, University of Warwick, Coventry, England.

M. C. Seibel, Chef du Service des Etudes Informatiques et Statistiques, Ministere de l'Education, France.

Dr. R. Sumner, Principal Research Officer, N.F.E.R. England & Wales.

Dr. M. Tyerman, Secretary to the Committee for Educational Research, Council for Cultural Co-operation, Council of Europe, Strasbourg.

Mr. L. Van Muskens, Research Officer, Research Institute, Amsterdam, Holland.

Mr. M. Van Tuyl, Research Officer, Research Institute, Amsterdam, Holland.

Dr. I. Wedman, University Teacher, The University of Umea, Sweden.

Dr. W. Westphal, Professor, Institut fur die Padagogik der Naturwissenschaften an der Christian-Albrechts-Universitat, Olshausenstr, Germany.

Dr. A. Wilmott, Principal Research Officer, N.F.E.R. England & Wales.

INTRODUCTION

The workshop was organised by the N.F.E.R. at the invitation of the Committee for Educational Research, Council for Cultural Co-operation of the Council of Europe. Like the later workshops in the series, it was intended to be a forum for the discussion of issues and problems relating to a theme of national concern and would, possibly, lead to the formulation of joint researches, or at least to the promotion of further contacts between research workers with problems in common.

A Steering Group was formed from researchers with experience of achievement surveys. Their ideas about the theme were sought before a planning meeting took place to decide upon the duration and content of a programme. These preliminary views showed that, whilst a number of topics were of common interest, a broad approach to the theme would be preferable. It was pointed out, for instance, that some European countries had never undertaken surveys of school learning. Others who had done surveys and who might plan to do more were becoming increasingly aware of a host of ideological problems raised by 'monitoring' in addition to the more familiar, yet unresolved, methodological issues. The Steering Group meeting itself was a miniature workshop at which the topics were discussed in detail as a means of deciding on their importance and sequence. A balance was sought between policy, educational considerations affecting pupils and schools and the technical problems of design and instrumentation.

A logical sequence of topics emerged from the considerations of questions along these lines:-

   What educational reasons are there for monitoring the performance of pupils
   in the school system?

   What have previous surveys discovered and what have been the consequences?

   Are there improved or new methods for designing surveys and obtaining
   relevant measures?

   How might the results from monitoring affect educational policy so as to
   produce desirable educational results?

Hence, the framework for the programme can be summarised as (1) issues, (2) instances, (3) techniques, and (4) consequences.

A list of provisional titles for papers and suggestions for speakers was drawn up, which, in the event, was adhered to with only four exceptions; this was a pleasing outcome for the Steering Group and for the Council of Europe official responsible for liaising with the various governments requested to nominate the speakers as participants. The invited speakers were informed that papers would be distributed in advance of the workshop so that sessions could be devoted mainly to examining the problems raised. It was not anticipated that papers would necessarily be conclusive or even have a close connection with existing practices for monitoring achievement. It was hoped, rather, that the synthesis and interplay of ideas would elucidate associated concepts and lead to new starting points for monitoring.

The N.F.E.R. had some credentials to act as convenors for this workshop. Since 1947, when the first national reading survey was organised in England and Wales, a number of attainment surveys have been carried out (e.g. Pidgeon, 1967; McEwen et al, 1975; Start and Wells, 1972; Horton, 1973) and other researches with national survey characteristics have been completed, (e.g., Ross et al, 1972; Barker Lunn, 1970; Burstall et al, 1974; Goodacre, 1967).

In recent years some preparatory work has been done for a national longitudinal survey of mathematics attainment (Sumner et al, 1975). Also the Foundation assited in the deliberations of the committee of enquiry into language and literacy (Bullock Report, 1975), being particularly concerned with records, screening and the monitoring of progress. It is currently represented at the Assessment of Performance Unit, set up recently by the Department of Education and Science. Additionally, there is an internal working group concerned with item banking which involves test constructors, statisticians and others investigating the comparability of differing school examinations taken by sixteen year old pupils.

Despite the N.F.E.R.'s manifest interest in the workshop theme - and its awareness that unresolved technical problems abound - its own resources do not permit the investigation of theoretical and empirical problems in any great depth. Like many other research institutions, adapted but ready-made solutions for jobs in hand are the rule; even though from the outside they may appear to be fully tailored! So the opportunity to meet with active and eminent researchers from countries in Europe was particularly welcome.

Before reviewing the workshop programme a few general points should be made. Most importantly, there is a lack of definition about the term 'monitoring' which was reflected in later discussion. As one French-speaking participant remarked "What are the differences between assessment, evaluation and monitoring? We would see them as the same". Yet, though the English-speakers might have made good attempts at semantic distinctions, there is virtually no body of practice <u>in educ-ation</u> to supply a context, provide models, set precedents, or otherwise establish an intuitive sense of its meaning.

Curiously enough, the most apposite illustrations would be found in the familiar micro settings of the classroom and school.   Unless pupils are left disorientated in their learning they require feedback on their immediate progress; and this erratic supply of information should be drawn together in some kind of periodic systematic review consistent with the methods of teaching and the pupil's individ-ual learning schemas.   The customary format, in the U.K., is the pupil's sessional or yearly report, though its information content is usually too slight and the timing inappropriate to assist much with learning.   In British schools, the terms formative and summative evaluation would not be applied to these sources of inform-ation, even if they were known.   But marking (i.e., giving a score, usually a value between 0 and 10) and commenting on work done in class or as homework is standard practice in the secondary stage and the later primary years.   For the most part, pupils and teachers alike find these procedures revelant to their joint activities; whilst parental concern to know how their child is 'getting on' seems to be higher than ever.   Some teachers eschew 'marks'; choosing instead to emphasise qualitative remarks as more informative and therefore superior in guiding the learner.   But the majority employ scores to convey both an idea of quality and to give an indication of merit on some scaled continuum.   In this latter usage both the work and its originator are graded.   It is that aspect which the objectors appear to abhor most, speaking of 'labelling' and fixing expectations so that pupils become predisposed to perform at a certain level which also is accepted as a pupil's standard by the teachers.

The ideal may, of course, lie in the goals implicit in self-criticism but, apart from the philosophical argument, which logically pursued would lead to the elimin-ation of the teacher (other than as a resource manager), the generation and testing of adequate criteria for evaluation simply lie beyond the capacities of all but the most mature school students.   Conversely, many pupils keep track of their own progress by comparing results with peers.

In the classroom then, monitoring involves keeping a watch on performance by using the feedback from teachers and peers as well as the pupil's own conceptions of criteria.   Praise and punishment as well as qualitative comments and scores and grades can figure in the process.   Its predominant feature is recurrence, daily or weekly for the pupil and at longer intervals in reports from the headteacher to the parent.   Done well it has the merits of aptness, flexibility and immediacy for the pupil; but it has the disadvantages of idiosyncrasy and vagueness wher released from its specific contexts.

It is becoming quite commonplace for schools (usually secondaries) to monitor successive intakes of pupils as an aid to curriculum planning and teaching group organisation.   Specialisation has now extended to the lower secondary school so that
besides having Heads of First Year, Second Year and so on there are other posts,
such as 'First Year Mathematics Co-ordinator'.   Clearly these teachers are concerned
with individual progress but to a lesser extent than class teachers.   They ought
to know the state of progress of groups in order to control resource allocation as
well as attending to the individual guidance of teachers and pupils.   The N.F.E.R.
now receives an increasing number of enquiries from teachers which illustrate that
formal assessment and course evaluation is being introduced.   Inevitably it would
seem that as schools become more complex in attempting to meet proliferating
expectations, each one must take steps to appraise its own performance as a self-
contained system.

The complementary relationship between pupils' learning and the assessment and
recording of progress is very obvious when practised in the school; it is less
clear when local authorities attempt to determine the state of knowledge or levels
of skill possessed by the pupils within the systems for which they have responsibility.   A range of sources other than tests can provide information about the
education service; for example, reports from inspectors or advisory staff; submissions from Heads, or even complaints from parents.   But obtaining up-to-date
information about attainment on a common baseline from such sources is virtually
impossible; so that authority-wide surveys are increasingly recognised as necessary
especially when screening every child for signs of learning difficulty.   As the
Bullock Report (op cit) noted, however, few of the local authorities (before re-
organisation in 1974) had adopted a regular pattern of testing.   The upshot is
that no widely agreed consensus on criteria for evaluating standards has evolved.
A major difficulty would seem to lie in the lack of clear understanding of the
merits and limitations of variously constructed and standardised tests; neither are
the purposes of examining attainment through surveys sharply defined or completely
spelled out for those with a stake in the results.   Nevertheless, locally drawn
patterns of achievement have served a number of educational ends, of which the most
noteworthy is the identification of schools experiencing particularly severe
problems yet reluctant to declare themselves or ask for help.   Hence, this
objective route to deciding on the allocation of additional resources and the associated intensification of teaching effort has certainly been of eventual benefit
to numerous children.

In the system of education where the responsibility for providing a publicly
acceptable structure of institutions rests with local bodies, it could be argued
that monitoring should be confined to the area of each authority.   At the very
least the politically elected respresentatives through their officials, have to
ensure that education in the community carries on.   But the massive costs of
education entail the use of funds drawn from the national budget and the notion
(in the U.K.) that each local authority is an entity, which may do as it pleases,
is merely an illusion.   Neither are they isolated culturally, as the tendency
towards the creation of regional and national social organs (literature, newspapers,
pop, magazine, sport, marketing, design, holidays, fashion, production, distribution, technology, academic journals....) strengthens at the expense of local ones.
Indeed, the struggle to preserve roots and maintain a distinctive identity has
moved to the political plane, though no doubt the educationists will continue to be
pluralistic in the process of conservation.   Mobility within and across national
boundaries is increasingly impinging on all but the most peripheral communities,
creating in its turn educational problems which span nations rather than localities.
In the absence of co-ordinated local authority activity, there would seem to be a
compelling case for enquiring nationally into the state of educational performance.
This conclusion does not preclude locally based enquiry or efforts at devising co-
ordinated schemes.   It is encouraging to note, for example, that one education
authority in England has recently written to others inviting them to join in the
creation of a national data bank.

Undoubtedly, the perspective achieved in the preceeding review is hazy in outline,
and drastically foreshortened.   It should, however, give some idea of the scope
of concern at each level and indicate some of the conditions which might influence
the scale of any monitoring activity.

The workshop theme was focussed on national standards, whatever these might be.
Here the questions must be asked about the performance of a national school system.
Each country could, no doubt, chart a variety of connected sub-systems of provision
and give the history leading to the current set-up.   There are few who can state
unambiguously, in detail, what each of the systems is expected to do, but none who
believe that improvements are impossible.   A totally centralized system can choose
to innovate by successively turning its creative resources from one aspect to another;
it may, in addition, plan to evaluate the effects of change even before an innovation is introduced.   Furthermore, the location of the evaluation, with respect to
policy affecting the structure of schools in the country and the prescribed curricula,
can be highly critical to decision taking.   This situation is illustrated most
clearly in the workshop's case study from France by Siebel and Bargas which describes some preliminary approaches towards establishing base-lines.

In contrast decentralised systems may well have many small teams of innovators producing variations in organisation and curriculum programmes, which are proffered as options to the authorities and schools.   The validity of innovators' claims is rarely tested; neither is the extent of the 'unadulterated' adoption of a new scheme known or its indirect influence ascertained.   These issues are discussed, by Rodmell, in the context of policy in the U.K.   Other fundamental considerations initiated the workshop's deliberations; with Kay asking for example, whether monitoring might encompass the moral side of children's development as well as the functional and cultural outcomes of schooling.   Here, in a sense, he is advocating a much wider view of the curriculum and casting the school as an agent of social change.

Our scientific colleagues at the workshop offered possibilities for measurement and analysis well beyond the levels of those used previously in surveys.   The essence of the linked presentations by Cardinet and Allal is that design procedures can both sharpen awareness of a survey's objectives and improve its effectiveness in controlling and differentiating the elements to be considered as contributing distinctively to school achievement.   The techniques they expound make parallel demands on measurement techniques.   But there is a prospect of meeting these demands: improved scaling methods, flexibility of item choice, better fidelity in curriculum portrayal and enhanced coverage of selected objectives are all on offer, according to the papers on item banking, by Choppin and by Wilmott.   The extensiveness of the performances to be examined is no particular obstacle, as James' review of item sampling principles shows.   More fundamental considerations of scaling were not ignored, however, though the logic, according to Scheibleschner, confirms that probabilistic scaling methods rather than attempts to provide absolute measures will prevail.   A hint of a new dimension for monitoring appears in Wedman's paper on the application of ability criteria to decision taking during a learner's progress. His methods would depend on the availability to schools of a high level of technology as would the sophisticated use by them of calibrated item banks, but nevertheless, the appraisal of effectiveness in taking learning decisions would appear to be important in assessing the performance of educational systems.

Another approach to national monitoring would be to shift the emphasis from the pupils' attainment towards a more global concept of achievement; that is from simply making appraisals of the state of performance (a difficult enough task) to explaining how the performance comes about.   Hitherto, the efforts in this direction on a national scale have been mainly cross-sectional and the methodology open to serious doubt.   Kellaghan's paper examines these issues in some depth and anticipates improved methods of analysis whereby contributing factors to achievement might be identified and compared over time.   The motivation underlying longitudinal studies is to study changes, and here Giesen's contribution illustrates that the assessment of gain (or loss) has not yet overcome the fundamental problems of the change itself affecting the very nature of the properties examined.   Burstall's account of the way national assessment proceeds in the U.S.A. shows that such difficulties need not deter and describes how the Americans have adopted a direct approach by asking whether specific objectives are being achieved by pupils in school or by young adults.

The American programme led to demands for localised monitoring schemes; often aimed at accountability but with an eye on the national picture.   These programmes have created a great deal of much publicised controversy, possibly because the interpretation of results is highly critical of schools and tends to ignore certain background factors.   Pollock's description of a survey in a Scottish County raises some optimism that the results can be presented and utilised in a constructive manner. It illustrates too, how the second of the two surveys could well have been mounted with relatively little effort if a thread of continuity with the earlier survey had been maintained.

The context for the use of survey designs and measurement devices is overwhelmingly societal.   Though the objectives of a survey can be defined impersonally, they cannot be achieved without the involvement of people; a self-evident fact but essential to reiterate when our jargon speaks of 'items behaving' and other such freaks of nature.   My own paper seeks to locate the activity of monitoring in the social functioning of the school system and attempts to conceptualise models for monitoring among these broader contexts.

This preview of the workshop has not taken the papers in the same order of presentation; an example to be followed by other readers, who will, in any event, find their own perspectives.   A quick skim through the abstracts is recommended, however, as a preliminary to serious reading.   Whether the concerns and backgrounds of the reader are pedagogical, administrative, research or political, it is hoped that the contributions in this volume will enable the practice of monitoring to be carried out in future with a clearer appreciation of issues, a firmer grasp of techniques and a better resolution of problems.   The discussions reported in the concluding remarks indicate, nevertheless, that a number of workshop participants were not sanguine on all points; but more of these later.

MONITORING: PURPOSE, DESIRABILITY AND SCOPE

B.W. KAY

Abstract - The allocation and use of society's resources is
taken as justification for controlling the processes and products of educational systems. In
the U.K. context only limited means for judgement exist and no appraisal of the overall effects
of the compulsory schooling period can be
attempted. Purposes for monitoring in relation
to educational standards, curriculum changes,
accountability, sorting of pupils, and decision
making are examined and the merits and shortcomings of a model of assessment based on objectives
are discussed.   Six lines of pupil development
are hypothesised as "permeating the whole curriculum" and the possibilities inherent in this
approach to monitoring are considered.

All communities exercise some control over the educational system they have set up -
naturally, since schools are one of the most important determinants of the future
pattern of society.   This control is in part unstructured and unco-ordinated -
public opinion, the demands of business and industry, the ideological stance of the
teaching profession - and partly structured, through the agency of national or
regional government.   The major instrument of government control is usually
finance - the money to train and subsequently to employ teachers, the money to build
and equip schools.   But governments are also interested in the content and quality
of education, in the outcomes of their investment of resources, and hence in the
curriculum.   There are a number of ways in which they, through their Ministries of
Education or their regional educational authorities, exercise some control over what
is taught in schools, and how.   Some countries prescribe in great detail what
subjects should constitute the curriculum, how much time should be devoted to each,
what should be the main contents and methods of teaching for each, and what books
may (or must) be used by teachers.   Some make use of an inspectorate whose task is
to visit schools to see what is going on, to ensure that statutory obligations are
being met, to assess and to advise.   Some rely on external examinations, under
their own control or delegated to universities or other examining bodies, to set

and maintain standards, and to encourage the development of sound curricula within schools. Some adopt a monitoring device such as the testing of pupils at certain stages within certain areas of their school curriculum. None of these methods is without its dangers and in practice few if any governments appear to rely on only one of them.

In this country for a long time there has been no central prescription of the curriculum and no control over the books or teaching materials used in schools. We have tended to use H.M. Inspectorate and the public examination system as the main organisational 'control' of the educational system. In recent years the conflicting attitudes to be found within public opinion in a pluralist society have increased and made education one of their battlegrounds. This has resulted in a wider diversity of practice within schools, and in turn has led to closer public questioning of educational practices.

The Inspectorate in England consists of under five-hundred men and women of whom only about three fifths are concerned directly with schools. There was a time when every school, in theory if not always in practice, received a full inspection at regular intervals of time. Over the years the numbers of schools have risen, the numbers of Inspectors have remained constant or even reduced, and their duties have multiplied. Consequently, first the regular intervals between inspections became longer and longer, and finally the idea of regular inspection of all institutions was dropped entirely. The Inspectorate has a role to play no less important than in the past, but that role cannot any longer include oversight over the educational standards in every individual school.

Public examinations have a more pervasive influence on the later years of schooling. Over the last year or two, especially following the raising of the school-leaving age, the number of pupils entering for at least one subject in the public examinations taken at the age of 16 or so has risen dramatically, and now amounts to about 86% of the age group.** Something like 80% of the age group is now being entered for public examinations in English, and 70% in mathematics. This means that some sort of final assessment of achievement is taking place for at least part of their curriculum in the case of the great majority of pupils before they leave school. But examination results need to be interpreted with care, especially for purposes other than those for which they were intended. Their purpose is after all to grade individual pupils in a number of subjects so as to provide information on

** These figures and those contained in the following sentence are derived from the Schools Council's report Examinations at 16+: Proposals for the future, 1975, Section 6.1 .

the basis of which they, their parents, their teachers present and future, and their future employers will be able to make decisions about their careers. However successfully they may be used for that purpose, and opinions vary about that, they are far less reliable as a measure of the success of either individual schools or of the educational system as a whole. After all there are some twenty-two different examining bodies, and despite efforts to ensure uniformity of standards, there are known discrepancies both as between one Board and another and as between one subject and another within the same Board and no doubt between one year and another. Many candidates choose only two or three subjects in which to be examined, and this hardly makes possible an assessment of the effects of their total educational programme. This assessment does take place only at the end of eleven years of compulsory schooling: it would appear at least prudent to monitor achievement before the point at which any deficiencies that are disclosed can no longer be remedied within the school system.

Thus, with one eye on what is taking place in the U.S.A., as so often in this country, we are asking whether it would not be a good thing to supplement these forms of quality control with some programme of monitoring; perhaps the continuous monitoring of a small constantly changing sample of pupils at certain ages, in those aspects of their curriculum which are deemed most important - the last few words being capable of a number of interpretations that we shall return to later. Meanwhile it would be well to list and comment upon some of the grounds that have been put forward, not necessarily in this country, for such a monitoring programme, and some of the uses to which its results might be applied. It will not pass unnoticed that the present writer would regard some of these purposes and uses as more desirable than others.

1. STANDARDS IN EDUCATION

There is in this and some other countries some disillusionment at present with public institutions of all kinds, and education has not escaped the general blame. The focus of discontent is two-fold, on 'standards' and on 'behaviour'. As regards standards, it is usually upon the 'basic skills', the 'three R's' that the complaint centres - 'pupils cannot read properly, they cannot write legibly, grammatically and intelligibly, and they are incapable of carrying out the simplest forms of computation correctly - and that despite the fact that a large proportion of our public expenditure goes on education'. The schools are also blamed, perhaps less justly, for the behaviour of delinquent teenagers, for vandalism and violence at one end of the scale, for work-shyness and unreliability at the other. In either case it is not uncommon for standards today to be compared unfavourably with those of earlier days - the critic being unfailingly a 'laudator temporis acti, Se puero'.

Regrettably such criticism can neither be advanced nor rebuffed on any safe grounds. It is better to know the truth of the matter than to be at the mercy of prejudice, and it would be valuable to know how the performance of pupils today does compare with their predecessors, not just in broad categories of reading or arithmetic, but in the various skills which each comprises. It is not much help to know that general standards in reading have risen or deteriorated or remained constant, but it would be useful to know what aspects of reading have improved and what have declined. This could then lead to an educational debate on whether those that have declined are in fact aspects that are no longer of such importance as at an earlier period of time. If so, they could be allowed to slip. If not they could be brought to the attention of teachers and teacher trainers, and one might hope for some change of emphasis in teaching to right the deficiency. The monitoring would thus serve as an 'early warning signal' that all was not well, and remedial action necessary. It might equally indicate strengths that later teachers or employers should be alert to utilise.

This leads to a further point: arguably what matters is not so much whether pupils today can read better or worse than pupils ten years ago - but whether pupils today can read adequately for their own personal enrichment and for the needs of their lives in the community now and in the future. Linear comparison with the past is in the end less important than present and future adequacy in terms of personal satisfaction and community need. If that is so, then monitoring must be flexible enough to reflect the changing needs of society, and the criteria on which assessment is based must be stated in terms of those needs.

It is also necessary to keep in mind, that though it sometimes appears that the public concern is solely with basic skills of literacy and numeracy in fact few people, if pressed, would limit their concern about standards to those; they would concede that an adequate monitoring of educational outcomes must go far beyond the measurement of reading and arithmetic. The additional areas they would suggest, however, would not normally, I suspect, be expressed in terms of the subject divisions of the ordinary school time-table.

2. CURRICULUM CHANGES

The public concern over standards is often associated with a concern about changing styles of education, comparing the progressive, freer pupil-centred approach with the traditional more rigorous teacher-directed style. This distinction is simplistic, educational change does not proceed along a single axis, but it remains true that different teaching styles, accompanied with different organisations of schools and different groupings of pupils within schools are all affecting educational performance in ways which we cannot at present quantify. Is it true that progressive methods or comprehensive re-organisation or open planned schools lead to lower achievement in the basic skills? It is widely believed that they do, but on remarkably little evidence either way. Monitoring will not establish a causal relationship, but it will offer some harder facts than are available at present, on which judgement may be based. What of those educational goals which have been thrown into greater prominence by these changes, goals which have perhaps been undervalued and therefore gone unassessed in the past? It is presumably desirable that some steps should be taken to identify and assess these, so that they can be included in any overall evaluation of curriculum change. So on both grounds, the concern about basic skills and the interest in new goals, educational change reinforces this need for monitoring.

3. ACCOUNTABILITY

Schools are accountable in at least two ways: they are accountable to society for the use to which they put the substantial resources of money and manpower which they enjoy; they are also accountable to society and particularly to parents for the welfare of those who by law must attend them for a period of eleven years. The concept of financial accountability can be interpreted in many ways. In its most extreme form it may mean that individual schools are set minimum achievement targets, which take into consideration as far as possible the differences between them and in particular the difference in the socio-economic status of their pupils. Where special grants of money are made for specific purposes, the continuance of such grants may depend on the achievement of these targets. In at any rate one State of U.S.A. this is (or was) nominally the case and is still believed to be so by many teachers, but no grant has ever in fact been removed from a school on these grounds. An alternative approach involves an element of devolution. Schools, or school districts, may evolve their own sets of objectives,which must be broadly in line with State policy, and the schools or districts themselves measure the extent to which they achieve them. In this way they set up their own criteria of accountability and are in a sense their own auditors. The notion of accountability can also be applied to the system as a whole, and for this purpose it would be possible by sampling to assess the extent to which the whole educational programme is successfully meeting present and future needs of society. In any case society's requirements are a combination of general quality and the meeting of certain specific needs.

The basis of schools' accountability to parents is different, and indeed more fundamental. Society has legislated that all pupils should have a substantial period of compulsory education and it is the responsibility of the schools to ensure that this enforced experience is not only beneficial rather than harmful, but more beneficial than other forms of experience which might have filled these years. Schools are accountable for the quality of the experience they provide, yet neither the criteria nor the way of rendering account have ever been clarified. If one listens to a headmaster's report on speech day, one comes away with the impression that the main criteria are: successes in many fields of old boys or old girls; examination successes of present pupils; sports successes; the number and prestige value of extra-curricular activities, including visits abroad; general 'tone' and standards of behaviour. These are perhaps not bad criteria, but they tend to rely disproportionately upon the performance of a minority of pupils. Perhaps some more structured form of self-evaluation might present a fuller picture.

4. SORTING PUPILS OR DESCRIBING A SYSTEM

A great deal of energy is devoted in the school system to 'sorting' children, though less at the age of eleven now than in the past, when in this country a universal and traumatic sorting used to take place. The public examination system, for mainly the 16-19 age group, is essentially a system of sorting, in particular for the filling of places in Higher Education which still do not fully match demand and for the selection of candidates for posts in business and industry, where competition is frequently fierce. Many schools also do a great deal of sorting internally to create relatively homogeneous groups for one reason or another. Most of the tests given in schools are used similarly for sorting pupils; they may take the form of end of term examinations used to allocate pupils to teaching sets for the following year, or standardised tests used to supply verbal reasoning quotients or reading ages, thereby rating pupils against a norm that has been set up by testing a sample of the whole population.

There is also, it is argued, need for a form of assessment that will describe aspects of the educational system rather than rate individual pupils. If, as has been suggested above, there are some reasonable expectations that society may hold in relation to the outcomes of education, then the statement about any one of those outcomes that '55% of the pupils achieve this at a satisfactory level' is potentially important. If one can further describe some of the characteristics of the 55%, and perhaps even more important of the remaining 45%, whether in terms of the sort of educational experiences to which they have been exposed or the social circumstances which affect them, this information is still more valuable. If further one can, by means of the assessment instruments, offer a preliminary diagnosis of the methodological elements which go to make up success or failure then one adds a further dimension of usefulness. This is the sort of outcome one would look to from national monitoring: not statements about the relative achievement of different pupils, but statements about the relative success of the system in achieving outcomes agreed to be desirable.

5. <u>DECISION MAKING AND EVALUATION</u>

Decisions have to be taken at both national and local level about the distribution of the total public expenditure as between education and the other services, since there will never be enough to meet all requirements, and some sort of priority must be worked out for sharing the limited resources.   But can such requirements be better identified and priorities established as a result of monitoring?   Can the social benefits of investment in education as a result be better balanced against those for a similar investment in health or housing?   If they can, it will be because the process of monitoring and the interpretation of its results has gone hand in hand with an analysis of what society requires of its education service.   Neither the monitoring nor the analysis is likely to be so precise as to offer irrefutable evidence, but they should help to inform the discussion.

Within education departments, again both national and regional; better evidence is sought on which to base policy decisions.   Currently two problems in particular face the administrator.   First how can he ensure, particularly when money is short, that limited resources are placed where they will produce the maximum benefits, and secondly, having made the provision, how can he be sure that the additional resources are in fact making any differences?   For example, if he is, as is quite likely, concerned about the educationally disadvantaged child, how can he best identify the child, the school or the area of special need, channel additional resources and satisfy himself that his actions have been effective?   It is no simple matter to use the assessment of pupils' achievement for any of these purposes.   The channelling of resources towards children shown to be performing poorly may penalise the conscient- iousness and skill of the school which has against all odds raised the standards of its pupils to an acceptable level, while rewarding the slack or inefficient instit- ution which has little or no excuse for not achieving higher standards.   The use of an assessment of pupils' performance to evaluate teaching methods, or classroom organisation, or curricular changes is fraught with dangers, though if handled with proper discretion it may be a serviceable tool in the hands of the teacher or evaluator.

If the reasons for introducing some form of national monitoring are diverse, the ways of implementing it are almost equally wide ranging.   One way is to respond to the most frequent expressions of public concern by limiting assessment to the basic skills and in them to defining minimum objectives that should be achieved by all pupils.   This has the advantage of requiring a relatively short and straightforward development programme for producing the necessary instruments, of being comparatively easy and cheap to carry out and of leaving the bulk of the school curriculum uninfluenced for good or ill by the testing.   But the testing of basic skills may in fact influence the rest of the curriculum indirectly, by conveying the message that

they constitute the most important part of the curriculum, and so potentially
distorting the overall curriculum balance.   This influence may well be strengthened
by the presence of a number of further conditions: a 'census type' testing
programme which makes it possible to identify individual pupils, teachers and schools;
the publishing of the results of such an assessment on a school by school basis; the
identification of schools that should receive additional resources to help under-
achieving pupils; the use of testing to evaluate the results of introducing
additional resources; the use of pupils' assessment for evaluating teachers.   Any of
these conditions is likely to create a feeling of anxiety on the part of at least
some teachers which may result in their adopting short-cuts to achieve good test
results, without necessarily using the best methods to ensure long-term improvement
in the pupil's performance; in their neglecting those parts of the curriculum that
are not tested; in their concentrating unduly on those who are likely through this
means to achieve the minimum objectives, and neglecting pupils who have little chance
of meeting even these, or who are already well above them, or both.

Basic skills may be enlarged to include 'basic competencies' or 'life skills' - i.e.
all those specific tests which an ordinary member of the community has to be able to
carry out; filling in the various types of forms that he meets from the income tax
form to hire purchase agreements, understanding the implications of insurance and
mortgage schemes, handling a cheque book, and so on.   Whether these are specific
skills that need to be taught, and ought to be mastered before a pupil leaves school
is a matter for debate elsewhere.

At the other end of the range of response to demands for monitoring is the attempt to
assess achievement in some way across the curriculum.   This is a challenging task.
The curriculum for any one pupil is the result of the complex interactions between
himself, his parents, his teachers, and the outside influences both local and national
which affect his school.   The curriculum is thus in a sense unique to the individual,
and any form of assessment which covers a number of pupils and a number of schools is
ruled out of court.   The more broadly a monitoring programme spreads across the
curriculum the greater the chance of conflict between society's demands and a school's
need to relate its teaching to its own pupils.   Assessment instruments that depend
heavily on the recall of information probably exert more pressure towards uniformity
than those concerned mainly with skills, a fact that is illustrated by the control
imposed by the largely syllabus-based public examinations upon the upper parts of the
secondary school.   Moreover a form of monitoring based on sampling, which is known
to preclude the possibility of judgements about individual pupils, teachers or schools,
will exert far less insidious pressure than one which can lead to such judgements.
Both of these implications should certainly influence the design of a monitoring
programme and the nature of the assessment instruments.

There are, however, at least two reasons why a measure of uniformity is desirable. Pupils and teacher mobility is much higher than it used to be in many countries, and wide diversity from school to school creates some very considerable problems both for pupils and the teachers. In some schools in Michigan, U.S.A. for example, apart from normal promotions from school to school as many as 30% of the pupils may move school in the course of a single year; and a lower but still substantial amount of movement is known to take place annually in this country.

The other reason arises from the second of the two interpretations of accountability mentioned earlier. When society requires boys and girls to attend school, it is presumably because there is some benefit to be derived which may be defined in common terms for all pupils. There is thus some core of experience which society may reasonably expect every school to provide for every pupil, whether it is defined in terms of basic skills or competencies, or in broader terms which include the affective, and this represents the desirable area of uniformity among schools. If one can define and then set up a means of assessing these common areas, then the tension between diversity and uniformity in education can be kept in equilibrium - there is still rich scope for every school to individualise its methods and programmes around an agreed core of experience which should be common to all.

It is by no means easy to identify that agreed core and to define it with sufficient precision for it to be assessed. In the U.S.A. a number of States started with ambitious schemes of monitoring the whole curriculum, and in particular of including the affective as well as the cognitive aspects, but faced with the problems that this raised, faced too with pressure from the Legislature to act quickly (one state was allowed six months to implement its accountability scheme from scratch!) and to assess all pupils in certain age bands, they fall back on the basic skills. Interestingly, while the sheer technical problems were the main reason for this limitation, another was an attack on the enquiry into pupils' attitudes on the grounds of invasion of privacy. This may have been because the enquiries did not stop short of testing pupils' attitudes towards school and the curriculum, but also included their attitude towards their family, politics and religion, and thus entered dangerous grounds. In this country, where the affective domain has always been regarded as a central part of education, the problems of assessment in that field are more likely to be those of overcoming technical problems than of facing parental criticism. Yet another reason for the giving up of more ambitious plans has been the lessening in public and political pressures - and therefore of financial support for monitoring - once it was felt that monitoring had adequately covered the basic skills.

Pre-eminent amongst attempts that have so far been made to monitor a substantial part of the curriculum is the work of the U.S. National Assessment of Educational Progress whose first tests, of a sample of pupils and young people of age 9, 13, 17 and within the 26-35 bracket, were administered in 1969. Test material has been developed in ten areas of the curriculum and the general plan so far has been to test in two areas each year on a rota. A number of outside influences has upset the tidiness of this plan, but all the ten areas have now been monitored, some for the second time. The areas include writing, reading, literature, science, mathematics, social studies, citizenship, career and occupational development, music and art. The suprising omission of any foreign language so far reflects both the diversity of foreign languages taught in different parts of the United States and the consequent difficulty of making a national assessment, but also the modest role that the teaching of foreign languages appear to play within American schools.

A number of important points emerge from the NAEP experience. The tests, or 'exercises' as they prefer to call them to emphasise their difference from the typical standardised test - are criterion - or objective-referenced, and a very substantial amount of work was done on clarifying goals and objectives in the year or two before the exercises were written; a wide programme of consultation formed an important part of this work. The exercises themselves are in many cases 'open-ended' and need to be hand scored - some requiring markers of considerable ability, a condition that has not always been met in practice. In order to exclude the influence of reading skills on the results, the exercises, which are administered either individually or to groups of not more than twelve, are tape-recorded and the students hear as well as see the questions. Some of the exercises taken by school-based students and all those taken by 'young adults' are administered individually. Results are reported as percentages of students giving satisfactory answers to individual items. The whole exercise is carried out on a small national sample designed to give information about the differential performance of students in terms of sex, colour, parental education, region (the U.S.A. is divided into four areas) and type of community (rural, inner-city, affluent suburb).

The NAEP is a most ambitious project and its achievement has been very considerable. It has done pioneering work in many new areas and has attempted to assess a broader range of achievement with a greater variety of methods of assessment in the more traditional areas. Where the tests have been administered for a second time, and in particular where preparation has been made for a third administration, there has been a remarkable development in the thinking which underlies the testing programme, and the quality of the material has greatly improved. It remains the case that there are areas where it has proved impossible to define objectives in other than somewhat trivial form, and where accordingly one is left with the feeling that part of the essence of the subject has not been identified and tested. Indeed there are many who would deny the possibility of fully describing the curriculum in terms of behavioural (and therefore assessible) objectives. Certainly there is a gap at present between even the most comprehensive framework of objectives for a subject and the concept of that subject that the best teachers hold. It may be that the gap exists partly because the writers of objectives have not pushed that model as far as it can go; it may be that there has been a certain wooliness of thought on the part of the teachers, that they have not fully thought out what to them is an art practised for the most part intuitively. Whatever the reason, the existence of that gap is the main obstacle to the assessment of a broad area of the curriculum.

The setting up of the Assessment of Performance Unit, with the task of promoting "the development of methods of assessing and monitoring the achievement of children at school", and of seeking "to identify the incidence of under-achievement" makes it necessary to face the dilemma underlying the last few paragraphs. We had to decide whether to play safe and concentrate solely on the basic skills, however these are defined, or to attempt to present a broader picture of the curriculum, whether to pursue a programme of assessment which assumes that it is possible to evaluate a pupil's performance solely in terms of his measured achievement of precisely defined objectives, or whether there is a further area which is highly resistant to quantif- ication but yet needs to be integrated in some way into any overall assessment of the curriculum; whether it is possible to find a relatively small number of areas the assessment of which would provide an adequate and balanced account of the whole curriculum, or whether it is necessary to assess every subject separately. The present author in an earlier article (1975) suggested a model of the curriculum for assessment purposes in terms of six lines of the pupil's development; linguistic, mathematical, scientific, aesthetic, moral and physical. It should be stressed that this was not intended either as a guide to curriculum construction, nor as a theoretical or philosophical account of the curriculum, but simply as a working hypothesis, a way in to the problem of monitoring the curriculum. The lines of development are not thought of as coinciding with any subject boundaries, but as permeating the whole curriculum to a greater or lesser extent. Since the publication of the Bullock Report, the concept of language development as taking place throughout the whole curriculum, while not in itself a novel idea, has gained much wider currency and is already proving influential in matters concerning the curriculum. Mathematics, which comprises many forms of non-verbal communication, similarly spreads across a considerable proportion of the curriculum. One may then define three ways of responding to the environment, each of which underlies substantial areas of the curriculum, and these may be somewhat inadequately labelled the scientific, the aesthetic and the moral or ethical. In relation to both the human and the physical world around us, the student asks how it functions and what are the causes of its present state, he appreciates the qualities of beauty and order which it shows, he makes judgements about the rightness or wrongness of what he sees. All three attitudes co-exist and influence each other. On looking at a red sunset over an industrial town one can simultaneously think 'how beautiful!', 'I suspect that the impurities in the air are in part responsible for suppressing the colours at one end of the spectrum and leaving the sunset predominantly red', and 'is it not wrong to pollute the atmosphere in this way, both in the interests of the people who must breathe it and because in some way we are spoiling something which we ought to preserve'.   Anyone who habitually fails to think in all these three ways is thereby the poorer and it is part of the job of the teacher to help pupils to handle all these ways of thinking in an increasingly confident and mature way.   No one of them is the sole concern of one subject specialist or even a group of subject specialists; they are all, to a greater or lesser degree, the responsibility of all teachers.

The problems of assessment in these areas are very considerable.   For one thing, the model stresses attitude and process rather than knowledge and informational content. It depends on the assumption that there is some form of behaviour labelled 'scientific' which may be observed and assessed, and that it may be identified not only in assoc-iation with the usual subject matter of science but also for example applied to the problems of geography or the design problems of metal work or technology. Consequently the assessment methods will need to be relatively 'content free', which makes the task much harder.   Similarly, one hopes to identify types of performance which could be labelled aesthetic, and which are observable not only in the art-room and music studio, but also in the literature class and the mathematics lesson.   Forms of thinking which can be labelled 'moral' must similarly be identified as a desirable outcome of the history or literature or science lesson as well as the religious education lesson.

The task of describing these forms of performance with sufficient precision for them to be assessed is a demanding one, and there are a number of working groups within the A.P.U. which have already started on this task.   The reconciliation of the forms of achievement that are identified as the most significant with the limitations of the technology of assessment will be a taxing problem, but one which cannot help but add greater clarity to the thinking about educational objectives, in the course of its solution.

The sixth line of development in the assessment model is the physical.   There is no doubt that education is concerned with the physical development of pupils. If any evidence were needed it is provided by the substantial proportion of school buildings devoted to laboratories, workshops, art and craft studios, home economics rooms, dance and drama studios and gymnasia, (not to mention the areas of outside playing space) and the amount of time which the curriculum devotes to activities carried out within these areas.   And of course activities calling upon physical skills are not confined to the so-called practical spaces.   In the primary school where specialism of function has not been carried so far in the planning of school buildings, the interpenetration of activities which combine the application of physical skills with the intellectual is reflected in the planning of working areas. The issue is not really so much whether education is concerned with physical development as whether this area should be identified, like those others so far considered, for purposes of assessment, on the grounds that an important element in the total educational process may otherwise be overlooked.

If it is to be included, then two aspects will need to be kept in mind, the development of physical dexterity, starting from the use of a crayon or the handling of simple apparatus in the infant school and progressing to the high degree of precisely controlled physical movement needed for dissection in the biology laboratory, carving in the art studio, or playing a keyboard instrument; and the development of the expressive use of the body in drama, dance, gymnastics and sport. In an area where the innate gifts of pupils differ much more visibly than in the intellectual field it will not be easy to find suitable forms of assessment which may be applied to all.

The attempt to put into practice this model for assessing the curriculum will not only be a long and difficult task, it will involve extending the limits of assessment technology as far as they will go, and it may also involve accumulating data some of which will carry a lower reliability factor than others. A recent article in the Times Educational Supplement suggested the need for tools of assessment "less complicated than the research worker would wish, but more sophisticated than the customary reliance on a warm feeling inside". There may well be room within some of the more elusive parts of the curriculum for some such intermediate scale of assessment scale, to supplement the more rigorous and precise instrument that can be applied elsewhere. It is difficult to see for example, how creative writing, the application of the scientific method of enquiry, or the aesthetic or moral response to a situation can be assessed without the involvement of a measure of controlled subjectivity in the process. And rather than omit these areas a greater degree of imprecision may need to be tolerated.

In the course of this paper the author has briefly surveyed the reason for monitoring the school curriculum, the different ways of responding to those reasons and, in particular, the way in which the Assessment of Performance Unit in Great Britain is approaching the problem. In so broad a survey much has had to be compressed or omitted, and in particular examples have been drawn mainly from this country and from the U.S.A. The purpose has been to set the scene, discuss the broad issues rather than to offer solutions. To that extent it may serve as a backcloth for the more detailed studies of this Conference.

THE AMERICAN SCENE

C. BURSTALL

Abstract - The measurement model adopted by the National
Assessment of Educational Progress programme
is described and developments in its procedures since the first surveys in 1969 are traced.
An alternative model, which examines only
'minimal' competence in the basic skills, is
also described and the critical reactions to
its effects are noted.   Finally, a number of
recommendations for the conduct of national
monitoring programmes are made.

In the field of large-scale assessment, the model which dominates the American scene
is undoubtedly that of the National Assessment of Educational Progress (NAEP). Although the prime purpose of NAEP is to monitor performance on a national scale, the NAEP
model has also been adopted or adapted for use in various statewide assessment
programmes and is thus extensive in its influence.

Planning for national assessment in America began in 1964 and the first survey of
performance was mounted in 1969.   A national probability sample was drawn at. the nine-
year-old, the thirteen-year-old and the seventeen-year-old levels and a stratified
sample drawn from the "young adult" population (defined as those falling within the 26-
35 age-range).   These sampling points were chosen to correspond with key stages in the
education of an individual: the end of primary school, junior high school, high school
and the period following the end of the formal schooling.   The decision was taken to
define the target populations by age rather than by year or grade in school and efforts
were made to secure an adequate sample of those seventeen-year-olds who had in fact
left school by the time of the assessment.

For the purposes of national assessment, America was divided into four geographical
regions: Northeast, Southeast, Central and West.   This strategy was deliberately
adopted in order to prevent the possibility of invidious comparisons being made
between standards of educational achievement in individual states.   In the event,
however, the growing demand for information to be provided at the individual state
level caused some modification of the original NAEP position: the sampling frame

was modified to provide at least one primary sampling unit within each of the 50 states and the District of Columbia and the NAEP staff came to play an increasingly active part in 'servicing' statewide assessment programmes: providing advice, technical assistance, NAEP test data and materials, and even constructing new materials to meet the assessment needs of a given state educational system.

The initial national assessment carried out in 1969 involved only three subject-areas: Writing, Science and Citizenship. The long-range plans for national assessment, however, called for the monitoring of achievement in seven other areas: Reading, Literature, Mathematics, Social Sciences, Career and Occupational Development, Music and Art. It was envisaged that no more than two or three subject-areas would be involved in any one year of the assessment programme and that achievement in each of the chosen areas would be re-assessed at intervals of approximately five years, the initial assessment providing the 'benchmark' against which subsequent change could be assessed. The possibility was also left open that subject-areas other than the ten originally chosen might be added to the cycle of assessment at a later stage.

For each of the chosen subject-areas, outside agencies under contract to NAEP were asked to develop a set of objectives to guide the subsequent development of the test items or 'exercises', as they came to be called. These objectives had to satisfy three criteria of acceptance: (i) they had to be seen by subject-matter specialists as satisfactory goals for each subject-area; (ii) they had to be accepted by teachers and other educationists as representing current goals for the American educational system; (iii) they had to be accepted by 'thoughtful lay adults' as representing reasonable goals for the American educational system. This third criterion was met by the setting-up of a number of 'review panels' whose task was to scrutinise the objectives as they were being developed and pronounce upon their acceptability. The panels were composed of lay adults judged to be knowledgeable about education and representative of the four geographical areas and the three types of community - large cities, suburban areas, small rural towns - involved in the plans for assessment. It was agreed that the sets of objectives, once accepted, should be reviewed periodically and revised as necessary in response to changes in the school curriculum.

Once the objectives for national assessment in the different subject-areas had been established, the same outside agencies under contract to NAEP began the development of the 'exercises' to be used in the assessment. (The term 'exercise' is used by NAEP to cover all questions, test items or tasks used for the purposes of gathering assessment data.) The model chosen to guide the development of the exercises was that of mastery learning, albeit at a group rather than an individual level, so that criterion-referenced rather than norm-referenced items were required. These could either be in the traditional multiple-choice format (initially, the predominant mode) or in open-ended form; they could call for a group rather than an individual response; they could call for interview data rather than responses to paper-and-pencil tests and questionnaires; they could even involve the direct measurement of a skill, such as the playing of a musical instrument. Whatever the format, the content validity of each exercise was determined by a lengthy process of review, again involving subject-matter specialists, other professional educators and lay people. Samples of those exercises judged valid were then given field trials (though these trials were some-times of a fairly limited nature) and, in the light of the item analysis of the field trial results, 'packages' of exercises were assembled for administration. Each 'package' intended for group administration would contain exercises from two or three different subject-areas, selected in such a way that the total testing time for any individual in the sample would not exceed 40-50 minutes. Some 'packages', particul-arly those involving the direct measurement of skills, would be composed entirely of exercises which had to be administered on an individual basis.

The administration of all national assessment test material is handled by NAEP staff, not by school personnel. This helps to alleviate the problems caused by the initial decision to sample within the school population by age rather than by grade, preclud-ing the possibility of using intact classes. Those to be tested have to be drawn from several classes and formed into appropriate groups for the administration of the test packages, a time-consuming and disruptive procedure without the availability of extra staff.

National assessment results are reported exercise by exercise, since the concept of a total score would be meaningless in this context. Each exercise is reported in relation to the scoring procedure developed in conjunction with it: some exercises are machine-scorable; some are amenable to scoring by relatively untrained personnel; some require specialist scoring. This last requirement is inevitably the most cumb-ersome and costly: indeed, some of the written material gathered during the last cycle of assessment still lies unscored, for want of further funds.

Results are normally reported in terms of the percentages of respondents giving correct responses or reaching some criterion of performance. Approximately half the exercises used in each cycle are 'released' by the process of reporting and become available for local use. The remaining exercises are referred to in general terms only and are retained for use in the next cycle of assessment, in order to provide a measure of change. They are supplemented by new material which, in turn, will be released for local use when it has served its purpose at the national level. Once a cycle of assessment has been completed, the results for each subject-area are reported at a number of different levels, ranging from weighty technical volumes through briefer statements of the main findings to chatty news-letters, each prepared with a different readership in view.

Since the early years of NAEP, a number of changes of emphasis have become apparent. The need to respond to the demands of local assessment has already been mentioned. Other discernible trends include the following: a shift away from the bald present- ation of data towards a more interpretative style of reporting; a move away from the use of commercial agencies for the production of test materials towards a concentrat- ion on the 'in-house' development of new material; a lessened reliance on the use of multiple-choice test items and a more vigorous attempt to develop new forms of assess- ment, particularly in regard to the direct measurement of skills; a greater concent- ration on the within-school sample (the 'young adult' sample, at least for the time being, having fallen a victim to a cut-back in funds); an attempt to improve the quality of 'change' data by breaking away from the previous policy of releasing half the exercises after only one administration and developing instead 'measurement modules' for each subject-area which would be kept intact for at least two cycles before release; and, finally, an increased awareness of the need to exert as much control as possible over the publicity accorded to the NAEP findings in the various media.

The NAEP model, test data and assessment materials are now being used in a number of statewide assessment programmes, either in their original form (but often applied to a total school population rather than to a sample drawn from it) or in local variants of the original design. In a number of states, comparisons of state and national data have led to changes in state educational practice. In Maine, for example, the finding that students were scoring significantly below the national level in Science led to an extensive re-training programme for elementary and secondary school Science teachers; similarly, the finding that Franco-American students in Maine were achiev- ing at a significantly lower level than other students in the state educational system led to the development of a series of television programmes designed to improve the Franco-American students' self-esteem and motivation for school learning. In Connecticut also, comparisons of state and national reading results have led to a new emphasis on the development of urban reading programmes: similar outcomes have been reported in a number of other states using the NAEP model.

Not all statewide assessment programmes are based on the NAEP model, however. Perhaps the best-known alternative to the NAEP model is the Michigan Educational Assessment Programme, based on the measurement of 'minimal' performance objectives in the basic skill areas. To date, the programme of assessment has been concentrated on students in the fourth and seventh grades, but there has also been some smaller-scale testing of first-grade students and plans have been announced to extend the basic skills testing programme to the tenth- and twelfth-grade levels.

The Michigan assessment programme was conceived within the conceptual framework of educational accountability and has aroused considerable controversy. Much bitterness and hostility was kindled within the teaching profession when the state educational authorities were pressured by politicians into releasing achievement test results for individual schools, having previously assured the teachers concerned that the test results would remain confidential to local school administrators. Complaints were made that the tests used did not adequately reflect the school curriculum, that there had been little teacher involvement in the development of the tests and that the concept of 'minimal' performance objectives was both nebulous and potentially stifling to all but the least able. The debate grew even more heated when it was announced in 1971 that a new compensatory education programme ('Chapter 3') would tie the distribution of funds to the achievement test results. The school districts with larger percentages of students scoring below the 16th percentile would be funded first, until the available funds were exhausted. Once the money reached the districts, the lowest-achieving children were to be identified on the basis of local test scores: those selected were to remain in the compensatory programme for three years. Each district was required to specify its own performance objectives: the most common response was to specify one month's academic growth for each month in the programme, as measured by locally-chosen standardised tests. Funds for the second year of the programme were to be allocated according to the first year's test results: for each pupil achieving 75 per cent of the specified objectives, the school district would receive a full per pupil allocation for the next year; for each pupil achieving less than 75 per cent of the specified objectives the school district was to receive a lesser amount, proportionate to the gains achieved. In the event, it proved impossible to implement this policy for the first year of the programme and, in 1972, 'Chapter 3' was amended by the inclusion of a first-year waiver. The law continued to stipulate, however, that the second-year performance results would determine the allocation of funds for the third year of the programme. In fact, when the 1972-73 test results became available, it was revealed that more than one third of the 'Chapter 3' students had fallen short of the 75 per cent goal, entailing a potential loss of five million dollars if the incentive provision were to be implemented. Again, there was intensive local lobbying to have the incentive provision waived and, again, the state education authorities and the legislature yielded to the pressure. The situation apparently remains unchanged today: the incentive provision has not been implemented; funds have not been withheld from low-scoring school districts. Nevertheless, the whole episode has left an aftermath of resentment among the teachers involved and a lingering belief that the attitude of the state education authority towards the teaching profession is a punitive rather than a supportive one.

Until now, this paper has concentrated on a discussion of large-scale assessment programmes in America: it would be wrong to give the impression, however, that the climate of opinion in American educational circles is uniformly in favour of such enterprises. There exists a body of opinion which condemns all attempts to monitor performance at the national or the statewide level. One of the most outspoken proponents of this point of view is Dr. Ernest House who, together with a number of his colleagues at the University of Illinois, has been vociferous in his criticisms of the concept of educational accountability and, in particular, of the way in which this concept has been put into practice in the Michigan assessment programme. Those who share these views tend to advocate self-evaluation at the individual school level as the only truly meaningful form of educational assessment.

What, then, can other nations planning a national monitoring programme learn from a contemplation of the American scene? The following recommendations would seem to emerge from a consideration of the successes and failures of the different American approaches to assessment.

i. Teachers and others concerned with educational planning and practice must be involved as active partners in the monitoring programme from the very outset. Consensus of opinion regarding the objectives of the exercise must be obtained before further developments are allowed to take place.

ii. Agreements entered into in good faith (such as those pertaining to the confidentiality of results) must be faithfully honoured. This implies the reporting of results at several different levels and the total rejection of the notion that test data could be made available for accountability purposes.

iii. National monitoring should ideally involve the assessment of performance in non-cognitive as well as in cognitive areas. This implies the need to accept means of assessment with differing degrees of statistical reliability.

iv. The most potentially fruitful approach to national monitoring would seem to be a multi-faceted one, employing the techniques of observation and simulation as well as gathering data by means of paper-and-pencil tests and questionnaires.

v. Recurrent monitoring implies the need to establish banks of items capable of renewal and expansion as objectives are up-dated in response to changes in the school curriculum.

vi. There is a need to consider from the outset the strong possibility that any national assessment model will eventually be expected to respond, at least in part, to local needs.

vii.   It must be recognised that the setting-up of a national monitoring scheme will inevitably demand a great deal of time and technical expertise, especially with regard to the establishment, maintenance and renewal of banks of valid, reliable and sensitive items.

viii.   From the earliest planning stages, it is important to recognise and make provision for the difficulties involved in the interpretation of test data and the reporting of results, whether at the national or the local level.

Editor's Note.   The National Assessment of Educational Progress in Denver, U.S.A.
(Postal Address: 700 Lincoln Tower, 1860 Lincoln Street, Denver, Colorado 80203)
A General Information Yearbook is published, which lists the extensive range of publications available.

MEASURING SCHOOL EFFECTIVENESS

T. KELLAGHAN

Abstract - The measurement of school effectiveness involves methodological problems related to the measurement of input variables, the measurement of output variables, the design of studies and the analysis of data. In the measurement of input variables, the need to develop techniques that will measure processes is indicated. In measuring output variables, account should be taken of a wider range of variables than has been the case in the past; furthermore, care should be taken to see that output measures are congruent with the objectives and curricula of schools. While cross-sectional surveys can provide some useful information about the functioning of schools, longitudinal and experimental studies are needed to supplement such information.

A case for examining critically the results of our educational endeavours scarcely needs to be made. It is something that educationalists and educational administrators have long been conscious of and various approaches, both formal and informal, have been employed to assess the effectiveness of schools. Throughout the history of state-sponsored education in western European countries, the performance of schools has been monitored continuously and informally through the inspectorial system and public examinations, while from time to time, more formal investigations have also been undertaken. As far back as 1858, the Newcastle Commission examined education in England and made recommendations that anticipated many present-day arguments about accountability. On the assumption that some 'free trade' in the educational system would be beneficial, the Commision decided that grants to schools would, in future, depend on the attendance record of pupils and on the results of annual examinations. While the system prepared by the Newcastle Commission came in for severe criticism from many sources, including later commissions (the Cross Commission in England in 1888, and the Belmore Commission in Ireland in 1898), it is an interesting example of an early attempt to make schools responsive to economic thinking and economic pressures. Several other government commissions have been assembled since these early ones; more recent ones have been more concerned with curriculum practices in schools.

Three general points may be made about educational commissions in Britain and Ireland over the past century and a quarter.   Firstly, they were concerned in a general and not very systematic way with the monitoring of national systems of education.   Secondly with some exceptions, the focus was more on input measures (e.g., teachers and curricula) than on output measures (e.g., student attainment).[1]   And thirdly, the bases for decisions were, for the most part, the opinions of committees of 'experts' and interested parties.   Sometimes, empirical data were collected.[2]   But, by and large, 'expert' opinions, rather than empirical data, were the bases for decisions.

Following the development of empirical procedures in the field of education around the turn of the century, various attempts have also been made by social scientists to examine the workings of educational systems.   These tended to be modest in scope and, while they often carried implications for policy, they were not usually commissioned by policy-makers.   Much sociological work on education in Britain over the last twenty years, for example, has been concerned with social class inequalities in educational institutions, the studies being based on the assumption that schools contribute considerably to the process of social stratification in society (c.f. Floud, Halsey and Martin, 1958).[3]   In these studies as in the deliberations of government commissions, the emphasis has been largely on input variables in, and access to, education (e.g., social class composition of schools) though the implications for output variables (e.g., attainment and job opportunity) they have not been ignored.

Studies more directly concerned with school output have also been carried out over the last thirty years.   For example, a series of studies of the reading standards of pupils, commencing in 1948, has been carried out in Britain (Start and Wells, 1972). Similar studies have been carried out in Ireland since 1964 (McDonagh, 1973).   In the United States, the National Assessment of Educational Progress studies have been measuring a wide range of attainments in the school system since 1969 (National Assessment of Educational Progress, 1974).

[1]   The concept of output or performance is relative to the level of generality on which one operates.   Thus, a measure of input at one level may be a measure of output at another (Carr-Hill and Magnussen, 1973).   For example, student attainment is usually regarded as an output measure but, it may also be regarded as an input to over-all social welfare.   In this paper we speak of inputs and outputs at a relatively low level of generality (involving relationships between school factors and student performance); we shall not be concerned with the level of generality implied by a concept such as 'over-all social welfare'.

[2]   For example, as far back as 1908, survey data were used to guide the deliberations of the Royal Commission on the Care and Control of the Feeble-minded in Ireland.

[3]   This view is now challenged both in Europe (cf Flude and Ahier, 1974) and in the United States (cf Jencks, Smith, Acland, Bane, Cohen, Gintis, Heyns, and Michelson, 1972).

In the 1960's, the traditional approach in which commissions or committees of experts examined the working of the educational system was combined with more empirical approaches when government agencies sponsored empirical research to throw light on problems facing administrators and policy makers.   Furthermore, these studies did not focus on input or output measures in isolation but on the relationship between the two,[4] presumably on the assumption that measuring either type of variable in isolation is not likely to increase our understanding of the working of the system to a level that effective action can be taken to instigate desirable changes. Indeed, it has been argued that output data cannot be adequately interpreted in the absence of input information (Sheldon, 1976).   The first major empirical investigation of the American school system undertaken in the interests of the policy formation of the United States' government was commissioned in 1964 and reported its findings two years later (Coleman, Campbell, Hobson, McPartland, Mood, Weinfield and York, 1966). At the same time, a similar survey was carried out in the United Kingdom (Great Britain: Department of Education and Science, 1967).

Part of the motivation for attempting to monitor the working of school systems has been basically utilitarian.   Education is a very expensive commodity; in most countries, the proportion of national income it attracts has increased steadily over the past thirty years, between three and five per cent of such income being devoted to education (Sheehan, 1973).[5]   Given expenditure of this magnitude, the demand for cost benefit analysis does not seem suprising.   Another purpose in evaluating school systems, that is also broadly utilitarian, is the perceived need to enhance the national interest, which is seen to be in competition with other national interests (Ianni, 1965).   This has given rise to concern about out-dated curricula and loss of talent, particularly among certain sections of the community.   Interest in the problems of the disadvantaged in the United Stated in the 1950's and 1960's grew partly out of such concern (Kellaghan, 1972).

Utilitarian reasons, however, do not constitute the sole basis of interest in the effectiveness of schooling.   Coleman et al. (1966), in both the title of their report (Equality of Educational Opportunity) and in outlining the rationale of their study, clearly indicate that they, and by implication their government sponsors, were concerned primarily with educational opportunity, particularly in the context of children of minority groups.   The concept of equality of educational opportunity, which in

---

[4]   There have, of course, been many individual studies which related output to input variables in education (c.f. Averch, Carroll, Donaldson, Kiesling and Pincus, 1972). Here we are primarily concerned with studies that have been undertaken in the interests of making policy decisions.

[5]   In the United States the figure is higher.   In 1973, expenditure on educat-ation amounted to 7.6 per cent of Gross National Product (United States: National Center for Education Statistics, 1975).

its traditional definition is taken to mean that all children - irrespective of creed, colour, class, sex, or financial resources - should have equal access to educational facilities, is basically a statement of a philosophical position, though it may also involve economic and political considerations. The position is one that is frequently presented by governments of western European countries as a basic tenet guiding educational policy and planning.

An interesting aspect of the concept of equality of educational opportunity is that its explication and development in recent years has contributed to the shift in policy attention from its traditional focus on comparisons of inputs in education to a focus on outputs and the effect of various inputs on output (Coleman, 1972). The concept itself has changed from one in which equality was considered to exist if children of all classes had equal access, or even more radically, equal participation rates in non-compulsory education (equality of input) to one in which equality of results (equality of output) is to be regarded as the criterion of equality.

Despite an increase in the number and scope of empirical studies of educational systems in recent years, we are still far from having a clear picture of what the outputs of various educational systems are. Much less do we know what factors in the school contribute most significantly to such outcomes. The guidance that research can provide in making policy decisions regarding increased efficiency or in the pursuit of the achievement of equality of opportunity is thus very limited. Part of the problem is a philosophical one; there is lack of agreement on what the goals of schooling should be. But there are also serious methodological problems relating to the measurement of school input variables, the measurement of school output variables (e.g., attainment), the design of studies and the analysis of data. The problem is complicated by the fact that the school does not operate in isolation from the background of students, and indeed some recent studies have indicated that the home background of the student may be a much more potent influence than the school in determining his level of scholastic achievement (e.g., Coleman et al, 1966: Great Britain: Department of Education and Science, 1967; Smith, 1972; Sohlman, 1971). Thus, if we are to understand the contribution of schools, and their limitations, it is probably necessary to take into account the background of students as well as the formal educational environment.

THE MEASUREMENT OF INPUT VARIABLES

A review of studies in which various school variables have been related to measures of school output (e.g., attainment) indicates that 'almost every study has identified one or more school characteristics that appeared to have a non-random effect on test scores or plans. On the other hand, the school characteristics that have appeared significant in one study have not been particularly likely to appear significant in other studies (Jencks and Brown, 1975).' It is difficult to impose order on the relative confusion that emerges from these studies. A basic problem is conceptual rather than methodological. Our lack of a satisfactory model or theory of school learning means we have little to guide us in the selection of variables or in the interpretation of relationships between variables. This situation had led to the inclusion of very large numbers of variables in some studies. While the problem is basically conceptual, methodological approaches, such as the use of path coefficients (Duncan, Featherman and Duncan, 1972; Hauser, 1969) may help in the establishment of a working model.

Part of the difficulty in interpreting studies of school effectiveness is due to the fact that studies were carried out in different school systems and used different measures of school input and output variables.[6] Furthermore, most of the variables used to describe school characteristics are probably best regarded as proxies for the variables which are causally related to attainment, but which are more difficult to measure. In addition to the normal sources of error to be expected in the measurement of any variable, there is an additional source of error in measurements of this kind, since the variable one is directly measuring is in itself a measure of another variable. Furthermore, it may also be that in choosing 'proxies' for more basic variables, researchers have chosen poorly. "The number of volumes in the library is presumably not as crucial as the choice of books and their accessability. A teacher's score on a verbal test may not matter as much as her sympathy, her sense of humour, or her confidence in her students (Rivlin, 1971, p.75)." What Rivlin is suggesting, and it is not a novel idea, is that educational practices are more important than physical amenities or educational programmes though, of course, amenities and programmes may well be prerequisites for practice.

An examination of studies of school effectiveness lends support to the view that process variables are probably more important than status ones in accounting for student achievement. For example, Dyer's (1968) examination of relationships in the Coleman et al. data led him to conclude that the great majority of items which are related to achievement have to do with the characteristics of people in the schools (e.g., race of teachers, racial mix of students, verbal ability of students and teachers) rather than with status and organizational factors (e.g., number of science labs, volumes per pupil in school library, teaching sets or tracking). Two more recent studies have indicated the importance of achievement-orientated values.

6   The tendency for researchers, in the social sciences, to construct ad hoc instruments for use in individual studies creates serious problems when one attempts to compare, generalize or synthesise research findings. The tendency is not confined to studies of school effectiveness.

In one of these studies carried out in boys' secondary schools in Ireland, classes that were most successful on public examinations tended to be characterized by high educational aspirations and expectations, conformity to academic press and strict discipline - in general, a climate in which there were social rewards for academic excellence, in which scholastic achievement is valued by teachers and students (Madaus, Kellaghan and Rakow, 1975). Similar findings are reported in a study carried out in England, which examined the relationship between background factors and students' performance on the General Certificate of Education (O-level). Again, process variables (such as peer group pressures to achieve academically) were found to be important predictors of examination success (Brimer, Madaus, Chapman, Kellaghan and Wood, 1976). These findings suggest that in future research, greater attention should be given to process-type variables in measuring the characteristics of schools.

It may be argued that process-type variables are not as amenable to policy manipulation as are status variables (c.f. Cain and Watts, 1970), and that there is little point in trying to assess the role of variables that cannot be manipulated by the policy-maker or administrator. This seems a rather short-sighted position to adopt. If our goal is a greater understanding of the educational process and in particular of the functioning of schools, then the variables one examines should hardly be limited to those that seem most amenable to manipulation. The policy-maker's vision does not always include all the options, and a deeper understanding of the educational process may in time lead to the identification of alternatives that had not previously been considered.

MEASUREMENT OF SCHOOL OUTPUT VARIABLES

The measurement of school output variables raises problems that range from the philosophical to the technical. The problems are philosophical in that they touch on issues related to the purpose of schooling. Since in the final analysis, objectives are matters of choice, they must be based on the value judgements of those responsible for the school (c.f. Tyler, 1949). There is considerable variety in the range of goals or objectives that have been set for schools. This range includes the transmission of the culture and accumulated knowledge of the society (including 'functional' literacy and knowledge of the basic disciplines of knowledge - mathematics, sciences, humanities), the preparation of students for life in a changing society (e.g., coping with the 'explosion' of knowledge as well as changing social and economic conditions), the preparation of students for the world of work (which may or may not be interpreted in a strictly vocational sense), the fostering of the personal development of students and the promotion of philosophical and social goals (e.g., equality of opportunity). It has been suggested that the logical approach in selecting from this vast range of goals would be to construct an appropriate classification of goal structures for a modern industrial society, based on an agreed analysis of social, political and economic phenomena (Carr-Hill and Magnussen, 1973). However, differences in basic philosophical positions about the nature of man and the function of education make it extremely unlikely that a set of goals, on which there would be a wide agreement, would emerge.

Empirical studies of school effectiveness have for the most part not concerned themselves with a broad range of outcome measures, with a few exceptions, preferring to focus on a very limited number of outputs. Furthermore, in most studies, the focus of concern has been cognitive development, partly perhaps, because it is easier to assess development in this area than in say the sphere of social or emotional development, and partly, because cognitive factors seem important in the public mind. They are emphasized in examinations and much of the recent criticism of schools has been not that schools do not foster emotional or social development, but that children leaving them cannot read or write.

Not only has cognitive development been the focus of most studies of school effectiveness, whether these were evaluations of compensatory education or surveys of differential school effects, but invariably the measure of cognitive development has been a standardized norm-referenced test (Averch et al, 1972; Cohen, 1972). For example, the IEA studies developed standardized tests, following normal psychometric procedures, over a range of subject areas. Coleman et al (1966) and Smith (1972) used as their main measure of school outcome a verbal ability test, while Mayeske, Wisler, Beaton, Weinfield, Cohen, Okada, Proshek and Tabler (1972) used an over-all achievement composite based on a factor analysis of five standardized tests. This is not to say that investigators were completely happy with the choice of outcome measure. Smith (1972), for example, noted that verbal achievement "may in no way be representative of the outputs that the resources are intended to affect" (p.314).

There were several reasons why standardized tests of ability and attainment were so widely adopted as criterion measures in studies of school or programme effectiveness. For one thing, such tests have an intuitive value. They appear to emphasize the skills of basic literacy and numeracy, which are perceived by policy-makers and parents as being important. People may argue about other potential school outcomes; most would agree that if the student has not certain basic skills related to literacy and numeracy, the school has failed. Not only had standardized tests an intuitive value, they also were readily available and, despite periodic controversies (c.f. Cronbach, 1975; Madaus, Airasian and Kellaghan, 1971) were widely accepted by educators and by the larger public since the early 1920's. Besides the availability of national norms and derived scores such as grade equivalents and reading ages, possessed an illusory simplicity of interpretation, particularly for those who wished to make national comparisons.

Even if we confine ourselves to the measurement of the cognitive outcomes of schools, can we be satisfied that standardized tests, of the kind that has been used in studies of school effectiveness, are the most appropriate instruments?   Such tests, it should be borne in mind, have been measures of general ability or of attainments in general areas, such as reading or mathematics (performance on which tends to be highly correlated with performance on the general ability tests).   There are a number of considerations which might lead us to believe that such tests may not be suitable measures of the effects of schools (Madaus, Kellaghan and Rakow, 1975).   Firstly, - and this point refers most obviously to the use of tests of general or verbal ability - the tests can be said to lack content validity if one takes as one's universe of attainment the variety of pupil achievements across subject areas and in the various behaviours, content, skills, knowledge and abilities that one finds in schools.   It can hardly be claimed that the behaviours demonstrated in a test of verbal ability constitute a representative sample of the domain of such school behaviours.

Secondly, and this point applies most obviously to many standardized tests of reading and mathematics - test constructors are concerned with achieving maximum applicability for their instruments across schools.   This is both in the interest of profitability and so that adequate norms for comparing the performances of individuals may be derived.   Through a review of textbooks and through item analyses procedures, the test constructor attempts to select content which is common to all or most schools, even though schools may be following different curricula, have different emphases in their objectives and use different methods of teaching.   The effect of selecting such common material in school content, and of ignoring in test scores the separate content areas and skills by using a summary measure of attainment, is to produce tests which are insensitive to the strengths, weaknesses and varying curricular emphases of schools.   Furthermore, having been developed on the basis of an individual differences model of behaviour with the purpose of maximizing differences between individuals, it is not surprising that performance on such tests is more closely related to personal characteristics than to school characteristics.   Indeed, it might be argued that tests of general ability (or tests that correlate highly with them) are more appropriately considered measures of school input than of school output,[7] particularly since the traits measured by such tests seem fairly stably established at a relatively early age (Bloom, 1964).

[7]   Wilson(1968), for example, says that 'the most conspicuous determinant of achievement which is not controlled in the analysis presented in the Coleman report is 'ability'. A decision to use ability as a measure of school output probably can be taken to reflect certain assumptions about the nature of ability and the functions of schooling.

If we are to assess the effects of schools fairly, our measures should reflect the work being carried out in them. When such measures, in the form of curriculum sensitive public examinations, are used to study school effectiveness, it is found that performance on them is more closely related to school variables than is performance on standardized tests of ability or of general achievement (Madaus, Kellaghan and Rakow, 1975). A major methodological task for the immediate future in studying school effectiveness would seem to be the development of measures that are congruent with the objectives and curricula of schools. In the absence of such measures, many of the statements about the effectiveness, or lack of effectiveness, of schools seem premature.

DESIGN OF STUDIES AND ANALYSIS OF DATA

In theory, one may use any standard design, from a survey to a strict experiment, in studying school effectiveness. The use of classical experimental design has many attractions. It allows inferences about causality which cannot readily be made on the basis of other designs as well as allowing the exploration of methods of treatment which may not already exist in a school system. The practical difficulties associated with such experimentation, such as randomization, sample maintenance, treatment implementation and the acceptance by teachers and the public of alternative approaches, however, are huge. It is not suprising then, that in practice, most studies of school effectiveness have adopted a survey or quasi-experimental approach rather than a true experimental design. Furthermore, most studies have been cross-sectional rather than longitudinal. Both factors limit the range of inferences that can be made on the basis of analysis of data.

Dealing with the cross-sectional aspects of studies, Rivlin (1971) has pointed out that this approach does not allow for cumulative processes to show. It cannot, for example, take into account the fact that students change teachers or may have different access to resources from year to year. For similar reasons, Leucke and McGinn (1975) have indicated that cross-sectional 'research designs have probably obscured the actual contribution that educational inputs make to student achievement'. Hence, the need for gathering longitudinal data has been stressed by several authors (Bowles and Levin, 1968; Hanushek and Kain, 1972; Rivlin, 1971).

Even the availability of longitudinal data, however, does not get over other basic problems associated with survey methods. In particular, the data one obtains from such studies can only relate to the situation as it is. This restriction gives rise to a number of problems. Firstly, lack of variance in variables will create difficulties in assessing the impact of those variables. The case has been made, for example, that the considerable uniformity in school variables - in facilities and in curricula - that exists in many school systems is an important factor in accounting for the low amount of variance in school outputs which is explained by such variables. And, of course, the survey tells us nothing about how expanding the range of facilities or how the introduction of innovations would affect the situation. Secondly, data obtained in surveys always presents problems in making causal inferences.

The most common technique used to analyse data collected to examine school effectiveness in large-scale surveys has been multiple regression. This technique attempts to analyse the collective and separate contributions of two or more independent or regressor variables to the variation in a dependent variable (c.f. Cohen and Cohen, 1975). The dependent variable in studies of school effectiveness has of course been some measure of output, nearly always as we saw, a measure derived from performance on a standardized test of ability or achievement. The regressor or independent variables have been various input measures such as indices of students' home background, teacher characteristics and school facilities (books in the library, etc.).

Problems in the use of regression analysis occur when one is dealing with a large number of independent variables which are intercorrelated among themselves. Such seems to be the case for variables included in studies of school effectiveness (Mood, 1971). For example, it is likely that the social class of students in a school will be related to school-based variables, such as per-pupil expenditure and teachers' perceptions of the vocational aspirations of the students. A perusal of correlation matrices derived from studies of school effectiveness brings home very clearly the extent of the relationships that exist between independent variables.

Two issues have received attention in the context of this problem. One has concerned the selection and grouping of variables for use in analysis and the other has concerned the order of the entry of the variables into the analysis. The problem of grouping has been dealt with in several studies by the establishment of 'blocks' of variables, each block being composed of a set of variables perceived as similar to each other and distinguishable from other sets. To be selected for inclusion in a block, a variable must seem conceptually appropriate. In addition, empirical relationships between variables are usually taken into account. Thus, variables are screened on the basis of their partial correlations with dependent variables, variables being retained in so far as they have significant partial correlation coefficients with a given number of dependent variables. In general, blocks were constructed to represent home background factors on the one hand and school factors on the other. Further specification varied from study to study. For example, the surveys of the International Association of Educational Achievement (IEA) used four blocks - home and student background, school placement variables (type of school and type of programme), school treatment or learning conditions, and personal attributes (Thorndike, 1973). Coleman et al (1966) also used four blocks, though they were somewhat differently constituted: home background, student body characteristics, school facilities and curriculum, and teacher characteristics.

On the question of the order of entry of variables into the final regression equations, a number of procedures have been adopted. Here, it will be recalled, that in regression analysis the first independent variable entered in the equation contains all the variance that variable can explain in the dependent variable, regardless of what common contribution that variable shares with other variables subsequently admitted to the equation. That is, it contains variance which overlaps with all other input variables with which it is correlated. Each additional variable which is added likewise pre-empts the variance it has in common with subsequently entered variables. Only the last variable contributes uniquely to the explained variance. Thus, the major analytic problem in using regression analysis has been how to separate the part of the variation in achievement due to variation in school resources from the parts due to variation in students' backgrounds or peer-group influences.

In the analyses of Coleman et al (1966), variables representing the student's background were first entered into the regression equations on the assumption that "the student's background is clearly prior to and independent of, any influence from school factors" (p.330). A similar procedure was followed in the IEA studies (Comber and Keeves, 1973). Thus, the effects of school variables (e.g., facilities, curriculum and teachers) were limited to those that could be demonstrated after variation explained by family background differences had been taken out. This procedure has the effect of assigning to the family background block both the explanatory power which it possesses uniquely and the explanatory power which it shares with the other blocks. Conversely, the school block is assigned none of the variances in achievement which it accounts for jointly with family background. Thus, the possibility of school effects being demonstrated is reduced very considerably.

To overcome problems associated with such techniques of asymmetric variance decomposition, a method of symmetric variance decomposition has been suggested (Beaton, 1973, 1974; Mayeske et al, 1972; Wisler, 1974). Its purpose is to partition "explainable variance in a dependent variable into the portions attributable to each independent variable and to all combinations of independent variables in order that we may better understand the interactions of predictors in estimating the criteria" (Beaton, 1974, p.63). A major virtue of this approach is that all possible orders of entering the sets of variables into the regression equation are examined and thus the partitioning of variance is not dependent on the order in which variables were entered. Thus, for example, no a priori decision is taken to assign to the home, variance which is jointly attributable to home and school factors.

The blocking of variables and the use of symmetric variance decomposition seem particularly appropriate when regression analysis is used to examine school effectiveness. Blocking has the effect of combining variables in conceptually meaningful categories, while symmetric variance decomposition allows the relationship between the variables represented in these categories and school achievement to be demonstrated in a manner that takes into account the complexity of the relationships between home, school and achievement. In particular, the method does not assume that home background ceases to have an effect at the time at which a child enters school. In fact, empirical findings when the method is used point to considerable over-lap between blocks of variables (Brimer et al, 1976; Mayeske et al, 1972).

CONCLUSION

This over-view has tended to raise rather than resolve issues related to the measurement of school effectiveness. While some progress has been made, it is clear that much remains to be accomplished in the area of methodology. As far as the choice and measurement of input variables are concerned, there is some evidence that process variables are more likely to be functional in student attainment than status variables. The strongest evidence for this comes from some European studies carried out in selective educational systems, though there are indications of it in American studies also. There is a need to examine this proposition more thoroughly with carefully chosen process variables and in more comprehensive educational systems.

The range of output measures that has been examined in studies of school effectiveness has been very limited. There is an obvious need to develop a much broader range of 'educational' indicators relating to output than has been discussed in this paper. Apart from developing measures in the cognitive area which will be more sensitive to school curricula, as indicated above, there is also a need to develop measures in non-cognitive areas of achievement and measures of aspirations and of the broader impact of schooling on individual life chances as well as on the social, economic and cultural systems of nations (Gooler, 1976).

Finally, the need to develop and implement research designs that will provide a sounder basis for making inferences about the effects of schools than surveys permit must be recognized. Experimental and longitudinal studies give rise to their own set of methodological problems. However, it must be recognised that despite advances in the use of regression analysis, the survey has in-built disadvantages in the identification of causal relation-ships. It may also be that regression analysis as an analytic technique in this context has reached the limit of its explanatory capabilities. While information derived from surveys can bring us some distance in understanding the functioning of schools and may be necessary to obtain in the future, the need for the development of alternative methodologies is also clear. In the meanwhile, general statements about the effectiveness or non-effectiveness of schooling in general or school practices in particular should be viewed with a healthy scepticism.

REFERENCES

AVERCH, H.A., CARROL, S.J., DONALDSON, T.S., KIESLING, H.J. and PINCUS, J. (1972). How effective is schooling? A critical review and synthesis of research findings. Santa Monica, California: Rand Corporation.

BEATON, A.E. (1973). Commonality. Unpublished manuscript.

BEATON, A.E. (1974). Multivariate commonality analysis. In: MAYESKE, G.W., BEATON, A.E., WISLER, C.E., OKADA, T. and COHEN, W.M. Technical supplement to 'A study of the achievement of our nation's students'. Washington, D.C.: U.S. Department of Health, Education and Welfare.

BLOOM, B.S. (1964). Stability and change in human characteristics. New York: Wiley.

BOWLES, S., and LEVIN, H.M. (1968). The determinants of scholastic achievement: An appraisal of some recent evidence. Journal of Human Resources, 3, 3-24.

BRIMER, A., MADAUS, G.F., CHAPMAN, B., KELLAGHAN, T. and WOOD, B. (1976). Sources of difference in school achievement. Report submitted to the Carnegie Corporation.

CAIN, G.G., and WATTS, H.W. (1970). Problems in making policy inferences from the Coleman report. American Sociological Review, 35, 228-242.

CARR-HILL, R. and MAGNUSSEN, O. (1973). Indicators of performance of educational systems. Paris: Organisation for Economic Co-operation and Development.

COHEN, D.K. (1972). Compensatory education. In WALBERG, H.J., and KOPAN, A.T., (Eds.). Rethinking urban education. San Francisco: Jossey-Bass.

COHEN, J. and COHEN, P. (1975). Applied multiple regression/ correlation analysis for the behavioral sciences. New York: Wiley.

COLEMAN, J.S. (1972). The evaluation of Equality of Educational Opportunity. In: MOSTELLER, F. and MOYNIHAN, D.P. (Eds.). On equality of educational opportunity. Papers deriving from the Harvard University faculty seminar on the Coleman report. New York: Vintage Books.

COLEMAN, J.S., CAMPBELL, E.Q., HOBSON, C.J., McPARTLAN, J., MOOD, A.M., WEINFELD, F.D. and YORK, R.L. (1966). Equality of educational opportunity. Washington, D.C.: Office of Education, U.S. Department of Health, Education and Welfare.

COMBER, L.C. and KEEVES, J.P. (1973). Science education in nineteen countries. An empirical study. New York: Wiley.

CRONBACH, L.J. (1975). Five decades of public controversy over mental testing. American Psychologist, 30, 1-14.

DUNCAN, O.D., FEATHERMAN, D.L. and DUNCAN, B. (1972). Socioeconomic background and achievement. New York: Seminar Press.

DYER, H.S. (1968). School factors and equal educational opportunity. Harvard Educational Review, 38, 38-56.

FLOUD, J.E., HALSEY, A.H. and MARTIN, F.M. (1958). Social class and educational opportunity. London: Heinemann.

FLUDE, M. and AHIER, J. (Eds.) (1974). Educability, schools and ideology. New York: Halsted Press.

GOOLER, D.D. (1976). The development and use of educational indicators. In: KRATHWOHL, D.R. (Ed.), Educational indicators: Monitoring the state of education. Proceedings of the 1975 E.T.S. Invitational Conference Princeton, N.J.: Educational Testing Service.

GREAT BRITIAN: DEPARTMENT OF EDUCATION AND SCIENCE (1967). Children and their primary schools. A report of the Central Advisory Council for Education (England). London: Her Majesty's Stationary Office.

HANUSHEK, E.A. and KAIN, J.F. (1972). On the value of Equality of Educational Opportunity as a guide to public policy. In MOSTELLER, F. and MOYNIHAN, D.P. (Eds.). On equality of educational opportunity. Papers deriving from the Harvard University faculty seminar on the Coleman report. New York: Vintage Books.

HAUSER, R.M. (1969). Schools and the stratification process. American Journal of Sociology, 74, 587-611.

IANNI, F.A.J. (1965). Research in education. In: HARRIS, S.E. and LEVENSOHN,A. (Eds.). Education and public policy. Berkeley, California: McCutchan.

JENCKS, C.S. and BROWN, M.D. (1975). Effects of high schools on their students. Harvard Educational Review. 45, 273-324.

JENCKS, C.S., SMITH, M., ACLAND, H. BANE, M.J., COHEN, D., GINTIS, H., HEYNS, B. and MICHELSON, S. (1972). Inequality: A re-assessment of the effect of family and schooling in America. New York: Basic Books.

KELLAGHAN, T. (1972). Preschool intervention for the educationally disadvantaged. Irish Journal of Psychology, 1, 160-176.

LUECKE, D.F. and McGINN, W.F. (1975). Regression analyses and educational production functions: Can they be trusted? Harvard Educational Review, 45, 325-350.

MADAUS, G.F., AIRASIAN, P. and KELLAGHAN, T. (1971). The effects of standardized testing. Irish Journal of Education, 5, 70-85.

MADAUS, G., KELLAGHAN, T. and RAKOW, E. (1975). A study of the sensitivity of of measures of school effectiveness. Report submitted to the Carnegie Corporation. Dublin: Educational Research Centre, St. Patrick's College.

MAYESKE, G.W., WISLER, C.E., BEATON, A.E., WEINFELD, F.D., COHEN, W.M., OKADA, T., PROSHEK, J.M. and TABLER, K.A. (1972). A study of our nation's schools. DHEW Publication No.(OE) 72-142. Washington, D.C.: U.S. Department of Health, Education and Welfare.

McDONAGH, D. (1973). A survey of reading comprehension in Dublin city schools. Irish Journal of Education, 7, 5-10.

MOOD, A.M. (1971). Partitioning variance in multiple regression analyses as a tool for developing learning models. American Educational Research Journal, 8, 191-202.

NATIONAL ASSESSMENT OF EDUCATIONAL PROGRESS (1974). General information yearbook. Report No.03/04-GIY. Washington, D.C.: U.S. Government Printing Office.

RIVLIN, A.M. (1971). Systematic thinking for social action. Washington, D.C.: Brookings Institution.

SHEEHAN, J. (1973). The economics of education. London: Allen and Unwin.

SHELDON, E.G. (1976). The social indicators movement. In: KRATHWOHL, D.R. (Ed.). Educational indicators: Monitoring the state of education. Proceedings of the 1975 ETS Invitational Conference. Princeton, N.J.: Educational Testing Service.

SMITH, M. (1972). Equality of educational opportunity: The basic findings re-considered. In: MOSTELLER, F. and MOYNIHAN, D.P. (Eds.). On equality of educational opportunity. Papers deriving from the Harvard University faculty seminar on the Coleman report. New York: Vintage Books.

SOHLMAN, A. (1971). Differences in school achievement and occupational opport-unities: Explanatory factors. A survey based on European experience. In Organisation for Economic Co-operation and Development. Group disparities in educational participation and achievement. Paris: Organisation for Economic Co-operation and Development.

START, K.B., and WELLS, B.K. (1972). The trend of reading standards. Windsor, Berks: NFER Publishing Co.

THORNDIKE, R.L. (1973). Reading comprehension in fifteen countries: An empirical study. Stockholm: Almqvist and Wiksell.

TYLER, R.W. (1949). Basic principles of curriculum and instruction. Chicago: University of Chicago Press.

UNITED STATES: National Center for Education Statistics (1975). The condition of education 1975. Washington, D.C.: Government Printing Office.

WILSON, A.B. (1968). Social class and equal educational opportunity. Harvard Educational Review, 38, 77-84.

WILSLER, C.E. (1974). Partitioning the explained variance in a regression analysis. In MAYESKE, G.W., BEATON, A.E., WISLER, C.E., OKADA, T., and COHEN, W.M. Technical supplement to 'A study of the achievement of our nation's students'. Washington, D.C.: U.S. Department of Health, Education and Welfare.

MODELS FOR MONITORING ACHIEVEMENT IN SCHOOLS

R. SUMNER

Abstract - Preliminary consideration is given to the
notions of 'monitoring', 'achievement' and
'model' as a prelude to adapting an analysis
of the features of a social system to the
circumstances of education. The types of
measures available are classified under the
headings of fields, structures, and sources
and a framework for the appraisal of systems
is exemplified. A parallel is drawn between
programme evaluation and monitoring, leading
to a paradigm for the systematic monitoring
of educational events and its relations to
the familiar input - output model. The
implications from treating monitoring in the
context of a social system are commented on,
and a 'minimal model' as proposed in the
N.F.E.R.'s Mathematics Attainment feasibility
study is described.

WHAT IS A MODEL?

Briefly, it can be defined as,

1.   a physically reduced replica of an existing object, usually with less detail than the original,

2.   a full-size or reduced prototype of an object aimed at simulating the major features of a product,

3.   an ideal of some kind, e.g. model community, which embodies desirable features, as in a 'model of behaviour' set as an example to others.

WHAT IS MONITORING?

Here there is no accepted definition, but examples exist; i.e.

1.   in education: 'the monitorial system' - when a teacher entrusted younger children's learning to an assistant who instructed in specifics,

2.   in a machine: when aspects of its performance are kept under review

whilst it is working or during maintainance; <u>examples</u>, speed of vehicle,
engine revolutions, petrol consumption; (rarely does the ordinary motorist
review braking power, acceleration, or thermal efficiency),

3.   in business: the periodic examination of cash flow, stock records,
salaries, personnel establishment, premises; exemplified in annual accounts
of assets acquired and disposed, profits and loss, etc.,

4.   in ideas: reviews of publications;authors; papers-speakers (scanning
contents pages, current research lists, i.e. keeping aware, alerting by
information services).

Its obvious features are   (a) keeping track of major events   (b) by observation
(c) of critical aspects   (d) given by small-scale indicators   (e) yielding reliable
readings   (f) of good quality data   (g) often at given intervals of time.

Common sense would seem to indicate that efficient monitoring requires
(a) identification of the purposes of the main activity,   (b) location of critical
points in the processes by which these purposes are achieved,   (c) instruments for
transforming activity at chosen critical points into contextual observations,
(d) criteria enabling instrument readings to be interpreted in relation to the achievement of the main activity,   (e) little or no interference with the execution of
the main activity.

WHAT IS ACHIEVEMENT IN SCHOOLS?

This 'global concept' enshrines several diffuse major purposes: e.g., transmitting the
culture; establishing basic educational skills; enabling pupils to earn a living,
enriching pupils' personal development; providing a variety of learned experiences;
enhancing capacity for choice; promoting social awareness and social behaviour; etc.

In a broad sense, achievement can be viewed as a relative term; i.e. the pupil at any
given entry point makes progress in respect of these overall purposes: <u>OR</u> in more
precise curriculum terms; i.e. within a specific course a pupil's gains' relate to his
starting and end points.   Thinking of 'knowing' certain facts and processes narrows
the idea of achievement to one of <u>attainment</u>; in this case there is no consideration
of starting position; the question is simply, has this pupil attained such and such a
specified state?   Defining <u>desirable</u> states has become standard practice so that it
is commonplace to distinguish between general goals, main aims and detailed objectives
- with rules for operationalising the latter as behaviour objectives.

Few schools in U.K. attempt to state their objectives or even their major aspirations;

in all schools the curriculum is controlled by the staff, with a great deal of dele-
gation in planning, execution and control.   Certainly particular materials are chosen
for use throughout an entire stage of schooling (e.g. The School Mathematics Project,
'Fletcher' Mathematics series, Humanities Curriculum Project, Project Technology,
etc.) and the producers of these courses intend to influence teaching by the contents
of guides.   But even in these examples of high prescription the individual teacher
retains the right to adapt, re-order, omit or extend topics according to his own
notions of sound practice.   'Achievement' can thus only be viewed as a consensus
arising from the widespread use of contemporary materials, the applications of
pedagogic process philosophies such as 'guided discovery' or 'independent reasoning',
or 'structured learning' (however received during training or translated into
strategies in the classroom).   Very recently, in the sphere of technical education,
a large number of modular courses each based on a structured set of objectives have
been produced (Technican Education Council).   When these are adopted by the technical
colleges (with pupils or apprentices aged 16 years and over) it will be possible to
express achievement as the attainment of precisely defined objectives exemplified by
a specific act of behaviour.   As far as is known, this is the only approach (in the
U.K.) to course planning which is 'objectives based'.

As distinct from a machine or business concern it seems obvious that the purposes of
'school' and their realisations as 'achievement' (or attainment) will be incapable of
concise, unambigious and all-inclusive definition.   The best that might be done would
be either a consensus statement (propounded as a basis for educational practice) or a
statement more focussed on the pragmatic issues alive in current educational debate;
either way, there will inevitably be objections and dissent.

FEEDBACK AND EVALUATION

Education can take on the concept of social system; specialised in function, carried
out in institutions by classified personnel, according to expectations ascribed by the
community which allocates a share of resources to it.   In this sense, it is but one
of society's many sub-systems; its own purposes ought, therefore, to be consonant with
society at large.

In his provisional structural description of a social system Parsons (1951), classified the sources of differentiation as follows:-

      1.   Relational Institutions (i.e., the individual's and collectives, their
      role orientation and distribution within the system).

      2.   Regulative Institutions (i.e. the 'economy' of instrumental relation-
      ships; resources and their distribution, organisation of the power system:

similarly for expressive relationships; classification and distribution of rewards and the organisation of the reward system):

3.   Cultural Institutions (i.e. patterns of cultural orientations including ideology, religious beliefs, expressive symbols):

4.   Relational and Regulative Institutions (integrative structures, including norms and their enforcement and roles institutionalising special responsibilities for collective interests).

For school education, these sub-system categories can be translated as follows:-

1.   the pupils, teachers, ancilliaries, advisers, inspectors and administrators, together with their expectations, intentions and functions both as individuals and as groups.   Essentially, these units (individuals) and collectives (groups) inter-act to fulfil their institutionalised purposes:

2.   the government machinery for gathering and allocating resources for education i.e., elected representatives and relevant committees, executives in ministries and local councils, administrative and clerical staffs and the local advisers, headteachers and teachers when dealing with resources:

3.   The cultural institutions are both reflected and directly presented by the curriculum or its agents (teachers, visiting lecturers, programme designers, visiting performers); less direct influence is exercised by common interest groups (e.g. Confederation of British Industries: The Festival of Light), and pressure groups (e.g. Confederation for the Advancement of State Education, teachers' unions, teachers' subject associations). More influent- ial perhaps, in the U.K. certainly, are the school examination boards which, at the Advanced Level, especially, through strong links with University faculties maintain the ideology of disciplined study about a corpus of knowledge.

4.   This fourth category (of Relational and Regulative institutions, which provide integrative structures) is most obviously represented operationally by the curriculum organisations and the examining boards, the former by seeking to prescribe what ought to be taught and the latter by attempting to measure the learning that has accrued.   Regulation is exercised in a number of ways (yet interestingly, the term regulation implies keeping order and balance in some on-going dynamic process) but control, i.e. the positive direction of affairs, is generally by consent (through the policies of elected governments) and most often focussed on the means rather than the ends.

Clearly the first three categories of participants in the educational system meet in this fourth and though the majority of recognised cultural institutions have not assumed a formal regulative role, they have a voice through their representatives on examining bodies and submissions to other commissions (e.g. 'Children and Their Primary Schools' (1966) Plowden B., Chairman - Evidence was given by 119 organisations, including the churches).

In England and Wales a form of regulation takes place through the activities of the school inspectorate who, at the national level, are charged with advising the Minister of State as to whether the local education authorities are carrying out their statutary obligations to provide education in accordance with government enactment. Their work ranges over 'full inspections' of individual schools, whereby a team of inspectors will observe all manner of school activity, and occasional visits to headmasters or assistant teachers. As well as inspecting, they organise courses for teachers and so can bring to a wide audience examples of 'good' practice or advances in curriculum or pedagogical theory. There are less than 700 inspectors and well over 30,000 schools and colleges; and though their reports are 'advisory' they are extremely influential (as regulators) in pin-pointing poor or outstanding features, and in promoting certain lines of development in teaching and school administration.

From the foregoing, it is plain that the educational system does have several forms of regulations and control, some of which are overt and comparatively direct (budgetary) whilst others are more subtle and indirect. There is, too, a great deal of information gathered and tabulated year by year, and from the achievement standpoint, in U.K., a wealth (or more aptly perhaps, a deluge) of data on externally administered examination performance at the age of 16+. Recently, these data have figured prominently in the debate on educational standards achieved by the comprehensive sector of Local Authority schools, as compared with the 'unre-organised' selective (11+ examination) sector, (e.g. Baldwin and Travers, 1975).

In spite of the inconclusive state of this debate, which completely ignores the fact that eight 'Ordinary' General Certificate of Education (University based) boards and 14 Certificate of Secondary Education (regional teacher-controlled) boards provide assessment in a range of subjects which has expanded markedly over the last decade, there is undoubtedly an evaluative use made of the data. It is perhaps reasonable, too, to overlook the difficulties of ensuring comparable standards between boards examining at the same level or in the alignment of standards between levels, (as illustrated by the reports from the N.F.E.R.'s Examination and Test Research Unit, (e.g. Nuttall (1968) : Nuttall, Backhouse and Wilmott(1974)); a crude indicator may be good enough. Hence, numbers of candidates per examination, average number of passes per pupil, and similar statistics based on aggregates can be quoted.

It is doubtful whether examination feedback has been used seriously for control, as applied to the curriculum; chief examiners reports are circulated to schools but little is heard thereafter. Hence, the balance between what pupils have learned (as evidenced by examinations) and what they should attempt to learn - as evidenced by the published syllabuses - is kept by periodic syllabus revisions, which, no doubt, take account of attainment in specific topics as well as evolving notions on the nature of the subject.

SYSTEMS IN EDUCATION

The previous discussion of relational and regulative institutions mentioned curriculum bodies, the local and national inspectorate, examination boards and commissions of enquiry: the Local Authorities act in the role of providers (though drawing on national as well as local funds): ancilliary provision, in the guise of advice, research, or in-service education is also provided by universities, teachers' centres and independent bodies (e.g. the National Childrens' Bureau). Each of these classes of organisation can be thought of as a social system: i.e. with individuals and groups performing ascribed roles interactively; with resources and power structures; with a particular cultural direction and external projections; and with integrative structures designed to pressure and extend the organisation in respect of ethos, influence and practice. By these criteria each school can be characterised as a system, with certain functions hierarchically distributed. Within schools there are sub-systems, though these may conveniently be described as 'routines' when the 'system' is a procedure for getting something done; e.g.'s record keeping, homework, or fire drill. Nevertheless, these procedures require organisation to translate intention into action, and because there is activity each one yields information which, in some sense, can be used as a measure.

TYPES OF MEASURE

A useful classification of institutional measures was derived by Barton (1961) when examining non-intellective factors as determinants of college success. His survey of literature was not confined solely to studies in educational institutions. The major fields he identified were measures of

i.	input,	iv.	social structure variables
ii.	output,	v.	attitudes
iii.	environment,	and vi.	activities

He saw distinctions between the structural attributes of measures as follows: additive (based on individual attributes), distributional (based on group and sub-groups), relational pattern (often called sociometric measures of group properties, e.g. communication nets), integral (e.g. programmes, possessions), and contextual (based on data on larger units to which the organisation belongs). Finally, he noted the source of basic data as (a) records, (b) direct observations, (c) informant's reports,   (d) reports (structured interviews or questionnaires) from samples, and (e) surveys of individual attitudes and behaviour.

Had Barton considered intellective determinants as well, he might have extended his categories to include:-

1.   the fields of scholastic aptitudes and scholastic attainments;

2.   a structure called, perhaps, 'analytic patterns' (arising from multi-variate analysis which condenses many associated variables into fewer over-riding relationships, e.g.'s cluster analysis, factor analysis, etc.): and

3.   the sources comprised of attainment tests and graded assessments. As it stands, without these additions, he quoted 109 references of which about 100 report the use of an organisational measure; many more could be listed nowadays.

Consideration will be given later as to which categories of measures distinguished above might be applied to monitoring school systems as well as to evaluating events in individual schools.**

CHANGES IN SCHOOLS

It is accepted that a changing social system is not necessarily disordered, and indeed a principal function might be to evolve specific strategies directed towards currently desired or projected ends; e.g. the N.F.E.R.'s Multi-racial Educational project.   In England and Wales there is a thrust towards a 'common curriculum' in the secondary stage (e.g. Hipkin, 1976) and the notion that central government should intervene is being voiced more frequently (e.g. Judge, 1976). The point now emphasised is that the issue of secondary selection is virtually settled and the trend towards mixed ability teaching is gaining ground even for older age groups, so that what ought to be taught to all pupils is of central concern if divisiveness is not to be perpetuated through selective course allocations.   Judge also makes the case for monitoring what pupils achieve so that the effects of innovation may become public knowledge.

There could be other good reasons for keeping watch on changes at the school, local authority or national level.   For example, a school could adapt its pedagogy and groupings if it were to detect new or unsuspected capabilities among its latest entrants.   However, a general aim, such as the appraisal of a sector of the

----

**   Barton did not use the terms 'field' and 'structure'; they are employed here for aptness and brevity together with the term 'source', which he did use.

educational complex, would be unsatisfactory.   For without an answer to the question 'Why are we studying the system?'   there is no context for the other questions to be posed when conducting an appraisal.   A framework for summarising systems is outlined by Jones (1972; who acknowledges R.L. Ackoff's, contribution entitled 'Towards a system of systems concepts' reproduced by Beishon and Peters, 1972).   The standard questions proposed continue along these lines:-

A.   What kind of system is it? (purposive, goal-seeking, homeostatic, ideal seeking).

B.   How can the system be characterised?   (abstract/concrete, open/closed, static/dynamic, adaptive/non-adaptive, an organisation).

C.   What is its goal/purpose/objective/ideal?

D.   What constitutes the system? (component, elements and sub-systems, the relevant links, the properties or variables of interest: these imply the system's extent and boundaries).

E.   What constitutes the system's environment?

F.   How do we measure the relevant variables?

G.   How does the system operate? (its response to normal inputs, its speed and flexibility of response).

H.   How does the system respond to abnormal situations?

I.   What future changes are likely in the structure of the system?

These are clarifying questions; though the answers may not be straightforward and tidy.   It becomes obvious, from question A, that the educational system purports to be purposive, goal and ideal seeking, and in some respects is homeostatic.   But our interest is educational achievement (question C), however defined, which the system ought to engender; though other properties may be advocated (e.g. adjustment). Recognising this purpose, however, sharpens considerably our perception of the components, (question D) or sub-systems which exist and thus can be studied as they operate.

This analysis may appear to be mere common-sense, partly because the organisation of school provision and schools themselves are familiar, as is the notion that pupils will learn subjects such as mathematics, English, German or French, geography, etc. A switch to less familiar territory: e.g. school achievement in morality would give rise to deeper thought.   The nub of the analysis lies in question D, especially in the identification of properties or variables relevant to the system or sub-systems of learning-achievement.   However, it is useful to be reminded that links are as important as components and that 'extent' and 'boundaries' will also require clear definition.   Here, perhaps, Barton's categories of 'field' variables are helpful, though some further differentiation of these might be useful by reserving the terms 'input' and 'output' for <u>phases</u> in the systems cycle; (adding 'throughput', for completeness).   Hence the list would deal with:-

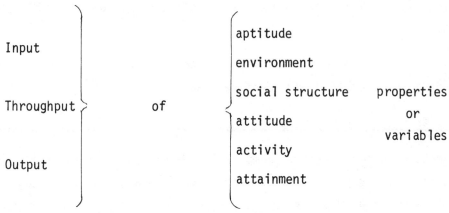

Input

Throughput   of

Output

aptitude

environment

social structure   properties

attitude   or

activity   variables

attainment

Question E, on the system's environment, will illustrate the context for the learning - achievement complex and pin-point helpful or obstructive features.   These may be incorporated in the analysis as measured variables or taken into account as background considerations when setting up an investigation (monitoring scheme) or when reporting findings.   The scale of enquiry may well affect the treatment accorded to certain environmental factors; at the school level, for example, distribution of capitation allowances between departments may affect the quality of learning experiences available to children; whereas at the national level, economic effects may <u>apparently</u> be less direct, for example limiting the school building programme or cutting out auxilliary help for teachers.

The question of how to measure relevant variables is, at first sight, less of a problem than finding agreement on what these variables are.   The scientific basis for measurement is being increasingly refined and the technology for carrying out measurement on practically any scale is available.   What is less known is how accept-able the established techniques are, in any given learning-achievement situation, and the extent to which the measures applied

(a)   do not distort the property under assessment   and

(b)   are valid for pupils in differing curriculum and pedagogic settings.

For instance, pupils accustomed to 'formal' teaching procedures may perform better on technically constructed measures than pupils whose routine is less structured with no 'testing' experience though familiar with 'continuous assessment' as practiced by their own teachers.   In respect of this question, perhaps more attention should be given in preliminary studies to construct validity in the context of aptness of of instrument in relation to learning experience; (Messick's, 1974, discussion has a bearing on this problem).

How a learning system operates (question G) is crucial to the notion of monitoring achievement because there may be highly effective or ineffective modes of response to new inputs, whenever these occur. Shayer (1972) for example, challenged the appropriateness of the Nuffield secondary science curriculum when it is delivered to the majority of pupils, as distinct from the highly able. His analysis revealed that abstract logical thinking was required to a large degree whereas a majority of young adolescents had yet to complete the transition from more concrete modes of conceptualisation: he now advocates adapting the curriculum to the pupils' capabilities. It would seem to be important to examine changes induced by attempts to follow new curricula or by the introduction of new learning strategies, such as 'mastery learning' (Bloom, 1973; Block, 1971; etc.): in such cases elements of the monitoring device might be inherent in the new scheme (e.g. additional hours of study required to reach mastery criteria following initial failure); but it would seem necessary for some elements to be independent of the new scheme. Also, knowing how and when a response becomes operative, and by whom, may indicate the most suitable position for a monitoring device. The mastery learning example, above, could show that the demands on some students are unrealistic relative to other commitments.

The remaining questions (H and I) are important, though it is to be hoped that 'abnormal' situations of a detrimental kind would not arise; nevertheless, a monitoring device should be sensitive enough to indicate departures from 'normal' states. Asking about future changes will set up a series of hypotheses about their effects and the adequacy of the monitoring devices to assess these effects.

AN APPROACH TO A MONITORING PARADIGM

It would be premature to claim that monitoring achievement can be placed on a theoretical footing. Firstly, the concept of monitoring is not fully elaborated; as indicated at the outset, it can mean simply keeping a watch on events by means of a sensory device or it can imply feedback and evaluation. In the case of a machine, simply keeping watch without taking action, if possible, would be pointless (if an aeroplane's height monitor reads zero, a pilot would expect trouble). But in a social system, the grounds for decision might not be as clear-cut. The values attached to the monitoring readings should be explicit if the analysis of the learning-achievement system has been done properly.

It may be the case that the purpose of monitoring is simply to describe pupils' achievement in unambigious terms across a given period of time. In a situation where the schools have genuine freedom to choose there would be no prospect of applying external decisions designed to alter the course of events, though the feedback to schools via the teachers' collective interpretation of the data may lead to changes intended to produce 'improvements'. One might speculate that one reason for the current expressions of dis-satisfaction with schooling, as voiced in the U.K. media, is the confusion created by the various idealogical factions and professionals with vested interests who can usually find an outlet for their views if they are suffic-iently extreme to be deemed newsworthy. The information on achievement has been gathered almost ad-hoc, with reading excepted by reason of the surveys done from time to time since 1948 (Start and Wells, 1972). Curiously enough, though the most recent survey of 1971 gave equivocal results it triggered off 'corrective' feedback on a massive scale via the mechanism of a government commission of enquiry, (the Bullock Report 'Language for Life' 1975). This report commented on the limited scope of the previous assessments and recommended that a widespread and systematic appraisal of language attainments be adopted.

The point to be made here is that time sampling may be integral to some monitoring schemes. On the other hand, monitoring could be event-sequenced. In this case the reason for monitoring achievement would be the incidence on learning of a sequence of events, such as the adoption of a new curriculum or the conclusion of a teachers' in-service training course, or the improvement of staffing ratio, or some other 'signi-ficant' occurence.

It will be instructive now to consider a particular scheme presented by its authors (Webster and Mendro, 1975) as a model for research and evaluation. This starts from a baseline of current information; a situation appraisal which (after Stufflebeam, et al; 1971) is called a 'context evaluation'. The context should make use of longitudinal information on matters such as "student dropout, attendance, achievement levels, drug usage, demographic and vocational patterns, community sociometric status and dominant value patterns, and teacher academic and demographic characteristics". It thus "provides the basis for formulating change objectives by identifying needs and, in some cases, outlining practical constraints in identified problem areas". Decision makers should now set priorities by establishing goals designed to realise the desired performances. These are merged at the planning stage with information from previous evaluations (of similar products), basic research, applied research and from other sources. The preliminary plan leads to a demand for resources which, if met, can be translated into an operational plan and this, in turn, provides interim evaluation and terminal evaluation of the product resulting from the revised learning programme. At this stage applied research and other pertinent factors are taken into account and a decision to continue or halt the programme is taken. Continuation can be either a repetition or a modified version of the learning programme. In the latter case an additional context evaluation may be carried out prior to re-shaping the operational programme plan.

Webster and Medro point out that information disseminations to those concerned is essential; they list the programme participant under six levels of management, i.e. Board of Education, upper project, building, teachers and parents/students. Each management class would receive information orientated to its own function. For example, the elected board members would receive summative product evaluation on the effects of the district's various projects and teaching programmes; they would also receive context evaluation data on the general state of the educational environment. The teachers would receive product evaluations of a formative and summative kind on the effects of programmes in which they are involved; likewise, context evaluation information would relate only to the student entry level. Additionally, the teachers would receive process evaluations (degree of programme implementation) on their projects and applied research information intended to improve instructional effectiveness. Interestingly, parents and students would receive feedback on individual student performance.

From the monitoring standpoint, the yearly context evaluation might be more than the minimum required. It could be sufficient to find just one critical variable to examine whenever a significant event has taken effect, though this procedure would call for the verification of certain assumptions, principally that the variable chosen as an indicator really is the most important in the field. It would have to be shown, too, that the index truly reflected the critical variable and that the trigger even led to non-trivial effects. There are further practical problems with such an approach, as it would require the monitoring capability to be 'on-tap', a situation that might be possible when the overall effort to carry through the procedure is relatively slight, needing little organisation and few resources. It is hard to imagine that the returns from such a procedure could be important enough to justify even the small effort involved. However, it represents a useful starting point for suggesting possible models for monitoring procedures. Stripped to its essentials the model would appear as follows:-

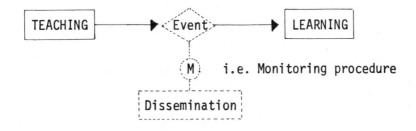

A more complete version would allow for an event to occur at any stage from init-
iation onwards,   thus :-

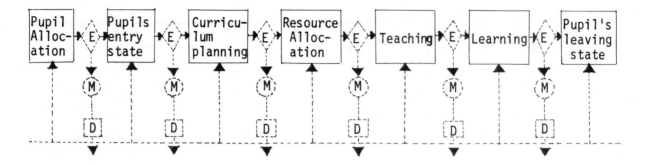

Quite clearly, the kinds of events that might occur in the curriculum implementation
chain will be different at the various points.   One can imagine prolonged school
closure having an effect on pupils at the start of a new school year, or a new head
of department taking over planning and resource allocations, new books could arrive
in mid-course and a faulty teaching machine guide pupils to erroneous concepts, after
initial learning a television series could convey a contradictory impression, whilst,
finally a summer holiday visit might re-inforce certain aspects of the programme.
Day to day events like these take place all the time and, no doubt, some notice is
taken according to the seeming importance of the consequences.   Also, dissemination of findings (from monitoring procedures, be they informal observations or tests
of attainment) could lead to corrective action or improved provision at any stage
upto the pupils' leaving.   However, it is emphasised that decision and action are
not necessary or desirable outcomes of monitoring as the information may be sufficient in itself.   Furthermore, it is doubtful whether such expedient responses to
random events could be called anything more than informal monitoring.

The notion of event sequenced monitoring is much more likely to appeal when an
occurence is of relatively great magnitude.   A series of comparable events, e.g.
lectures by visiting experts, might lead to repeated appraisals of effects on course
achievements.   The cause of any improvement might actually be of boost to morale
and a lift in aspirations rather than the relevance of lecture content or a lively
presentation of recent knowledge.   However, the point remains that mid-course events,
whether or not their timing is regular, may warrant monitoring simply for confirmat-
ion that the strategy had led to an effective result.

On the national scale, or even at district level, monitoring process effects of this
kind might not, at first sight, appear to be worthwhile.   However, if a strategy has
been taken up on a broad front, as in the Humanities Curriculum Project (where the
teacher has a neutral role in group discussions) a check on the maintainance of basic
skills or pupils' morale might be revealing: (the project's own evaluation showed that

project groups had improved more in these respects relative to controls). A special-purpose evaluation study may produce Hawthorne effects, whereas more widespread and continuous assessment, as for monitoring, would be less prone to temporary backwash of this kind; in any case, sustained positive backwash would add up to permanent improvement which would simply result in the monitoring instrument 'settling down' on a new normative reading.

Given that a course (i.e. curriculum programme) was to be repeated in the same sequence of stages, regular periodic monitoring would offset or control certain effects, such as length of time spent on study. Thus it would be possible to make direct comparisons between achievement in successive years or keep track of trends over several years. Schools would find such a procedure most informative with intakes transferred from a preceding stage. Hence, the monitoring would be on input and would function as a reassurance that teaching plans were realistic. When the reassurance was lacking a more complete procedure would be required: that is to say that diagnostic assessments or allocation to teaching groups could not be done properly with a monitoring device. Input monitoring makes sense when a small amount of information is sufficient; for transition between stages it would be preferable to use more complete end-of-stage assessments as the input appraisal for the subsequent stages (e.g. the N.F.E.R.'s development project report in preparation, Sumner and Bradley, 1976).

Terminal or summative assessment seems to fit the concept of achievement monitoring more comfortably than assessment done at the outset or during a phase of education. Its major drawback is that any feedback can only apply to a following cohort; nevertheless, it would answer the question of what are the products of the school system. In this respect, the opening paper issues a reminder that a narrow view taking only basic skills or 'important' subjects into account would be misleading and mistaken.

Schemes for input, through-put and output monitoring can be seen to relate to a specific feature appropriate to each phase; i.e. entry behaviour characteristics, processes and their effects, and curriculum objectives, respectively. The U.S. model for the National Assessment of Educational Progress programme is of objectives-based assessment conducted with four age-levels of student at periodic intervals of time. The purpose is to discover the extent to which desirable objectives have been attained, and the crucial assumption is that the objectives are indeed capable of attainment by the population for whom specified.

Returning to the extended (Barton's) 'field' categories, it can be seen that input, throughput and output may more aptly be applied to various global features (e.g. input of teachers, hours of preparation, class journeys, etc.). For achievement the

the pattern would thus become:-

Field \ Learning Phase	Entry Characteristics	Processes and Immediate Effects	Curriculum Objectives Eventual Effects	
Aptitudes				Direct Achievement
Attainments				Direct Achievement
Attitudes				Direct Achievement
Activities				Direct Achievement
Social Structures				Background
Environment				Background
MONITORING STAGE	INPUTS	THROUGHPUTS	OUTPUTS	Background

This is an assessment framework which corresponds to a 'teaching - learning - reporting' paradigm as follows:-

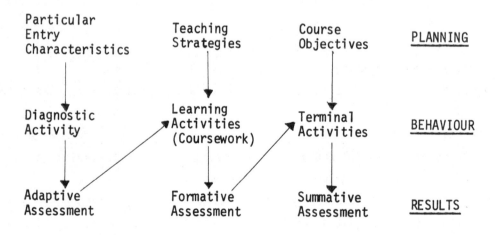

It has been made clear that monitoring results will feedback into the system in some way, either as an alerting signal, a token of reassurance, or as a regulator, or much more prescriptively, as a control. In a school system (district, region, nation) the cycle of provision and enablement might be crudely represented as shown overleaf:

In this layout

Ⓜ stands for monitoring reports,

Ⓡ is regulation, and

Ⓒ represents control

School System Structures

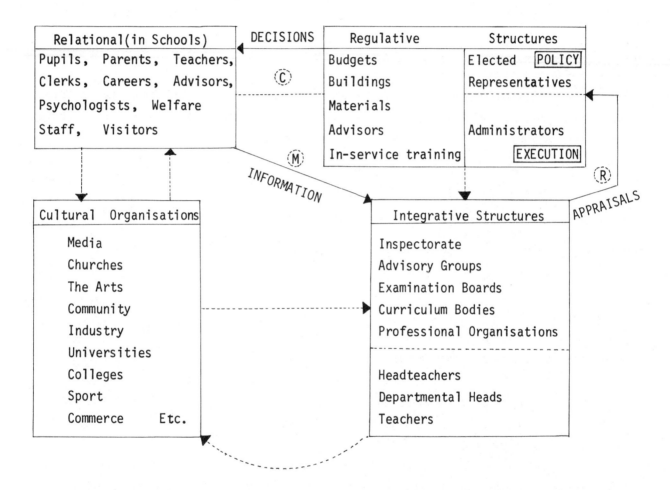

The diagram brings the various agents to the fore in turn, and also shows that monitoring, like other kinds of information on school performance could produce effects throughout the system. It implies too that preparatory consultation and reporting will require careful channelling; also that particular considerations may arise with respect to the choice of instruments. The systems behaviour scheme outlined previously will highlight potential problems by sharpening awareness, re-defining potent issues and spotlighting sensitive areas.

Planning for monitoring might proceed from this broad contextual stage, then through a system behaviour analysis, concluding with a precise programme for conducting assessment and reporting (similar to the Webster and Medro scheme). The purpose or purposes of monitoring will determine the field of interest, which will lead to the selection of learning phase and field.   At this stage the technical problems of measurement and sampling have to be anticipated and the resource constraints taken into account.   Beyond this point are questions of administration, data gathering, analysis and reporting (with consideration given as to the regulative or control out-comes before, during, or after the next cycle of monitoring).   Planning would, of course, be recursive such that every stage would be subject to review and ammendment as the plan is developed.

A MINIMAL MODEL

Over the last few years the N.F.E.R. has been engaged on a feasibility study to inves-tigate the application of mathematics test materials in a continuous monitoring survey (Sumner and others, 1975).   The results were twofold;

> i.   two sets of items, for 10-11 and 14-15 year olds respectively, organised in categories, mainly by content,   and

> ii.   a scheme for their use in monitoring.

Most of the categories are composed of items with provisional scale values derived from the Rasch technique.

For example,   the categories include 'properties of numbers and operations', 'geometry',   'sets and relations',   'problem solving',   'attitudes',   'visual representation of three dimensional shape',   'practical mathematics' and 'creat-ive extension'.   Administration would utilise a 'light sampling' scheme (initially propounded by G.F. Peaker - source unpublished) whereby only a fraction of the pupils in any one school would receive a given set of items.

For any particular size of sample, this scheme would involve a relatively small number of pupils per school; or alternatively, permit several sets of items to be given to a class at a single session.   The numbers of item or sub-scales available are in excess of 600 per age group and because the administrative and technical resources would, most likely, be limited it would be preferable to obtain measures for each category using a small selection of its items; but to do so at relatively frequent intervals; e.g. termly.

After an initial start-up period, it would be possible to report on attainment by producing detrended running means for each of the scaled categories.   Other mater-ials would be reported in a more basic way, perhaps by percentage of sample correct. All materials, both item and response, would be subject to qualitative comment, though the amount treated in this way would be comparatively small.   A scheme for item-sampling by rota, with rules for avoiding biases towards 'hard' or 'easy' sets has been suggested; this scheme is purely pragmatic and though its implementation appears straightforward, there would be a number of statistical problems (which a well conceived pilot study would help resolve).

The categorised item material was not created to assess attainment relative to defined objectives. The intention in creating the category materials was to produce items that reflect what is taught to the majority of pupils in the age group. A great deal of primary source material was consulted (i.e. text books, workcards, teachers guides) and advice was taken from a panel of mathematics educators and the project consultant.

It can be appreciated that the assessment model is quite basic, taking up only a small part of the 'field' and 'learning phase' set out in the foregoing analysis: i.e.

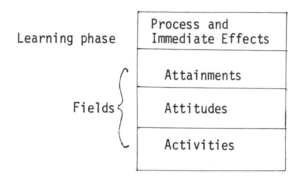

The project initially was about attainment; attitudes and practical activities were added later. The monitoring model is event-sequenced; but again very basic in that the event would be the occurrence of each school term. This makes for interpretation over specified periods of time though with considerable flexibility in the magnitude of time-slices. Another kind of data interpretation would be of 'gain' between primary and secondary stages (on the assumption that each sample item-category group would be equivalent because of random selection). This application would differ from the usual gain score but the light sampling procedure could be expanded, if required, to repeat assessment of a larger number of the same pupils at the primary and secondary stages. The administration of this type of longitudinal sampling might only be warranted if a special study including background variables, were mounted in order to go beyond monitoring into explanation.

CONCLUSIONS

Hindsight now shows that progress would have been enhanced by some knowledge of the issues discussed here. For example, the project staff often found themselves defending the idea of a monitoring survey.   It would have been especially helpful to have had a better awareness of the possible regulative functions of monitoring information and of the groups who would have a close interest in its (presumed) benefits.   These, in fact, are not impossible to forecast.   Technical questions are of little interest to the potential participants; they wish to know in advance what the consequences of _their_ idea of the data might be.   It is now clearer what kind of planning is necessary and that a more advanced modelling than the approach described here for mathematics attainment will be helpful in setting up a monitoring survey if one is commissioned.

REFERENCES

ACKOFF, R.L.   'Towards a system of systems concepts' reprinted in BEISHON, R.J. and PETERS, G. (Eds.) (1972). Systems Behaviour. Harper and Row

BARTON, A.H. (1961).   Organisational Measurement and It's Bearing on the Study of College Environments.   New York: C.E.E.B.

BLOCK, J.H. (Ed.) (1971).   'Mastery Learning: Theory and Practice' New York: Holt, Rinehart and Winston, New York.

BLOOM, B.S. (1973).   'Individual differences in school achievement: A vanishing point'.   Phi Delta Kappa address to AREA Conference in New York.

BULLOCK, A. (Chairman)   'A Language for Life' Report of the Committee of Enquiry commissioned by the Department of Education and Science. London: H.M.S.O.

JONES, L. (1972).   'Systems Behaviour, Module 1; Deep Sea Container Ports; Systems Appraisal and Simulation Modelling' Milton Keynes: The Open University Press.

JUDGE, H. (1976).   'To each according to his needs' Times Educational Supplement of 23. 4. 76.

MESSICK, S. (1975).   'The standard problem: Meaning and Values in Measurement and Education' American Psychologist, Vol. 30, No.10.

SCHOOLS COUNCIL (1975).   The Whole Curriculum 13-16.   London: Evans/Methuen.

SHAYER, M. (1972).   Piaget's Work and Science Teaching. Unpublished M. Ed Thesis, Leicester University.

START, K.B. and WELLS, B.K. (1972).   The Trend of Reading Standards: Slough, N.F.E.R.

STUFFLEBEAM, D.L. et al (1971).   Educational Evaluation and Decision Making
   Hasca, Illinois: Peakcock Publishers Inc.

SUMNER, R. and BRADLEY, K. (1976).   'Techniques for Appraising Pupils' Knowledge
   and Understanding on Transition from Primary to Secondary School'. Project
   Report.   Slough: N.F.E.R.

WEBSTER, W.J. and MEDRO, R.L. (1975).   'A pragmatic Model for a comprehensive
   public school research and educational system'.   The Journal of Educational
   Research,   Vol.69, No.4.

AN ASSESSMENT OF STANDARDS IN PRIMARY SCHOOLS IN A SCOTTISH COUNTY

G.J. POLLOCK

Abstract - The Research Services Unit of the Scottish
Council for Research in Education advised the
County of Stirlingshire on the design of a
survey intended to examine the effects on primary education of the 1965 Primary Memorandum
advocating a move towards the methods of discovery learning.   Tests in Reading and Mathematics were administered to approximately 500
pupils chosen by a two-stage sampling procedure
and examples of childrens' work were collected
from a small number of schools.   Additionally,
video tapes and slide cassettes were made to
illustrate pupils' learning experiences and a
written report on school life was prepared. This
paper, concerned mainly with the test data, illustrates how detailed analyses can inform judgements about the curriculum and so make possible
the constructive rather than critical use of
survey results.

Three years ago the Scottish Council for Research in Education set up a Research
Services Unit within its organisational framework, the aim of which was to serve
educationists in Scotland in a variety of ways including, e.g., consultancy and
advice on research techniques and methods for teachers, local authorities etc. and,
if need be, undertaking research work on a commissioned basis for such bodies.

The work reported in this paper is one example of the type of service provided by the
Research Services Unit and arose from an approach made to the Council by one of the
educational authorities in Scotland.

Stirlingshire Education Committee was anxious to make an assessment of the state of
primary education in the County.   Since 1966 the primary schools had been encouraged
to adopt as far as possible the principles and practices recommended in the 1965
Primary Memorandum published by the Scottish Education Department.   This had meant
changes in both the content of the curricula and in teaching methods.   The emphasis
had moved away from the learning of factual material towards a fostering of curiosity
in the child and the development of a child's capacity to discover things for himself/

herself. It takes time to introduce such changes of course and, by 1974, it seemed appropriate to consider such an assessment, since the primary pupils of 1974 could be considered to have had all their schooling under the new set-up. At the same time the Memorandum also stressed the need to ensure that the basic skills involved in the three R's should remain as basic elements of the school course. However, not for the first time, secondary teachers in Stirlingshire were voicing criticisms of the product they were receiving from their primary colleagues in terms of these basic skills and again it seemed appropriate to the Committee to examine these criticisms.

Accordingly, for both the reasons outlined above, Stirlingshire considered it desirable to carry out a review of work in progress in its primary schools with a view to answering the questions "What is happening to standards in Primary Education?"

A special Standards Committee was set up in Stirlingshire to consider ways and means of carrying out the review and initially it was proposed that some tests used by the Research Council in 1953 and 1963 in surveys of the Attainments of 10 year olds in English and Arithmetic be administered to the 1974 pupils in order that a straight comparison of attainments might be made. It was at this stage that the Council became involved and our advice sought on the desirability of such a procedure. Immediately we had to indicate that, in our view, the changes in curricula and in emphasis on content and methods rendered such a suggestion inappropriate for a number of reasons. In the group teaching situation now prevalent, children are learning at different rates and different levels and this makes evaluation and assessment of pupils' work more complex and difficult. Decimalisation and metrication have changed the pattern of number work considerably. Much more time is expected to be devoted to practical problems in arithmetic involving, e.g., the use of weights and measures and less to theoretical problems. 'English' has become 'Language Arts' and less time is devoted to the analysis of language and much more to the use of words and development of, for example, creative writing.

Acting on our advice it was accepted that the previous tests could not be used again. and alternative approaches were looked for. We recommended, e.g., in Mathematics the preparation of criterion referenced tests in various topics e.g., Basic Number, Sets, Shape but exigencies of time and finance prevented such an approach being adopted. We also indicated that, in our opinion, it was insufficient to restrict any assessment to the purely basic skills of Number and Language and that some form of "illuminative evaluation" also be adopted.

This meant that observation of the children in the classroom was required as a complement to the basic test data in order to provide additional descriptive and background material against which to judge the test data and to provide a fuller and more profitable discussion of the matters under investigation.

After further discussions it was eventually decided to restrict the work to an examination of the performance of Primary 6 pupils in session 1973-74 (again for financial and time reasons).   The Standards Committee proposed:-

1.   To carry out a formal assessment in Arithmetic using a test devised by members of the Standards Committee

2.   To carry out an assessment in Reading using one of the recently published Edinburgh Reading Tests

3.   To provide video-tapes and slide-cassettes with associated commentaries representing the variety of experience open to children in Stirlingshire schools

4.   To collect work-folders of individual children from a limited number of schools (in fact 5 in all)

5.   To provide a written report on children's life and learning in the county's schools.

As mentioned earlier the Reading Test used was the Edinburgh Reading Test for children aged 10.0 to 12.6.   The Arithmetic Test was devised by the Standards Committee appointed by the Education Committee.   The test itself comprised fifty items and was essentially a test of basic computational skills.

The work was carried out in the period from February to June 1974.   The evaluation of the test materials in Arithmetic and Reading was undertaken by the Research Services Unit of the Council.   The preparation of the video-tape and slide cassettes was undertaken by staff of Callendar Park College - one video-tape concentrated on a week in the life of children in a small two teacher rural school, the other on life in a three-stream town school.   The slide-tape programme set out to show something of the range of activities available to Primary 6 children in 1974 and to bring out the colourful nature of much of the work done.   The classroom observation and report on the schools was undertaken by a local headteacher seconded for this purpose by the authority.

It was agreed that a sample of approximately 500 pupils was sufficient for the purposes of the investigation and the Research Services Unit selected 20 classes (in 20 schools) from the 139 Primary 6 classes available in the county.   516 children in all were involved; 264 boys and 252 girls.

Although it was not felt possible to test any other subjects in the curriculum because of the difficulty of finding a common ground of basic knowledge and also because of the lack of standardised tests in these areas it was agreed that it was important to assess the work done in these subject areas. Accordingly a sub-sample of five classes was chosen from the twenty previously selected and the teachers asked to prepare dossiers of each child's work in all subjects over almost a term. It was stressed that the dossiers should contain examples only of ordinary classroom work and not specially prepared items. These dossiers were eventually used to provide materials for an exhibition of the work of pupils at various levels of ability.

I. THE SAMPLE OF PUPILS

The mean age of the pupils was 10 years 7 months. In general we had approximately 40 pupils in each monthly group from 10.2 to 11.1. However, features of the age sample were (a) a small group of 8 children less than 10.2 and (b) a similar group of 11 pupils aged 11.2 and above. Both of these groups it transpired later had anomalous results in the various tests. The younger group proved very able and the older group less able than average and presumably indicated groups advanced one year and retarded one year respectively. The average V.R.Q. of the groups was 97.2 (SD 12.7) but we were unable to check this against a figure for the county as a whole although we have no reason to doubt the representativeness of the sample. When we examined the mean V.R.Q.'s of the 20 classes we found considerable variations in the ability levels of the selected classes (See Table I).

TABLE I - Mean V.R.Q. Scores of Sample Classes

School	Mean V.R.Q.	S.D.	Number of pupils
A	90.6	22.2	5
B	101.9	10.8	24
C	97.8	15.0	9
D	89.8	13.2	8
E	98.3	15.5	17
F	87.6	17.7	8
G	96.3	16.0	26
H	95.6	8.3	36
I	90.0	6.3	30
J	95.3	9.0	33
K	93.6	12.0	28
L	103.2	9.8	39
M	101.6	10.0	26
N	105.8	8.5	30
O	101.0	12.7	31
P	94.1	14.3	32
Q	98.1	10.9	34
R	90.4	14.3	24
S	95.2	14.5	34
T	98.8	13.0	36

The mean V.R.Q.'s ranged from 87.6 to 105.8. These differences are no doubt a reflection of the wide variety of catchment areas from which the schools involved draw their intakes but these wide variations must be borne in mind when considering any between class analyses. Particular note, in this context, should be made of the extreme homogeneity of classes N and I (see column headed SD). The lower the value shown in this column the more homogeneous is the class in terms of ability. These two schools obviously drew pupils from very uniform areas but with very different social backgrounds.

2. THE READING TEST RESULTS

2.1   The mean Reading Quotient was 100.6 (SD 15.0) which corresponds very closely to the 1972 sample of Scottish children on which the norms of the Edinburgh Reading Test are based.

2.2   The data indicate that 29.3 per cent of the children were more than twelve months behind in reading vis-a-vis chronological age and 10.5 per cent were more than twenty-four months (two years) behind. On the other hand 33.9 per cent were more than twelve months ahead in reading age and 18.4 per cent two years ahead. These figures appear to indicate that problems of 'illiteracy' and 'semi-illiteracy' are much less serious here than in the English situation, as reported by the N.F.E.R. in a survey of "The Trend of Reading Standards" carried out in 1970 and published in 1972.

In that survey 'illiteracy' was defined as a retardation of reading age of 4 years and 'semi-illiteracy' as a retardation of reading age of 2 years. On this basis Start and Wells estimated 24% of their sample aged 11 as semi-illiterate and 9% as illiterate. The corresponding figures for Stirlingshire on this definition (although not on the same tests) were 10% and less than 1%. 1% of an age group corresponds to 900 children on a Scottish basis and therefore gives an estimate of perhaps 50,000 illiterate adults in Scotland. Such a figure serves to suggest caution in accepting estimates of much larger numbers published elsewhere which have possibly been extrapolated from English figures to a Scottish situation.

2.3   No significant difference in performance were found between boys and girls although boys showed a greater spread of scores or a greater variation in performance than the girls.

2.4   While wide variations in the reading performance of classes were found, the mean class quotients ranging from 88 to 111, we attributed most of these differences to the differences in catchment areas previously mentioned. Nevertheless they do show the wide variations which actually exist in schools.

2.5   Although the Edinburgh Reading Test provides five sub-scores based on Reading for Facts, Comprehension of Sequences, Retention of Main Ideas, Comprehension of Points of View and Vocabulary, which were designed to permit analysis of the relative strengths and weaknesses of individual pupils, we found little evidence that these sub-tests do in fact provide meaningful scores.   The inter-correlations of the sub-tests (none below 0.7) appear to indicate that the tests really provide only one measure and that pupils who score highly on one aspect of the test generally score highly on all the other aspects predicated in the sub-test structure.

3. THE ARITHMETIC TEST

3.1   The maximum mark was 50.   No child achieved 50 but one reached 49 while 4 children scored no marks at all.   The mean mark was 28.   The test was deliberately designed to be within the capabilities of primary 6 pupils and the items were such as could reasonably be handled by such children, in the opinion of the constructors (i.e., the Standards Committee).   As a consequence one would expect the distribution of marks to be highly skewed and this was indeed the case with 60% of the children having marks greater than 25, and 30% marks greater than 35.

FIGURE I -   Arithmetic Test Results for Individual Items

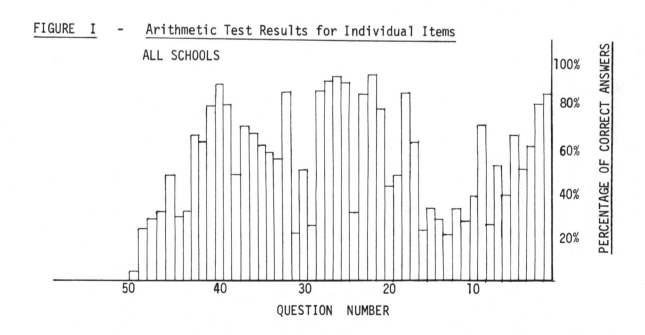

3.2   The performance of the sample on each of the 50 items is given in Figure I. Nine items mainly involving decimals or weights and measures were answered correctly by less than 30 per cent of the sample.   On the other hand eleven items involving mainly simple mechanical work or notation were answered correctly by more than 80 per cent of the sample.

3.3   No differences in performance were found between boys and girls.

3.4   Again there were wide variations in performance of the classes, the mean marks ranging from 18.7 to 40.9.   The average score of the best three classes was 38.2, that of the lowest three 19.5.

3.5   The test items could be grouped into various sub-sets measuring competence in various aspects of arithmetical skill (see Table 2).

TABLE   2   -   Summary of Responses to Items grouped by Arithmetical Content

Items	Sub-Set	No. of Questions in Sub-Set	Mean No. Correct	Mean Percentage Correct
1-5, 22, 23, 25, 26	Basic Rules	9	7.2	80
6-8	Fractions	3	1.3	43
9-13, 24	Decimals (Four Rules)	6	2.2	37
17-21	Money (Mechanical)	5	3.0	60
27, 28, 32-38	Notation	9	6.3	70
30, 39-43, 49, 50	Money Problems	8	4.6	58
44-48	Time and Speed	5	1.7	34
9-21, 24, 30, 38, 49, 50	All Decimals (Mechanical + Problems)	18	7.3	41
8, 17-21, 30, 39-43, 49, 50	All Money (Mechanical + Problems)	14	8.0	57
14-16, 29, 31	Length and Weight	5	1.3	26

The children, as a whole, proved most capable in dealing with items involving the basic arithmetical rules, notation and simple money sums.   On average approximately three quarters of such items were answered correctly by the sample while half of the children got all but one of them correct.   However, about 7% of the sample (35 children) got none of these items right.

The group were less successful with fractions and decimals answering approximately 40% of these correctly.   As compared with the 21% who got all the fraction questions correct only 5% answered the simple decimal items correctly.

The poorest performance was shown on items involving timetables, length and weight. The proportion of correct items was about 30% in these groups.   Few children (less than 15%) got all the items correct and a large number (45%) got none right.

3.6   Consideration of the results raised the possibility that, since the testing was carried out in February, some children might not have been given sufficient practice at that time in areas such as decimals, percentages etc.   We checked this by asking the class teachers to indicate which items in the test involved processes not reached by the majority of the class until later in the year and (b) which items were too advanced for the majority of the pupils.   The replies indicated some support for the view that some of the poor performance in certain areas, in particular Decimals, Time and Speed, Length and Weight, might have been due to unfamiliarity with the process involved on the part of some of the children.   Class teachers did show considerable divergence of opinion as to the appropriateness of some of the test items for primary 6 children.   On the other hand eleven of the twenty teachers indicated that none of the test items involved processes not covered by the majority of their class and eight indicated that none of the items was too difficult for the majority of their pupils.   Thus approximately half of the twenty teachers supported the view of the Standards Committee while the remainder disagreed to differing extents. To some extent these conflicting views probably reflect differences in ability levels among the classes under assessment.   However, in the absence of formal schemes of work, it is clear that no general consensus has emerged among teachers regarding standards of work to be expected at this level.   This divergence of views must be taken into account by any Education Authority in scrutinising work in its schools.

3.7   In order to bring out more clearly the details of the children's performance five sub-samples,of 25 children each,were selected from the original group. These pupils had test scores corresponding to ability levels varying from very able to poor and their performance in the various facets of Arithmetic is presented in Table 3.   If we label the groups   A to E those in groups A had marks close to 42 while those in group E were close to 11.

The characteristic performances shown by these groups are described in detail in order to show the strengths and weaknesses to be expected of children in the resultant score bands.   The groups are described in ascending order of accomplishment, beginning with group E.

TABLE 3 - Percentages of Correct Responses by Groups to Sub-sets of Arithmetical Items

Sub-Set of Items	GROUP				
	A	B	C	D	E
Basic Rules	97	93	88	76	53
Fractions	89	75	40	20	3
Decimals (Four Rules)	68	53	25	17	9
Money (Mechanical)	94	80	68	40	19
Notation	98	94	71	52	30
Money (Problems)	80	71	65	40	24
Time and Speed	71	44	27	8	2
Decimals (All)	73	57	39	19	9
Money (All)	85	74	65	39	21
Length and Weight	63	38	21	5	2

The performance of each group can be summarised as follows:

Group E

This group is at a level of ability which only 10 per cent of the sample failed to attain.   The average score of the pupils in this group was 11.   There were fifteen questions which no one in the group could answer and a further sixteen which were answered correctly by less than six of the group.   Only eleven questions were answered correctly by a majority of the group.   These items fall mainly into two of the sub-sets in Table 3, i.e., Basic Rules and Notation.   Only in 'Basic Rules' did the level of performance reach more than 50 per cent.   Inspection of the individual item performance indicates that the group could handle addition and subtraction better than multiplication and division but found decimal notation very difficult.   Performance on items involving fractions, decimals, time and speed was very poor indeed.

Group D

This group is at a level of ability which only 25 per cent of the sample failed to attain.   The average score of the pupils in this group was 19.   There were twenty-two items in the test which were answered correctly by less than six of the group.   On the other hand eighteen questions were answered correctly by a majority of the group.   Again these items, as for Group E, fall mainly into the two subsets 'Basic Rules' and 'Notation'. The level of performance in 'Basic Rules' was considerably better than for Group E, reaching 76 per cent. Multiplication by two figures, however, still caused some difficulty to more than half of the group. 'Notation' was handled by the group provided no decimal quantities were involved. Performance level in money reached 40 per cent but only some of the simpler bill items were handled satisfactorily. Overall performance in decimals, fractions and time and speed was still relatively poor, in no case exceeding 20 per cent.

Group C

This group represents the level of ability reached by the average child, i.e. by 50 per cent of the sample. The average score of the pupils in this group was 28. Only seventeen items in the test were answered correctly by less than eleven of the group. These items fell mainly into three sub-sets; 'Decimals (Four Rules)', 'Length and Weight' and 'Time and Speed'. Performance in these three areas, as a whole, was poor ranging from 21 per cent to 27 per cent. However, in most other areas the group showed a reasonable level of competence and particularly so in the case of 'Basic Rules' (88%), 'Notation' (71%) and 'Money' (65%).

Group B

This group is at a level of ability reached by the top 25 per cent of the sample. The average score of the group was 36. Only ten items were answered correctly by less than eleven of the group. On the other hand twenty-six of the items were answered correctly by over 80 per cent of this group. Only in the two sub-sets 'Length and Weight' (38%) and 'Time and Speed' (44%) did the level of performance fall below 50 per cent. 'Basic Rules', 'Fractions', 'Notation' and 'Money' were all at a high level of performance ranging from 71 per cent to 93 per cent. About half of the group could handle basic operations with decimals.

Group A

This group is at a level of ability reached only by the top 10 per cent of the sample. The average score of the group was 42. Only two items were answered incorrectly by more than half of the group. On the other hand thirty-six items were answered correctly by more than 80 per cent of the group. The competence of the group in most aspects of test content was very good. Only in 'Decimals (Four Rules)' (68%) and 'Length and Weight' (63%) did the level of performance fall below 70 per cent.

While all groups exhibited some competence in the application of the 'Basic Rules', 'Money' items were handled competently only by pupils at or above the average level of ability and 'Decimals' and 'Fractions' only by the top 25% of the sample. On the other hand 'Time and Speed', 'Length and Weight' items proved difficult for most pupils and only the A group could handle them competently,

The results taken as a whole indicate a need for a re-appraisal of the teaching of decimals, fractions, and weight and measures to Primary 6 children, with a view to improving performance in these areas.

3.8   On the basis of the results, we were able to produce a table of norms for arithmetical attainment which can be used as a basis for relating other Primary 6 children to the standards achieved by Stirlingshire pupils in February 1974 or indeed for comparisons in future years if required.

4. COMPARISONS ACROSS SUBJECTS

Our results show that in general pupils who did well on one test did well on the others.

However, one interesting finding in comparisons of classes was that while the relative order was reasonably similar, one class was ranked fifth in Reading and eighth in Arithmetic while another was ranked twelfth in Reading but second in Arithmetic.

One can only conjecture whether such differences are to be attributed to teacher's degree of enthusiasm for each subject - or was one subject not being taught competently or what?   The answers to such questions were however not part of our remit and cannot be dealt with here but they do pose problems for headteachers and advisers and must not be ignored.

In this article I have deliberately restricted my comments to the work undertaken by the Research Services Unit of the Council which was largely concerned with evaluation of basic skills in two subject areas.   However, it would be inappropriate not to refer again to the work carried out by Callendar Park College of Education on the production of the slide-tape and video-tape programmes and to the observational work of the Co-ordinator of the project.   These additional materials provide a wealth of background information and detail about life as it is in a primary 6 classroom today and provide a fabric against which to judge the picture of basic skills drawn above.

Mention should also be made of the assessment of the work contained in the school dossiers.   The assessment was carried out by panels of experienced teachers and involved grading the work of the pupils concerned in order of merit in various content areas such as Creative Writing and Art.

Having agreed an order of merit, several scripts were extracted around points corresponding to the tenth, twenty-fifth, fiftieth, seventy-fifth and ninetieth percentile levels.   These selected scripts then served as standards in each of the content areas which could be exhibited to teachers, parents and others interested in education and against which the work of other pupils at the same stage of education could be judged.

The display of work and its association with the report of survey results apparently evoked a thoughtful and favourable response from the teachers in the county and has led to renewed efforts to appraise the curriculum especially in defining priorities and appropriate emphases for certain groups of children.

MEASURING CHANGE IN LONGITUDINAL STUDIES AND THE ESTABLISHMENT OF CONFIDENCE INTERVALS

H. GIESEN

Abstract - A description is given of the research design
for a longitudinal study of student counselling
undertaken initially during the late secondary
stage and subsequently in the earlier stages of
university education.   The effects of altera-
tions in educational circumstances and the
practical constraints on repeated longitudinal
studies are discussed.   Some statistical
problems relating to difference scores are considered and certain methods for examining these
are illustrated.

THE OBJECTIVES OF OUR STUDY

First, I would like to introduce the objectives of the research project of a team at the Deutschen Institut für Internationale Pädagogische Forschung in Frankfurt. The title of the project is: "Pilot study to survey and analyse educational and vocational careers of secondary school pupils' (Bartenwerfer & Giesen 1973, 1974, 1975).   The purpose of the study is to develop and check a counselling test battery designed for two phases of education in schools.   Counselling should first take place on transition from the 11th to the 12th grade in secondary schools; in the German school system this would be about two years before the end of this educational phase.   The second point of time for counselling is planned during studies at university in the second to fourth term.   In order to research these goals the study is based on two major requirements:

i.   Epochal changes in educational conditions and on the part of the students are to be included as a trend in order not to endanger the app-lication of results in practical counselling situations.   Therefore, repeatedly, new generations of pupils are included in the study.

ii.   The study is to accompany education and thus is to directly en-compass the crucial stages of an educational career in its state and conseq-uences.   Therefore, at certain intervals, the pupils will be tested for a post study.   An important stage in education for all pupils tested is

about two and a half years after the first test.   At this time, most of
them have finished secondary school with their matriculation and must have
decided on their further education.   The second to third term of studies
at university is another important stage in students' educational careers.
At this point students find it difficult to solve problems regarding their
studies and to a certain degree, this is reflected in quitting the course
or in changing courses.   A further crucial stage is reached in some
subjects with the intermediate examinations.   In these subjects intermediate examinations are very often more important for the successful conclusion of studies than the finals.   In subjects without intermediate
examinations success is mostly not recognizable until the final examinations.
About 20 to 30% of the pupils at school in the first study will not begin
the third educational phase.   They will mostly finish a shorter spell of
education which is related to a certain profession.   This group should be
post-studied after the transition into the profession selected.

This research project has been aided by the Federal Minister of Education and Science
since 1972.   Up to now, the work has concentrated on the development and internal
analysis of the counselling test battery and on the appraisal of the initial data.
During the years to come research work will concentrate on method and the empirical
problems of predicting the intermediate and final criteria for success in educational branches after completion of secondary schools.   Another crucial point in
the research will arise from the second detailed study of students.   In this
counselling test battery parts of the battery from the first study will be used
again as far as they seem important at this point of time to forecast the successful
completion of studies.   In addition, new tests will be used to measure those
prognostic traits which now show up.   This will allow for the comparison of
constancies and changes in the personality structure of the majority of the students
tested in relation to age, the passage of time and specific educational conditions.
The purpose of the research design can be summarized as follows: To assess the
uncertainty of prognosis for success in education following secondary school, in
relation to duration of prognosis and time of measurement and under due consideration
of epochal trends.

DETAILS OF RESEARCH DESIGN AND SAMPLES

Up to now samples of the cohorts of 1972, 1973 and 1974 have been tested; this year
a sample of the generation of 1976 pupils will follow (Table I).   The samples are
random samples of pupils from the 11th grade attending Gymnasiums in states of the
Federal Republic.   The 1972 sample was smaller and does not represent all Federal
States.   This sample is considered as a pre-study in which the organizational

problems of a data survey and data evaluation as well as the criteria of test construction can be checked. The test battery for the secondary pupils is comprised of individual tests and lasts for about five hours. It includes biographical data, intelligence and knowledge tests and marks at school, personality questionaires as well as attitude and interest inventories and questions about studies and professional desires. Most tests were modified and analysed for the 1972 administration according to the rules of classical test theory.

The test battery for university students takes about three hours and can be given in small groups. Further characteristics of the group are obtained from a written questionaire in which the students tested are requested to state everything relevant to their education which has occurred since the first survey. By extensive and expensive measures a high access rate and willingness to cooperate has been achieved. The refusal quotas for samples in the first studies vary between 3.6 and 5.5 %. After one year it was 1.8 %. For the most part the remaining refusals among the samples are not maintained, so that the drop-out does not accumulate.

TABLE 1   -   Schedule and Sample Size

Time of Measurement	Cohort			
	1972	1973	1974	1976
1972	$N = 500$			
1973	$N = 492$	$N = 1000$		
1974			$N = 1000$	
1975	$N = 492$			
1976	$N_1 = 219$	$N = ?$		$N = 1000$

ADVANTAGES AND DIFFICULTIES OF LONGITUDINAL STUDIES

There is no doubt that the repeated use of longitudinal experimental designs is the best method to measure change in the course of time.   This not only applies to the presentation and interpretation of developmental curves but also to the estimation and interpretation of relationships between individual differences covering certain life spans (e.g., Nunnally 1973).   The problems of cross-section designs are mainly those of comparability of samples, the identity in meaning of measurements from the samples, and the confounding of age and generation at the time of the measurement.   For the research in question, the comparability of samples is one obstacle.   This applies to all studies in which the chronological age is not a characteristic of the cohort but a different criterion which exercises a selective influence on the cohort in the course of time.   The training effect and the con-founding of a genetically based differentiation of behavioural criteria with cumul-ative interaction effects between organismic variables and environmental conditions are considered to be problems of a single longitudinal study.   Experimental designs which combine cross-section designs with short longitudinal designs do not seem suitable to define the correlations between individual differences over longer periods of time (e.g., Schaie 1965; Baltes 1968).   They combine the disadvantages of both methods and do not allow a forecast over and above the period of the long-itudinal studies.   As far as the results are concerned, successively starting longitudinal studies of large samples over long periods of time are therefore the optimum.

On the other hand, in longitudinal studies difficulties can be found which are caused by the duration and high cost of the design (e.g., Wall and Williams 1970).   For example, in the course of time hypotheses, experimental designs, test batteries and evaluation possibilities change.   These changes may be subsequent to the investigator's experience and results or to new understandings in the literature. In 1972 we had to make up our minds either to start the first survey as soon as possible or to postpone it in order to try out alternative construction models for the tests.   In the interest of our sponsor and to ensure continuity of finding we relied on the construction principles of classical test theory.   As a second example of the difficulties arising from the experimental design I would like to mention environmental influences which make the original questions unnecessary or suspect.   During the last years in the Federal Republic the entry qualifications for universities became more and more rigid.   Many pupils of secondary schools could not study those subjects at universities which they actually wanted because they did not reach the average of marks necessary in their leaving certificate from secondary schools.   They chose different educational careers or they studied other subjects and dropped those subjects after some time, once they got a place

in the subject they desired.   This outside control seems to decrease the efficiency of an individual counselling.   The transfer of the empirical results to a
following generation not subject to the same outside influences will become dubious.
It should be noted that:-

i.   The samples mentioned above are selected in the course of their
educational career according to criteria for which validity has to be
checked in regard to a successful educational career;

ii.   The sub-groups,which are defined according to subjects studied and
other educational objectives, differ in criteria which directly or indirectly are subsequent to the entry qualifications of university.

THE PROBLEMS OF MEASURING CHANGE

Apart from these problems of time and cost, at least since 1963, experts are
familiar with a further methodical problem (Harris, 1963): the measurement of
change.   This problem stems from the fact that in a longitudinal study at least
two data surveys of identical samples at a defined interval are necessary.
Statistics for measuring change must correspond to this design.   Significant
measuring operations can only be achieved if the values of the variables measured
can change quantitatively within the defined period of time and when the quality of
the variables are kept constant.   Hardly anyone will be satisfied by simply
stating a change.

It seems more interesting to find out the reasons for these changes in general, or
the conditions for different quantities of change, or the direction of change in
different sub-groups of the tested sample.   In an example from the literature and
from my own empirical results, I would like to point out some difficulties arising
in this respect.

Amelang and Hoppensack (1975) studied students from five different courses of studies
at an interval of about five years with the same tests in regard to ability,
personality and interests.   They compared the scores of the five groups at both
times of measurement with a 2 x 5 analysis of variance and, generally, found a
decrease in the amount of interest regarding the subjects of their studies.   For
instance, the interest of biologists for biology, or of mathematicians for mathematics decreased.   They summarized the findings as follows: "Originally relatively
significant interests, which probably played a role in the choice of the respective
subject, obviously decreased by extensive scientific study of this subject."

This summary seems dubious in consideration of the following.   Simply put, change is defined as the difference between the test scores at the first and the second time of measurement.   Such a change in score depends on the initial score.   The further an initial score is deviant from the mean of the total sample the greater the probability that it will change towards this mean.   The error concept of classical test theory, the ceiling effect of a test and the regression effect serve as explanation for this negative relationship between change and initial score (Helmreich, 1975).

It is hardly ever possible to isolate these effects; the regression effect, however, can be in effect even if the test scores are undistorted and free of error.   The difficulties arising from this phenomenon are irrelevant when analysing the change of the test values of a sample from one time of measurement to another.   The problem is only relevant when in addition to the time of measurement another variable has to be taken into account.   It is particularly difficult if the sub-groups already differ at the time of the first measurement.   The principle is that different initial scores imply different final scores.   The interaction effect is over-estimated because the factor 'time of measurement' and the other factors correlate (Helmreich, 1975).

Only if the results are completely opposite to the regression effect, is the inter-action not due to the regression effect, but to a certain treatment.   In this case, a sub-group with high initial scores must achieve an increase in their scores and another group with low initial scores must achieve a decrease.   The results of Amelang and Hoppensack (1975) do not meet these requirements and it cannot be decided whether their interpretation is correct or whether it is a statistical artefact.

In order to illustrate these problems, I would like to refer to my own studies. From the study, which has not yet been quite completed, covering the students of the 1972 samples I have taken two sub-groups: i.e.,

(A)   Students of engineering, mathematics and natural science,   and

(B)   Students of arts and languages.

I chose the following variables: for intelligence the sub-test arithmetical problems (RA) from the IST 70 by Amthauer (1971), for interests three sub-tests from the DIT by Todt (1967), namely engineering and exact natural science (TN), mathematics (MA) and literature and language (LS).   In Table 2 the sample sizes, the means and the standard deviations of both sub-groups as well as the significances of differ-ences between the groups and the times of measurement for each variable are given separately.

TABLE 2   -   <u>Means and Standard Deviations of Four Variables in Two Study</u>
<u>Groups and Two Times of Measurement</u>

IST-RA

	N_A		N_B		ρ
	$\bar{x}$	S	$\bar{x}$	S	
T_1	11.5	3.5	10.6	3.8	-
T_2	12.7	3.4	11.4	3.7	x
ρ	xx		x		

DIT-TN

	N_A		N_B		ρ
	$\bar{x}$	S	$\bar{x}$	S	
T_1	37.9	10.1	28.8	9.0	xx
T_2	35.1	9.8	27.6	9.5	xx
ρ	xx		-		

DIT-MA

	N_A		N_B		ρ
	$\bar{x}$	S	$\bar{x}$	S	
T_1	37.5	9.3	28.9	10.1	xx
T_2	34.7	10.4	26.7	9.8	xx
ρ	xx		x		

DIT-LS

	N_A		N_B		ρ
	$\bar{x}$	S	$\bar{x}$	S	
T_1	36.7	7.9	43.1	7.6	xx
T_2	34.3	9.4	43.4	6.4	xx
ρ	xx		-		

N_A = 61 (Engineering, Mathematics and Natural Science)
N_B = 63 (Arts and Languages)
T_1 = First Time of Measurement (1972/3)
T_2 = Second Time of Measurement (1976)
ρ = Probable Error; xx $\leqslant$ 0.01; x < 0.05

All variables within the groups were normally distributed and, with one exception, the variances were homogeneous. The t-test for independent samples was used for testing the differences of the means between the groups; between the times of measurement the t-test for dependent samples was used. In the intelligence RA subtest, Group (A) at the second time of measurement achieved higher values; both groups achieved higher values after an interval of three years. In all three interest tests the groups differed considerably at the two times of measurement; but in Group (A) only all three areas of interest decreased from the first to the second time of measurement. For the interest tests TN and MA, Group (A) was significantly above the total mean for all students; for the LS test it was below the total mean. Interaction effects were not figured out. These results, however, suggest an interpretation along the same lines as Amelang and Hoppensack (1975): that the interests of engineers, mathematicians and natural scientists decrease after the start of their studies in those areas related to their studies.

In order to take the regression effect into consideration, we made a linear transformation of the scores of the first time of measurement.

The formula is as follows:

$$\widehat{X_1} = r_{tt} (X_1 - \overline{X}) + \overline{X}$$

$\widehat{X_1}$ = estimated score at first time of measurement

X_1 = observed score at first time of measurement

$\overline{X}$ = mean of all students (N = 208)

r_{tt} = coefficient of reliability

For the coefficient of reliability we have used two different estimates (Lienert, 1967):

(i.)   A coefficient of consistency following a formula of Gulliksen, which is equivalent to the Kuder-Richardson-formula 20 and which states the measurement accuracy of the tests.

(ii.)   The retest-coefficient between the first and the second time of measurement which additionally takes into account the instability of the characteristic under assessment.

The coefficients gained from the data of all students are given for all four tests in Table 3.

TABLE 3 - Coefficients of Consistency and Retest-Coefficients After Three Years of one Intelligence Test and Three Interest Tests with Students

	IST-RA	DIT-TN	DIT-MA	DIT-LS
Consistency N = 218	0.76	0.92	0.93	0.86
Retest-Reliability N = 208	0.74	0.64	0.77	0.71

Next, we computed the comparisons of means for each student group and each variable between the estimated scores derived with coefficients (i) and (ii) and the actual scores at the second time of measurement (B), Table 4 gives the exact t-value. As a comparison, the exact t-values for the comparisons of means of the observed scores have been included. Except for minor deviations the significance values of the three computations regarding the mathematics sub-test coincide. As far as the three interest tests are concerned, some dramatic changes can be observed. Regarding the student group of engineers, mathematicians and natural scientists the differences between the two times of measurement in those areas related to their studies become unimportant. However, the significance of the differences regarding areas unrelated to their studies increases in both groups. What is the proper answer to our question then? I would like to leave it open.

TABLE 4 - Significance of Means Between Two Times of Measurement (A & B) and Two
Groups of Students (N1 and N2)
(Exact T-Values from T > 1.96)

		1ST-RA	DIT-TN	DIT-MA	DIT-LS
Observed Scores	N1 A v B	3.59	2.58	2.84	3.46
	N2 A v B	2.16	-	2.50	-
Estimated Score (i) V Observed Score (B)	N1	4.27	2.21	2.49	4.24
	N2	2.07	-	2.88	-
Estimated Score (ii) V Observed Score (B)	N1	4.32	-	-	4.83
	N2	2.05	2.22	3.63	-

THE PROBLEM OF ERROR MEASUREMENT AND CONFIDENCE INTERVALS

Finally, I would like to mention the problem of error measurement and confidence intervals in regard to our study. Our statistical knowledge for the design of the study was sufficient to convince our client that we needed random samples to answer our questions. The classical methods of statistical interference are based on random samples in which each and every element of a population can be included independently of others and with equal probability.

These two assumptions do not apply to probability sampling or to stratified sampling (Hays, 1963). As mentioned above, we exercised great care to limit the drop-out rate to a minimum in order to avoid a systematic distortion of the random sample. According to the law of large numbers, closely allied to the Tchebycheff-inequality, and with the central limit theorem, the size of a sample can be defined in order to achieve a certain accuracy in estimates of the population parameters. According to the maximum likelihood principle with sample statistics a range of values (the confidence interval) can be specified which covers the true value of the population with high probability. Each estimate of population parameters from sample statistics is subject to errors of measurement. This also applies to standard-isation values, which actually are not available as parameters, but as estimates from sample statistics. For the expected value and for the standard deviation of estimated standardisation values Huber (1973) has given confidence intervals relating to the sample size. He could show that only standardisation samples above 500 could deliver practicable approximations to the size requested of the standardisation values.

The size of our annual sample of N = 1000 meets these requirements. The literature and our own results, however, show that there is more than one pupil population of secondary schools, and more than one successfully completed subject of study. The variable 'sex' alone or the different areas of study compel us to make separate analyses. We therefore hope that the differences in generation between the cohorts are minor so that the accuracy of the estimate of sub-sample statistics can be increased by pooling sub-groups of the cohort.

We are familiar, from classical test theory, with the fact that not only estim-ates of population parameters, but that also individual scores are subject to errors of measurement. False decisions can be the result of two kinds of error when at the point of the decision on the classification both errors are significant. The formula for the standard error of measurement for standardised scores in the popul-ation is as follows:

$$\sigma_e = K \sqrt{(1 - P_{tt})}$$

K is the desired standard deviation for the standardised test. Only statistics with an error are available for K and P_{tt}. In order to secure the estimate of reliability P_{tt} at least to the first decimal digit, the empirical coefficient of reliability must be gained from a sample of N > 400 (Huber, 1973).

As far as measuring changes is concerned, the problem of the error of measurement has led to desperate attempts to correct it. The problems arise from the fact that the reliability of change values tend towards zero the nearer the estimates of consistency and the retest-reliabilities are. This can easily be seen from the following formula:

$$r_D = \frac{r_{11} - r_{12}}{1 - r_{12}}$$

r_D = reliability of the difference values

r_{11} = estimate of consistency at the first time of measurement

r_{12} = retest reliability

This formula only applies if the variance and the reliability of the measurements are equivalent at both times of measurement. It must be assumed that changes can only be reliably measured if, measured against the accuracy of the test, a major fluctuation of characteristics in the course of time has taken place.

Lord (1963) and McNemar (1958) have developed the best-known correction methods for the estimate of difference values which are exempt from their errors of measurement. Helmreich (1975) discussed these correction methods and other similar suggestions in detail in his dissertation. He concludes that from a pragmatic point of view they are only of little value, especially since hardly any practical examples can be found in the literature.

REFERENCES

AMELANG, M. and HOPPENSACK, Th. (1975). Persönlichkeitsstruktur und Studienerfolg. Hamburg: Unveröffentlichter Zwischenbericht.

AMTHAUER, R. (1971). Intelligenz-Struktur-Test I-S-T 70. Göttingen: Hogrefe.

BALTES, P.B. (1968). Longitudinal and cross-sectional sequences in the study of age and generation effects. Human Development 11, 145-171.

BARTENWERFER, H. and GIESEN, H. (1973, 1974, 1975). Pilotstudie über die Beobachtung und Analyse von Bildungslebensläufen. Berichte-über die Arbeiten des ersten, zweiten und dritten Projektjahres. Frankfurt: Deutsches Institut für Internationale Pädagogische Forschung.

HARRIS, C.W. (Ed.) (1963). Problems in measuring change. Madison: University of Wisconsin Press.

HAYS, W.L. (1963). Statistics for psychologists. New York: Holt, Rinehart & Winston.

HELMREICH, R. (1975). Strategien zur Auswertung von Längsschnittdaten. Konstanz: Unveröffentlichte Dissertation.

HUBER, H.P. (1973). Psychometrische Einzelfalldiagnostik. Weinheim: Beltz.

LIENERT, G.A. (1967). Testaufbau und Testanalyse. Weinheim: Beltz.

LORD, F.M. (1963). Elementary models for measuring change. In: HARRIS, C.W. (Ed.). Problems in measuring change. Madison: University of Wisconsin Press.

McNEMAR, Q. (1958). On growth measurement. Educational and Psychological Measurement 18, 47-55.

NUNNALLY,J.C. (1973). Research strategies and measurement methods for investigating human development. In: NESSELROADE, J.R. and REESE, H.W. (Eds.). Life-span developmental psychology. New York: Academic Press 87-109.

SCHAIE, K.W. (1965). A general model for the study of developmental problems. Psychological Bulletin 64, 92-107.

TODT, E. (1967). Differentieller-Interessen-Test. Bern: Huber.

WALL, W.D. and WILLIAMS, H.L. (1970). Longitudinal studies and the social sciences. London: Heinemann.

HOW TO STRUCTURE AND MEASURE EDUCATIONAL OBJECTIVES IN PERIODIC SURVEYS

J. CARDINET & Y. TOURNEUR

Abstract - Periodic surveys require tests of a different
nature from the usual ones, as their judgement
is collective rather than individual. The
questions become the objects to be studied and
the pupils represent the instruments of this
study. We need a better knowledge of the
sources of difficulty that are present in the
questions. Surveys can also help us structure
the domain of educational objectives.

INTRODUCTION

It is hoped that a methodology for conducting national surveys designed to measure the evolution of scholastic attainments will emerge from our discussions. We wish to examine a particular stage of this general methodology: that of the development of instruments. We put forward two ideas:

- one very general idea: the formulation of test questions depends directly on the purpose that the test is intended to achieve. In the present case, it is the school system, rather than individual pupils, that is under study.

- a more specific idea: the study of the factors determining the difficulty of problems is a theoretical and practical question of vital interest for the development of educational practice. One must determine the underlying structure of the educational objectives in order to know what one is measuring.

(We wish to thank L. Allal and J. Brun for their remarks and suggestions, which were very helpful to us in preparing this text.)

We develop these ideas in the two parts of the report as follows:

In Part One, we present a three-dimensional model of the data collected by periodic surveys.

First, we show that these three dimensions (persons, activities, conditions) have symmetrical roles.

As a result, we can transpose the conventional model of aptitude tests to the design of tests of other kinds.

We consider the conclusions that may be drawn from this principle in order to adapt survey tests to their specific purpose.

In Part Two, we try to discover how to stratify an educational field in order to draw valid samples of questions from it.

First, we propose a choice of scientifically elaborated constructs.

These scientific concepts may then turn the survey into a project of basic research, with the test structure embodying the factors to be monitored.

Statistical methods are available for estimating the effects of the factors introduced and for validating the hierarchies of objectives postulated at the start.

In conclusion, we discuss the place of studies of this kind in the whole scientific approach to the study of education.

PART ONE: ADAPTING THE QUESTIONS TO THE OBJECTIVES OF THE SURVEY

1.1. To define the various possible types of test, bring out the symmetry of the data.

1.1.1. Tests supply information which can be represented in the three dimensions of persons, activities and conditions.

These are characteristics that are necessarily present in each assessment situation. In an examination or test, certain students are given activities to perform, and their performance is affected by the examination conditions.

Each dimension may be structured further:

- On the <u>persons dimension</u>, the pupils may belong to classes and the classes to schools etc. (i.e., the pupils are nested in classes and the classes in schools). The pupils may also be divided into groups which are <u>crossed</u> with those above: sex or socio-economic background, for example.

- On the <u>activities dimension</u>, the questions may relate to different chapters (i.e., they are <u>nested</u> in chapters), or they may correspond to definite levels of complexity (which thus form a facet <u>crossed</u> with that of questions).

- On the <u>conditions dimension</u>, a whole series of situational characteristics may be taken into account in accordance with nested or crossed designs. How much time is allowed for the test? Who gives the instructions or asks the questions? What time of day, or what day of the week, is chosen for the test? At what stage in the pupils' learning process does the examination occur? In what year is the survey conducted? Each of these questions opens up a series of possibilities which constitute as many 'facets' in structuring all the possible observations.

The cube in Figure 1 illustrates the way in which the various data facets are arranged. In fact, it constitutes a concise representation of any set of observations. Other facets (crossed or nested) can be added to those represented, for example, various treatments:

FIGURE I - <u>Data Facets in a Typical Observation Design</u>

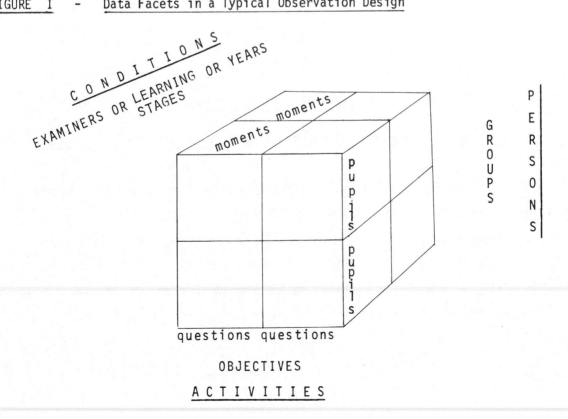

OBJECTIVES

<u>A C T I V I T I E S</u>

- Any variable that can be considered as a set of treatments applied to independent groups will appear on the persons dimension, with the subjects nested in treatments.

- Treatments applied to a group with repeated measurement will appear on one of the other two dimensions. If the treatments are simultaneous, they will be located on the activities dimension, the pupils being crossed both with the treatments and with the activities. If the treatments are consecutive, they will appear on the conditions dimension (the pupils being crossed with the treatment as before).

A representation of this type is convenient for examining the various possible observation designs and analysing the biases specific to each.

     1.1.2.   Different types of tests are distinguished by their allocation to three types of facets; i.e., differentiation facets, generalisation facets and fixed facets.

The Three types of Facets

The arrangement of the data into crossed and nested facets, as illustrated in Figure I, constitutes an observation design. In order to effect a measurement, the problem must be narrowed down further and a measurement design established; all facets under investigation being partitioned into the three categories described as follows:

- A differentiation facet represents the 'objects under study'. Usually, in the assessment of scholastic attainment the objects under study are the pupils, but one can conceive of other objects. The word "differentiation" is used because measuring objects means separating them into a series of classes of equivalence, and to do so one must be able to discern differences between them.

- A generalisation facet corresponds to a set of randomly chosen observational conditions. Normally, the questions constitute a generalisation facet (when the reliability of a test is calculated by comparing the results of two parallel forms, for instance). The moments (time of testing) may also constitute a generalisation facet (if the reliability of a test is calculated by administering the test twice in the same week). It is also possible to have the pupils' essays evaluated by several judges (to determine the reliability of the grading). In each case, the intention is to formulate a 'general' judgement on the pupil, irrespective of the particular questions, moments and judges. We aim at generalising about these conditions by considering that the particular sample of conditions we have used is representative of the universe of possible conditions.

- A facet is _fixed_ when the instruments or conditions used exhaust the universe considered and we can no longer talk of a choice of sample or, consequently, of sample fluctuations.   For example, if an inquiry is conducted in Belgium, France and Switzerland, no other French-speaking European country can be found to which the results can be generalised.   Similarly, if we measure attainments before and after the learning process, these are two quite definite stages and we cannot speak of a sample of stages.   Nor can inquiries which are conducted every year or at regular intervals be regarded as random investigations.

Combinations of these three types of facet

There is no necessity to treat pupils only as a facet of differentiation.   In developing a curriculum, one inevitably differentiates the levels of difficulty of the objectives and the moments at which the objectives are mastered (stages of learning).   In this case, the pupils are the instruments used for the study of the objectives and of the stages.

The symmetry of the cube means that any facet can play the same role as any other, so that all combinations of differentiation and generalisation are theoretically possible.   We may wish to differentiate questions, years, etc. by generalising over some, or all, of the other facets or by fixing some of them.   The usual purpose of a survey test, for example, is to differentiate the levels of success attained for each of the objectives, whilst at the same time generalising over questions within objectives and also over pupils and moments (within a particular stage of learning).

Just as we can generalise over several facets at once, we can also differentiate along several dimensions at the same time.   A survey test designed to detect the differential mastery of objectives over a period of time must be capable of distinguishing between the success on various objectives (facet O), success during various years (facet Y) and success on certain objectives in certain years (interaction OxY).

It is even possible to differentiate singly the interaction of certain facets: for example, the purpose of a professional interest test is to reveal motivational polarities, disregarding differences in the general level of interest of individuals or in the social prestige that attaches to the professions concerned.

If we consider all the possible sources of variation (main effects and interact-actions) and all the conceivable permutations of variances attributable to differentiation, generalisation and fixed facets, we find that the number of possibilities is vast.   Each practical problem doubtless reveals a particular combination.   The only restrictions are the following: there must always be differentiation variance (corresponding to what we are measuring) and at least one second source of variance (that of the measuring instruments).   If this second variance is fixed, the model makes no provision for error of measurement. An assertion of a scientific nature assumes at least one source of generalisation variance.

A general typology of tests cannot be formulated exhaustively.   Even so, the fact of taking relevant variances into account in each case and dividing them into differentiation, generalisation and fixed variances constitutes a general methodology.   We shall now take a closer look at the ways in which this methodology can be applied to typical survey tests.

1.2   To define the specificity of survey tests, investigate the differentiations which they imply.

1.2.1.   Periodic surveys differentiate activities, years, schools, etc. rather than pupils.

With the results of a survey, one can establish which items of knowledge have or have not been assimilated.   The purpose is to focus on the success rate of the various objectives or questions.   The object under study is the school system, and the pupil samples are selected in order to reveal the level of operation of this system.   No decisions about individuals are taken on the basis of this information.

In conducting periodic surveys, we must not overlook the temporal dimension. We must know which objectives are attained in relation to successive years.   Differentiation in this case relates simultaneously to the objectives, the years and their interaction.

In the case of international surveys of the IEA type, there is a third purpose in addition to the above.   This is to compare the performances of various teaching systems defined in terms of country, academic structures etc.   Here, differentiation relates to groups.

1.2.2.   The method used for devising tests which classify pupils can be transposed to tests which classify questions.

Classical methodology for ability tests

If we differentiate the pupils, generalisation relates to the questions: in other words, we consider that the problems chosen constitute a random sample of all problems of this type.

The error of generalisation associated with a question may be estimated as the difference between the student's result for that question and the average result he obtains on all the questions selected.   The variance of generalisation errors is the variance of these deviations, i.e., the within-row variance (if a row represents a pupil and a column a question).   It has two components: between-column variance (due to the differences in difficulty between one question and another) and the pupil-question interaction variance.

The experimental design is very simply illustrated in Figure 2A.   The first circle is the pupils facet (E), the second is the questions facet (Q), and the overlapping area represents the interaction QE.   The absolute error of gener-alisation is dependent on the Q and QE variance, as we have seen.   On the other hand, the relative error depends solely on the QE variance.

FIGURE 2 -   Measurement Designs to Differentiate:

A. the pupils   B. the questions

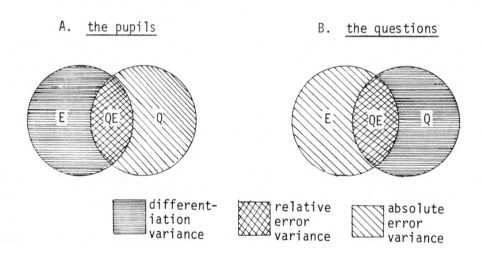

In these diagrams, each circle represents the variance of a facet.   It encompa-sses the sources of variance responsible for the differences between the levels of the facet.

The logical consequences of this design (type A, for pupil classification) are easy to draw.   To reduce the relative error, we reduce QE as far as possible by choosing a sample of highly correlated questions.   If we also wish to reduce the absolute error, we must reduce Q by selecting questions of the same average difficulty. Thus, we shall retain very homogeneous questions. This is the principle of the conventional methods of item analysis.

Simple transposition of this methodology

If we wish to differentiate the questions, our generalisation will relate to the pupils: in other words we shall estimate, on the basis of the observed sample, the mean of the population of all pupils. The absolute generalisation error now corresponds to the within-column variance (between-row variance and interaction). The experimental design is illustrated schematically in Figure 2B.

The conclusion to be drawn is that, in order to reduce the relative errors, we must reduce the QE variance as far as possible, that is to say limit the differences of pupils' reactions to a single question by selecting a group of pupils of homogeneous background. If we also wish to reduce the variance of absolute error we must try to reduce the variance E by choosing a sample of pupils of the same standard of ability.

Further extension using generalisability theory

The procedure described above is not easy to apply. Moreover, there is a risk of restricting unduly the population of pupils under study. (Item analysis is subject to a similar risk where the questions are concerned.) The introduction of other facets into the data makes the principle of transposition more interesting. Generalisability theory (Cronbach, Gleser, Nanda, Rajaratnam, 1972) may then suggest new procedures, as we shall see in applying it to the data of the cube in Figure I (conserving the facets E, G, Q, O, M, and S, for pupils, groups, questions, objectives, moments and stages, respectively).

We start by determining, as above, the sources of generalisation error when we wish to differentiate the objectives. Figure 3 enables us to locate them. The six facets (nested and crossed) enable us to analyse 26 sources of variation. Only the dotted area corresponds to differentiation variance in the case of a simple survey test aiming at distinguishing the objectives that have and have not been attained. The other 25 areas represent sources of absolute error which must be minimised. The relative error, corresponding to the various portions of the circle O outside the dotted area, comprises 17 sources of variation. We shall now examine the indications that can be drawn from this diagram, first for the factors crossed with the objectives and afterwards for the questions nested in the objectives facet.

There are two crossed facets, i.e., the minor facets (moments and pupils) on which intervention is virtually impossible; the moments and the pupils are assumed to be simply chosen at random.   The major facets (stages and groups), on the other hand, could be manipulated in order to reduce generalisation errors.   The absolute error would diminish if the range of stages and groups taken into consideration were reduced.   For example, we could consider only the last two years of compulsory schooling (instead of a longer study cycle) and exclude the pupils in special classes.   (It is clear that what we gain in accuracy we shall lose in generality, but there may be good reasons for making this choice.)

To reduce the relative error we must diminish the interactions OS, OG and OSG. By studying the averages of the groups and years in relation to the objectives we shall perhaps discover a source of heterogeneity that could be reduced.   For example, let us suppose that one group has not studied the same learning objectives as the others (OG interaction) or does not approach them at the same time (OS interaction): we may either exclude this group from the survey and so achieve greater accuracy, or we may consider it in isolation in order to discover what distinguishes it from the others.

The questions facet nested in the objectives facet affects the generalisation error in two ways.   Firstly, its own variance (heterogeneity in the difficulty of questions) is added to the variance of objectives and thus constitutes a source of error.   We must, therefore, devise the questions with sufficient precision to ensure that the fluctuations of difficulty of the items can be kept in controlled limits within a single objective.   We shall go into this point more thoroughly in Part 2.   Secondly, the variance of interaction of questions with stages or groups (OQS, OQG, OQSG) may reveal variations in the training given to one group or another at one stage or another.   Unless we deliberately attempt to detect these differences, we must select the questions which highlight the type of knowledge we are really seeking.

Periodic surveys should differentiate objectives and periods simultaneously. They should also differentiate groups, if it is desired to compare school systems. There would still remain three facets of generalisation to which the above type of reasoning would continue to apply.

FIGURE 3 — <u>The Components of Variance Determined by the Data Facets of Figure I</u>

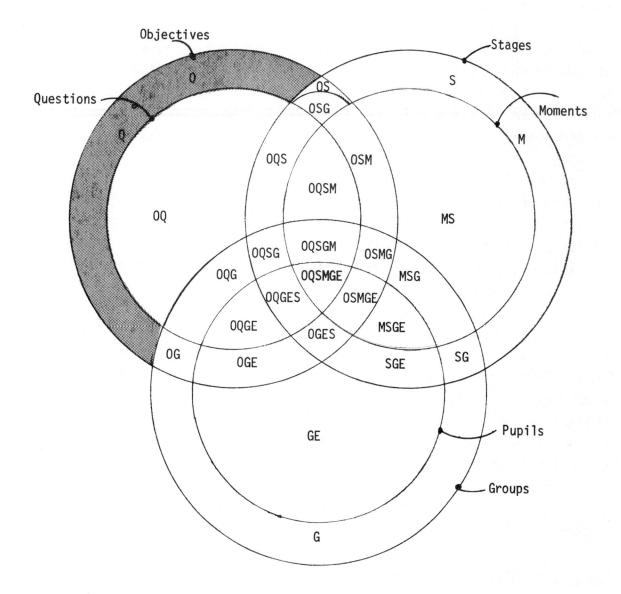

<u>Note:</u> In each sub-area we have indicated only the component of variance corresponding to the interaction of highest order, so as to avoid having to mention the 63 possible components of variance with a 6-factor design. For this reason, the components of variance of the nested facets E, Q and M appear as GE, OQ and MS, for example.

1.3   To adapt survey tests to their purpose, draft the questions to suit the planned analyses

1.3.1.   It is not sufficient to devise questions that focus on precise learning objectives.

Obviously, the questions that are included in a survey must be related to well-defined objectives.   However, it is not enough simply to re-affirm this requirement.   Years have elapsed since the term criterion referenced tests was introduced, but no agreement has yet been reached either on the precise definition of the concept or on the way in which such tests are to be devised.

The typology of tests offers an explanation for this difficulty.   A test related to a learning objective may be used for totally dissimilar differentiations: to classify the pupils according to their overall success on the objective or according to their level of attainment (in terms of time); to classify the questions according to difficulty; to differentiate the successive stages of comprehension (for the average of pupils); and so on.

The purpose of the test is defined by the differentiations required.   These appear in the planned analyses.   It is advisable at the outset to identify the differentiation, generalisation and fixed facets.   In this way, serious errors in the experimental design are avoided, such as the absence of generalisation facets (which removes any possibility of judging the value of the results) or the use of the same facet, to differentiate and generalise (as when the 'less successful' questions are eliminated from a survey).

1.3.2.   The questions must be sensitive to the differences to be measured, but little affected by the generalisation facets.

The persons dimension

Once we know how to attribute clearly each source of variation to the differentiation, generalisation and fixed variance, we can review the questions and investigate whether the content of each is consistent with the measurement design selected.   For example, let us suppose that on the persons dimension the pupils facet is a facet of generalisation.   We deduce that it is unnecessary to make provision for a total score per pupil, that we can disregard the stability of the pupil classification and that there is no need for comparability of contents or of the difficulties of the parallel forms used, etc.

If the classes' facet is also a facet of generalisation, we must avoid questions interacting with this factor (in other words those which are affected by the teachers' pedagogical options, such as knowledge of dates in history).

If the sex facet is to be used for analysis, the questions must cover fields in which differentiation of the success of boys and girls is plausible. On the other hand, if no such analysis is contemplated, this source of interaction must be avoided. The same line of argument applies to the socio-economic background of the pupils or any other principle of grouping.

The most common grouping on the persons facet is that which distinguishes pupils who have followed different curricula. In this case, because differentiation is sought, we shall introduce measurements of the desired objectives. We must, however, refrain from adding the results of the various objectives together (no generalisation on objectives), because the objectives-treatments interaction would then be regarded as an error instead of being examined on its own account. We must instead differentiate treatments, objectives and their interaction. (Care must then be taken to ensure that there remains at least one other facet of generalisation.)

The conditions dimension

The moments facet being normally a facet of generalisation, we must ensure that the questions are not affected by the time of the examination. This might happen if the pupils were prepared specially in order to sit the examination on a certain date (the moment would then be a source of systematic variance by virtue of its main effect) or if they had studied the sections of the curriculum in different orders according to their class (the moment would then be a source of interaction).

We must avoid other sources of interaction with the moment that are caused by the appearance of certain themes in the mass media; atomic energy, the space age, etc. These themes may well be replaced by others at the time the survey is repeated (interaction with the period of examination).

The stages, on the other hand, are generally fixed, since provision is made in the survey for a measurement either at the end of primary schooling or at a particular age, for example. They may even be a facet of differentiation if the investigation is a longitudinal one. In this case, care must be taken to ensure that the questions are capable of detecting developments in the mastery of concepts.

PART TWO: IMPROVING THE STRATIFICATION OF OBJECTIVES

2.1.   To extract more information from survey results, analyse the activity facet according to scientifically formulated constructs

2.1.1.   A survey aimed only at isolated items of knowledge would fail to take account of essential educational outcomes.

Almost as soon as tests began to be devised, it was proposed to choose questions according to a predetermined design or specification table.   The purpose was to ensure more balanced representation of the areas of content covered by the examination.   However, the conventional level of analysis in the formulation of school curricula was seldom exceeded.   Education, like the curricula, was regarded at that time as an accumulation of elements of knowledge.

Bloom and his colleagues (1956) proposed to place the abilities achieved as a result of school learning in a hierarchical order.   The advantage of their taxonomy was to recognise various types of mental activity carried out by the pupil, irrespective of the particular subject matters studied.   On the basis of their work, research has continued in two directions, one psychological (Aebli, 1977; Gagne, 1965; Hontarrede, 1975; Bruner, 1973) and the other logical (Vandevelde, 1975; De Landsheere and De Landsheere, 1975; D'Hainaut, 1970; Vergnaud, 1975).

It is possible to define precise educational objectives even in the case of higher levels of cognitive functioning.   Care must therefore be taken not to confine study to mere recognition of the concepts taught.   It would be regrettable if the survey gave too weak an image of the educational field under review. We know all too well how tests influence educational practice.

2.1.2.   The division of knowledge into items must be supplemented by a description of the psychological processes demanded and of the mode of communication between the examiner and the examinee.

No taxonomy of mental activities is really usable today.   Even so, partial descriptions are better than total ignorance.   We can draw on the work of Piaget, as did Brun and Guignard (1975) when learning is of the logical-mathematical type.   We may create ad hoc categories: e.g., direct operation/ inverse operation, number of stages of argument, length of verbal formulation etc. as attempted by Jaquet (1976).   The important thing is to describe what the pupil must do with the concepts he learns and to try to find classes of activity which reflect the complexity of the tasks proposed.

In discerning an objective we must distinguish, as Mager states (1972), between the mental activity demanded by the question and the activity involved in answering (underlining one of the proposed answers, writing the code number of the chosen answer, etc.). Only the first activity has any real importance, but the second characteristic must be considered: it should not affect the level of difficulty of the question to any appreciable extent. In order to control its effects, facets must be introduced relating to the mode of communication between examiner and examinee.

2.2. To exploit the possibilities of the scientific method, introduce a predetermined structure into the questions facet

2.2.1. Scientific teaching methods must offer the means of accounting for degrees of learning acquisition. The main purpose of surveys is to determine the success rates achieved with respect to each question.

The procedure we suggest is to consider the survey as a form of multifactorial research designed to investigate the underlying structure of the problems presented. Its aim would be to give the best possible account of the pupils' acquisitions by adding to the usual facets relating to periods and persons (treatments, social levels, etc.) as many facets as possible relating to the activities proposed.

Some tentative steps in this direction are described below.

2.2.2. We may choose between several types of design in order to organise the content of surveys.

Complete factorial designs

If the area of study is sufficiently limited, it is sometimes possible to make all the relevant factors vary simultaneously. This may be the case in an attitude survey. Foa (1965) like Guttman before him, proposed a number of examples of such systematic surveys in social psychology.

Incomplete balanced designs

In most cases, the number of factors to be controlled is too large for each to be varied separately, independently of the others, as a complete factorial design would require. We can therefore choose incomplete experimental designs which

make it possible at least to control the main effects and to know which interactions are confounded in the results.

An example is a reading test (Succession of Phonemes) given to children learning
to read (Cardinet and Weiss, 1974).   Half of the syllables began with a vowel
and the other half with a consonant; half of the vowels were double ("ou",for
example), as were half of the consonants (for example, "st").

A total of seven factors, each having two levels were introduced, the entire set
of questions being drafted to satisfy one of the incomplete factorial designs
proposed by Cochran and Cox (1957).   A test based on a complete factorial
design would, of course, have been too long for such young pupils.

In this particular example, the test made it possible to discover what influence
the various factors had for each child individually.   If the purpose of the
survey had been collective assessment, it would have been possible to use a
series of parallel forms and to present each one to different pupils.   Knapp
(1968) was the first to suggest using a balanced incomplete block design to
allow an item to be replicated on different groups of people.   Each test form
would represent a still more economical fraction of the complete factorial design.

Incomplete and unbalanced designs

It may not always be possible to fill all the cells of a predetermined design.

There remains the possibility of introducing mini-comparisons into the survey.
The influence of a hypothetical factor is tested in this case by the introduction
of some parallel questions differing only with respect to the variable whose
effect is to be judged.   (It is clear that these questions are then put to
different pupils.)   An example from the research work of Mai Tra (1976) is
given in Figure 4.   It was not possible to fill all the cells of this table,
but it was possible, in each row, to vary at least one of the hypothetical
factors of difficulty represented in the columns.

FIGURE 4 - Design of a Mathematics Test for the First Primary Year;
SETS - RELATIONS

Sources of difficulty / Topic	Order of Presentation		Degree of difficulty of the wording			Number of different logical operations			Size of numbers used (number of elements to be treated)			
	direct	inverse	1	2	3	1	2	3	1 - 5	6 - 9	10 - 15	16 - 20
Representation of set												
Symbols												
Complementary set: "no"												
Intersection: "and"												
Cartesian table												
Venn diagram												
Caroll diagram												
Tree												
Relation within a set												
Seriation												
Relation of order												
Relation of equivalence												
Other relations												
Relation between two sets												
From set A to set B												
Relation within a collection of sets												
As much. as....												
Less..... than...												
More..... than...												
=												
≠												

<u>2.2.3.</u>   Knowledge of the various sources of difficulty would make for more accurate estimates.

Stages in the determination of sources of difficulty

It will not be possible, in a single operation, to divide up the domain of activities under review into homogeneous sub-sets structured according to facets which reflect the successive thresholds of difficulty in the universe of questions.

First, we must locate the sources of difficulty from a qualitative standpoint and then check them and estimate their importance by means of more structured surveys.

Benefits likely to be derived from this knowledge

Better prior knowledge of the factors that affect pupil's success would naturally be of great pedagogical importance.   Even from the sole standpoint of the efficiency of the surveys, a number of benefits could be derived from better knowledge of the area.   It would be possible:

-    to centre the formulation of questions on the measurement of factors whose effects is likely to be important, at the expense of those whose effect is known to be insignificant;

-    to estimate these effects more accurately by means of a measurement design built up around them;

-    to include the least marked effects within the generalisation facets, and thereby limit the number of distinct educational objectives;

-    alternatively, to constitute different objectives, if one source of special difficulty makes it necessary to draw distinctions between questions previously thought to be homogeneous;

-    to offset the effect of accessory factors (by keeping them constant, sampling them systematically or calculating corrected averages);

-    to make a more valid assessment of the margins of error that effect each of our estimates.

In this way it should be possible to obtain universes of questions in which the items are genuinely interchangeable and where the estimates of an average success rate is really meaningful.

2.3.   To attain more generalisable results, define the objectives 'under control' with ever-increasing accuracy and introduce stronger models.

The possibility of generalising (from the results found with a few questions to the average of the objective) must be the goal.   Since the examiner cannot change the pupils' actual results, his only way of achieving this goal is to classify the questions correctly into homogeneous sets.   By attempting various methods of formulating or presenting the questions according to a systematic experimental design, he will obtain a clearer view.   Of course, he must first ascertain the item-objective concordance, that is to say the content validity of the questions, by having the semantic aspect monitored by qualified examiners.   It now remains to mention the statistical procedures that are available for testing the hypotheses relating to the objectives or for formulating others.

The simplest means of validating an objective is to calculate a confidence interval around its average difficulty.   If certain questions thought to belong to this objective fall outside the interval, the hypothesis must be rejected.   The definition of the universe we wish to sample must be formulated differently so that it can be given homogeneity and be considered 'under control'.

This of course assumes that the confidence interval is reasonably narrow, for example $\pm 10\%$.   If it is not, it means that a source of heterogeneity has not been controlled.   We must, for example, fix certain facets or divide the objective into more homogeneous sub-objectives.

This first criterion that an objective must satisfy does not automatically turn it into a psychological reality.   If we wish to be able to measure an individual trait (to take pedagogical decisions adapted to each personality), the correlations between questions within the objective must be significant and fundamentally amenable to explanation by a single factor.

At this point we leave the ANOVA model and use the word factor in a different sense. The fact that a single factor suffices to account for the correlations between questions is not incompatible with the idea that multiple sources of variance help to determine average success with each question.   By factorial analysis we can investigate whether this second criterion, that of factorial simplicity, is satisfied.

The relations between objectives may in turn satisfy theoretical models.   The simplest is that of an order structure.   We may assume that the objectives are classifiable in a certain order of difficulty defined according to the characteristics of the activities proposed. The test of this hypothesis is a problem of linear regression.

If we assume that there can be no success with a higher objective unless the objective immediately below has been attained, we postulate the existence of prerequisites. This characteristic cannot be tested without examining the patterns of individual responses.

CONCLUSION

Urgency of the problem - Permanence of the question

We cannot evade the obligation to work out genuinely relevant educational objectives. We might, doubtless, be tempted, for periodic surveys, to use the same questions over again. This would make it possible to camouflage the problem of objectives by taking as a point of reference the questions regarded as fixed (which would indeed make the temporal development more visible). But there are practical reasons for not re-using the same questions: they are inevitably used in the classes by teachers. There are also theoretical reasons for rejecting this easy way out. How can development be properly interpreted without a basis for regrouping questions of identical significance? How are general tendencies to be identified? How are averages to be calculated?

The preparation of surveys therefore implies that we have found the means of forming interchangeable groups of questions. But we still do not yet know on what criteria it might be possible to build up classes of equivalence. On the contrary, in each experiment we find that problems of apparently identical logical structure elicit very different success rates. Why calculate averages for each objective if the results vary as widely within an objective as between one objective and another, because the way of stating the question completely alters the difficulty of the problem?

The cause of these vast differences should be determined as a matter of urgency, not only in order to stabilise the averages for each objective, but chiefly because factors that determine such a proportion of success in school activities are necessarily of vital pedagogical importance. It would be worth taking the trouble to examine them on their own account.

This explains the proposals set out above. It will not be possible to improve the methodology of surveys as long as the questions dimension remains as inadequately structured as it is now. However, if we view the problem before us in perspective, we see that we are dealing with a general difficulty in the history of science. To find relevant descriptive variables in order to establish a classification is a problem that can be solved only by progress in the discipline as a whole.

Only gradually will it be possible to identify less superficial criteria capable of explaining the more general differences. The great advantage of generalisability theory is that two areas of research that have hitherto been kept too far apart can be brought closer together. One is the definition of educational objectives and the other the construction of measuring instruments. The criterion derived from the theory of generalisability (i.e., the proportion of variance explained by the facet under consideration) seems, on present evidence, to be a reasonable indicator as to how objectives can be defined and measured more accurately. Better indicators may be identified later, after more progress has been made in the psychology of learning.

REFERENCES

AEBLI, H. (in press 1977). 'Von Piagets Entwicklungspsychologie zur Theorie der kognitiven Sozialisation' In: STEINER, G. (Hrsg.) Piaget und die Folgen. Munchen: Kindler.

BLOOM, B. et al (1965). Taxonomy of Educational Objectives: Volume I - The Cognitive Domain. New York: Longmans.

BRUN, J. and GUIGNARD, N. (1975). Mathématique et Raisonnement. Geneva: Service de la Recherche Pédagogique, Départment de l'Instruction Publique.

BRUNNER, J.S. and OLSON, D.R. (1973). 'Apprentissage par expérience directe et apprentissage par expérience médiatisée', Perspectives, 3, 21-42

CARDINET, J. and WEISS, J. (1974). L'enseignement de la lecture et ses résultats, Expérimentation neuchâteloise 1971-1973. Neuchâtel: Institut romand de recherches et de documentation pédagogiques (IRDP).

COCHRAN, W. and COX, G. (1957). Experimental Designs. 2d ed. New York: Wiley.

CRONBACH, L., GLESER, G., NANDA, H. and RAJARATNAM, N. (1972). The Dependability of Behavioral Measurements: Theory of Generalizability for Scores and Profiles. New York: J. Wiley.

DE LANDSHEERE, V. and DE LANDSHEERE, G. (1975). Définir les Objectifs de l' Education, s.l.: Ed. G. Thone.

D'HAINAUT, L. (1970). 'Un modèle pour la détermination et la sélection des objectifs pédagogiques du domaine cognitif', Enseignement Programmé, 11, 21-38

FOA, U. (1965). 'New developments in facet design and analysis', Psychol. Revue, 72, 262-274.

GAGNE, R. (1965). The Conditions of Learning. New York: Holt, Rinehart and Winston.

HONTARREDE, G. (1975). 'Les niveaux d'assimilation et leurs applications', Psychologie scolaire, 13, 45-54.

JAQUET, F. (1976). Les connaissances des élèves romands après 4 ans d'étude de l'arithmétique. Neuchâtel: Institut romand de recherches et de documentations pedagogiques (IRDP).

KNAPP, T.R. (1968). 'An application of balanced incomplete block designs to the estimation of test norms', Educ. Psychol. Measurement. 28, 2, 265-72.

MAGER, R. (1972. Goal analysis. Belmont, California: Fearon.

TRA, M. (1976). Elaboration d'un test de contrôle des connaisances mathématiques en première primaire. Travail de diplome en psycho-pédagogie. Univ. de Génève: Faculté de Psychologie et des Sciences de l'Education.

VERGNAUD, G. (1975). 'Calcul relationnel et représentation calculable'. Bulletin de Psychologie, 28, 378-387

VANDEVELDE, L. and VANDER ELST, P. (1975). Peut-on préciser les objectifs en éducation ? Paris: Fernand Nathan.

APPLICATION OF GENERALIZABILITY THEORY: ESTIMATION OF ERRORS AND ADAPTATION OF MEASUREMENT DESIGNS

L.K. Allal & J. Cardinet

Abstract - The achievement of pupils in mathematics has been surveyed in Switzerland. The data are used to illustrate the various directions of analysis that are possible, depending on whether pupils, classes, cantons, questions, series of tests or objectives, are considered. The principles that underlie the formulas for the computation of error variances are presented. An application is made to the data of the survey.

Generalizability theory was introduced over ten years ago by Cronbach, Rajaratnam and Gleser (1963). Although the power of the theory as an analytical tool has been widely recognized, application of the theory has not yet become wide-spread in the field of educational programme evaluation. If one views programme evaluation as a 'one-shot' procedure (having introduced an innovation, one conducts a 'post-mortem' evaluation), only limited application of generalizability theory can be made. It serves merely to determine the adequacy of the measurement design already employed, and thus to introduce a certain degree of confidence - or caution - in the final conclusions. More and more, however, programme evaluation is viewed as the setting up of a system of data-gathering and data-interpreting procedures that will permit an on-going monitoring of a programme and its consequences. In this case, generalizability theory may be used not only to determine the adequacy of the current measurement design, but also the adaptations needed in order to assure the optimality of subsequent designs.

In this paper we will be concerned with two aspects of generalizability theory:

    1.   estimation of the margins of error related to various types of

---

We are indebted to Y. Tourneur for his helpful comments on earlier drafts of this paper.

comparisons which the researcher may wish to carry out,   and

2.   adaptation of an initial measurement design in order to improve the precision of the comparisons of interest.

Our presentation of these topics will be illustrated by a concrete example; i.e., data obtained in the first phase of a survey of mathematics achievement in the French-speaking cantons of Switzerland.   On the basis of this example, we will attempt to demonstrate the different lines of analysis that can be conducted within the framework of generalizability theory, and the different types of decisions that may be made regarding subsequent data collection.

Before examining the survey data, we will briefly review certain basic principles of generalizability theory.

1. ESTIMATION OF ERRORS OF MEASUREMENT: BASIC PRINCIPLES

In generalizability theory, an observed score obtained under one set of measurement conditions is considered to be a sample from the universe of scores that could be obtained using equivalent sets of measurement conditions.   Generalizability theory provides a conceptual and analytical framework for estimating the degree to which observed score variation may be attributed to errors of measurement (i.e., sampling fluctuations in the measurement conditions used to obtain observed scores).

1.1.   An illustrative example

Since the design of the mathematics survey was quite complex, we will begin with a simpler example in order to demonstrate the basic principles of error estimation. Let us suppose that at a given university all first-year students in psychology attend the same courses. At the end of the year, the students rate each of their professors with respect to a series of teaching qualities.   The observation design includes three facets - E (students), P (professors), Q(qualities) - which are completely crossed.[1]

1.2.   Facets of differentiation, facets of generalization, fixed facets

In any measurement design it is necessary to distinguish two major aspects:
(a) the objects under study, and (b) the instrumentation used to study these objects. The objects under study correspond to the facet(s) of the design along which comparisons are to be made, and are thus termed the facet(s) of differentiation of the the design.   In our example, P (professors) is the facet of differentiation.

---

[1]   In this text, we will use the same symbols to designate facets as those used in the French-language version (E- etudiants, P-professeurs, etc.)

E (students) and Q (qualities) are the facets of instrumentation used in evaluating P.

When estimating errors of measurement, it is necessary to distinguish between two types of instrumentation facet:

> i.   When an instrumentation facet constitutes a random sample from some definable and potentially infinite population and one wishes to draw conclusions that are generalizable to the population, the facet is termed a facet of generalization.

> ii.   When a facet has not been constituted by random sampling and/or one is not interested in generalizing to a larger population, the term fixed facet is applied.

In our example, if the aim is to draw conclusions about professorial teaching competency that are generalizable (i.e., replicable using another random sample of students and another list of randomly sampled teaching qualities), E and Q would be facets of generalization.

If, on the other hand, one wished to limit his conclusions to the particular group of students present in the study, or if the list of teaching qualities used included all qualities of interest, E or Q would be fixed facets.   When a facet is fixed, sampling fluctuations do not intervene in the measurement process.   Error of measurement is reduced, there is relative gain of precision, but a corresponding loss in the generalizability of the results.[2]

1.3.   Estimation of variance components

Applying the usual procedures of analysis of variance, one calculates the observed variance (mean sum of squares) associated with each facet and combination of facets in the design.   One then identifies and estimates the component of variance that may be attributed to each source of variation in the design.   This procedure may

---

[2]   In applications of generalizability theory, it is generally assumed, at least implicitly, that a facet of differentiation is constituted by random sampling. Although this assumption is tenable in most measurement contexts, there may be cases where it would be appropriate to consider a facet of differentiation as fixed.   For example, if one wished to evaluate the adequacy of a survey design for assessing levels of attainment for specified educational objectives that are to remain the same over repeated periods of a survey, it would be appropriate to consider objectives as a fixed differentiation facet.   In the present paper, our aim is to illustrate the use of generalizability methods for evaluating measurement designs which could be applied in various educational settings. Thus, in evaluating the adequacy of a design with respect to a given class of objects (pupils, classes, cantons (as representative of 'school districts' responsible for classes), questions, objectives or test forms), we have considered the facet(s) of differentiation as random.

FIGURE 1 - Variance Components in the Three-Facet Design Q x E x P

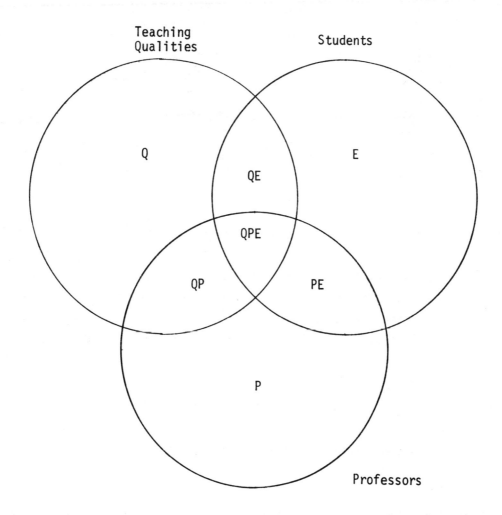

be represented by a diagram (Figure I, above).   The observed variance of each
facet is represented by a circle.   Since the three facets in our example are
crossed, the circles intersect.   The observed variance of each interaction of
facets is the area formed by the intersection of the corresponding circles.   Each
of the seven distinct sub-areas in the diagram corresponds to a component of variance
attributable to a source of variation in the design.

Examining the diagram, we are able to identify the variance components which are included in each observed variance.[3]

The observed variance:	is composed of the variance components(s):
Q	Q, QE, QP, QPE,
E	E, QE, PE, QPE
P	P, QP, PE, QPE
QE	QE, QPE
QP	QP, QPE
PE	PE, QPE
QPE	QPE

1.4.   Variance of differentiation

The variance of differentiation is the variance due to 'genuine' differences among the objects under study.   In generalizability theory, the classical notion of true score is replaced by the notion of universe score, defined as the expected value of observed scores obtained under equivalent conditions of measurement.   The variance of differentiation estimates universe-score variance.   It is composed of the components of variance attributable to differences in the universe scores of the objects under study.

In our example, professors are the objects under study.   If our aim is to differentiate professors on the basis of their mean scores (across Ne ratings of Nq qualities), the variance of differentiation is composed of a single variance component, P.

If, however, we wished to differentiate professors with respect to their scores on each quality (i.e., Np x Nq observations are to be differentiated), P and Q would be combined in a single facet of differentiation, and the variance of differentiation would include three variance components, P, Q and QP (see Figure 2A on the next page).

---

[3]   The following definition of components of variance is based on the random model of analysis of variance (i.e., both Q and E are treated as facets of generalization).   If Q or E were fixed, the mixed model would be appropriate, but, as Cronbach et al (1972, pp. 58-64) demonstrate, it is always possible to estimate mixed model components on the basis of components obtained in a random model analysis.

FIGURE 2 - Partition of variance for the estimation of errors of generalisation

| | Facet | | | Variance | | | | Diagrammatical representation |
	Differentiation	Generalization	Fixed	Differentiation	Generalization Relative	Generalization Absolute	Fixed	
2A	PQ	E		Q P QP	QE PE QPE	QE PE / QPE E		
2B	P	QE		P	QP PE QPE	QP / PE QPE Q / E QE		
2C	P	E	Q	P QP	PE QPE	PE QPE / E QE	Q	

Variance of differentiation — Fixed variance

Variance of generalization: relative error — Absolute error

1.5.   Variance of generalization: relative and absolute errors of generalization

The variance of generalization is the error variance introduced by random sampling fluctuations in the conditions of measurement.   The variance of generalization can be defined in two ways, depending on the type of differentiation one wishes to make.

The first is the error that occurs when one estimates the relative positions of the objects that belong to a differentiation facet.   It is the error that would occur, in our example, if we wished to determine the relative positions of the professors on the scale used to rate teaching qualities.   The relative variance of generalization is composed of the variance components attributable to the interactions between the facets of differentiation and the facets of generalization.   In making relative estimates, the variance of these interactions constitutes error variance, but the variance specific to the facets of generalization does not.   If the professors are rated by different random samples of students, the interaction between the professors and the students will vary from one replication to the next. This variation will cause fluctuations in the relative observed scores of the professors.   On the other hand, since in any given replication all professors are rated by the same student sample, the mean level (i.e., overall leniency or severity) of these students' ratings does not affect the relative positions of the professors.   The same arguments could be applied with respect to fluctuations provoked by random sampling of qualities.   Thus if both E and Q are considered to be facets of generalization, the relative variance of generalization is composed of three variance components, QP, PE, QPE, (See Figure 2B).

When estimating the absolute values of scores, the sources of error are greater than when estimating the relative positions of scores.   In other words, there is a greater likelihood of error if we want to draw conclusions about a professor's absolute level of teaching competency (i.e., his universe score), than if we want to draw conclusions about his relative level of teaching competency (i.e., his deviation universe score).   The mean level of the ratings furnished by a student sample (with respect to a sample of teaching qualities) will fluctuate from one sample of students (or of qualities) to the next, and will therefore cause fluctuations in the absolute values of the professors' observed scores.   Thus, in making absolute estimates, error variance is composed of the variance components due to interactions between the facets of differentiation and generalization plus the variance components due to the facets of generalization themselves.   In our example, the absolute variance of generalization would include the variance components of relative error (QP, PE, QPE) plus the variance components Q, E and QE – in other words, all variance components except P (see Figure 2B).

1.6. Fixed variance

If an instrumentation facet is fixed, it does not contribute to the random sampling fluctuations which constitute error variance.   In our example, we could decide to fix the facet Q, thus leaving a single facet of generalization E.   This means that ratings of the professors, by different random samples of students, would be based on the same (fixed) list of teaching qualities.   Fixing an instrumentation facet has several important consequences (see Figure 2C):

    i.   The components of variance attributable to fixed facets constitute fixed variance, and thus do not intervene in either the variance of differentiation or the variance of generalization.   Thus, in our example, the absolute error of generalization no longer includes the component Q.

    ii.   The components of variance due to the interaction between fixed facets and facets of generalization are included in the variance of generalization. Thus, in our example, the components QE and QPE remain part of the variance of generalization.

    iii.   The variance components due to interaction between fixed facets and facets of differentiation are included in the variance of differentiation. Thus, in our example, the variance of differentiation now includes the components P and QP.

1.7. Generalizability coefficients

A generalizability coefficient (ρ^2) indicates the precision with which the objects under study can be differentiated, given the conditions of measurement over which one wishes to generalize.   For differentiation along a given facet G, ρ^2 can be defined as the ratio of the variance of differentiation associated with the facet G to the total expected variance associated with the facet G.

$$\rho^2 = \frac{\text{variance of differentiation}}{\substack{\text{variance of} \\ \text{differentiation}} + \substack{\text{variance of} \\ \text{generalization} \\ \text{(error variance)}}}$$

The value of ρ^2 will differ depending on the type of differentiation to be made, and, consequently, the type of error variance (relative or absolute) to be considered.

1.8. Calculation of margins of error

Error variance is estimated by means of a weighted sum of variance components.
Each component of variance is divided by the number of observations (having the same
subscript(s) as the component) that enter into the mean score whose error variance
is being estimated.   In our example, a professor's overall rating is a mean score
averaged across Ne ratings of Nq qualities.   If Q and E are facets of generalization, the relative and absolute error variance for the mean score of a professor would be calculated by the following formulas.

$$\hat{\sigma}^2(\delta_p) \quad = \quad \frac{Vpe}{Nq} \quad + \quad \frac{Vpe}{Ne} \quad + \quad \frac{Vpqe}{Nq\ Ne}$$

$$\hat{\sigma}^2(\Delta_p) \quad = \quad \hat{\sigma}^2(\delta_p) \quad + \quad \frac{Vq}{Nq} \quad + \quad \frac{Ve}{Ne} \quad + \quad \frac{Vqe}{Nq\ Ne}$$

where   V = variance component δ - designates relative error

N = number of observations Δ - designates absolute error

Having obtained estimates of relative and absolute error variance, it is possible
to calculate the margins of error that exist in comparing two scores.   The variance of a difference between two independent variables is equal to the sum of the
variances of each variable.   Thus, the error associated with the difference
between two scores has a variance twice as large as the error variance associated
with any single score:

$$2\ \hat{\sigma}^2(\delta) \quad - \quad \text{for comparisons of two relative scores}$$

$$2\ \hat{\sigma}^2(\Delta) \quad - \quad \text{for comparisons of two absolute scores}$$

The corresponding standard deviations may be used to define the margins of error
that exist in making comparisons of two relative scores, or two absolute scores.
These margins of error will be designed as ErR and ErX, respectively.

$$ErR = \sqrt{2\ \hat{\sigma}^2(\delta)} \qquad\qquad ErX = \sqrt{2\hat{\sigma}^2(\Delta)}$$

2. THE SURVEY OF MATHEMATICS ACHIEVEMENT

2.1.   The purpose of the survey

A new 'modern mathematics' programme was introduced in all first-grade classes of
French-speaking Switzerland in the fall of 1973.   Since that time a number of
questions have arisen concerning the effects of this programme as compared to those
of the traditional programme.   In the fall of 1975 a survey was conducted in
order to examine the mathematics achievement of fifth-graders who belong to the
next-to-the-last cohort to be taught under the traditional programme.   The second
cohort of fifth-graders following the new programme will be examined in fall 1978.
After both phases of the survey have been completed, a comparative analysis of
mathematics achievement under the two programmes will be carried out.

2.2.   Design of the survey

The design includes three major dimensions - persons, tasks, treatments.

The person dimension is represented by three hierarchically nested facets: cantons
(K), classes nested in cantons (C:K), and pupils nested in classes and cantons
(E:CK).   These facets were constituted by randomly selecting fifth-grade classes
in each of the French-speaking cantons of Switzerland.   Selection of a class
implied selection of all pupils in the class.   The relationships among these
facets are shown in Figure 3A (on the next page).

The task dimension corresponds to the testing instruments used to assess mathematics achievement.   Eight parallel forms of a mathematics test were constructed.
Each form (termed a 'series') included eight questions.   The first four questions
concerned primarily the application of basic mathematical procedures, while the
second four questions implied higher-level mathematical reasoning.   It was
therefore decided to consider each set of four questions as representative of one
of two educational 'objectives'.   The task dimension of the design was thus
structured in terms of three facets: series (S), objectives (O) crossed with
series, and questions nested in series and objectives (Q:OS).   The relationships
among these three facets are shown in Figure 3B.

In each class one of the eight series was administered to each pupil.   Depending
on the size of the class, a variable number of pupils received the same series.
This means that the facet pupil (on the person dimension) is nested in the facet
series (on the task dimension).

FIGURE 3 - Partial Representations of the Survey Design

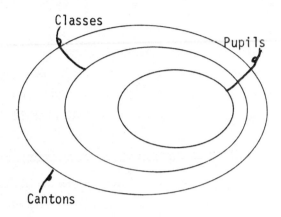

A. The facets related to the dimension Persons

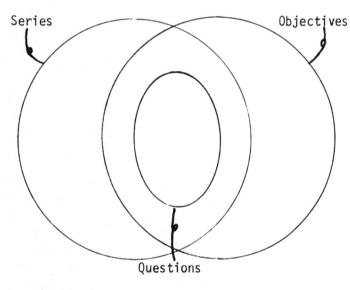

B. The facets related to the dimension Tasks

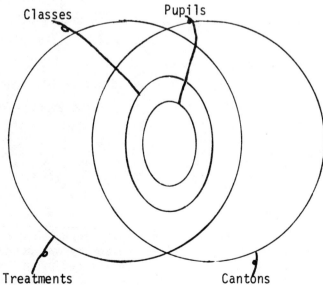

C. The relationship between the facet Treatment and the facets persons.

The dimension treatments includes a single facet: mathematics programme (modern or traditional). Once the second phase of the survey has been completed, data will be available for both treatments in five cantons.[4] In the complete survey design, the facet treatment is crossed with the facet canton, but not with the facets class and pupil. Since in the second phase of the survey new classes and pupils will be sampled, the facets class and pupil are nested in the facet treatment (see Figure 3C). The complete designations of these facets are therefore C:KT and E:CKST, respectively. Since the same testing instruments are to be applied in both phases of the survey, the facet treatment is crossed with the facets O, S and Q:OS.

When the survey is completed, the design will include seven facets: K, C:KT, E:CKST, S, O, Q:OS and T. A total of 27 variance components may be estimated for this design.

3. DIRECTIONS OF ANALYSIS

In the presentation of generalizability theory by Cronbach et al. (1972), it was assumed that persons are always the objects to be differentiated, while generalizing over instrumentation facets such as items, raters, occasions. However, as we have argued in a previous paper (Cardinet et al., 1976) it is possible to apply the principles of generalizability theory to determine the precision of differentiation along any facet of a design.

When conducting an educational survey, it is often useful to estimate margins of error for various sorts of comparisons that may be of interest. In the present survey, although comparisons of treatments is obviously of major interest, other comparisons may also be of interest to educational decision-makers. Comparisons of the achievement levels of classes or cantons may be of interest to educational administrators who are concerned with the supervision and co-ordination of programmes in the French-speaking cantons. Comparisons of the overall achievement levels for different questions, or groups of questions (objectives), may be of interest to curriculum committees concerned with any modifications (of content, of organization, of pacing across grade levels) that may be needed. By

---

[4] In one canton, Geneva, the new mathematics programme was introduced earlier than in the other five cantons. When the first phase of the survey was conducted, all fifth-grade classes in Geneva were already following the new programme. This means that the comparative analysis of the two programmes, after completion of the second phase of the survey, will be based on data from five cantons. The data from Geneva are highly useful, however, since they provide a basis for making certain preliminary estimations, at the end of the first phase of the survey, regarding the precision of differentiation along the facet treatment.

conducting successive analyses along the different facets in the survey design, it is possible to determine:

    i.   the adequacy of the survey design with respect to different sorts of comparisons of potential interest,

    ii.   the adaptations of the present design that would be required in order to improve the precision of any given comparison of interest.

3.1.   Analysis along the treatment dimension of the survey design

Since data on achievement under both mathematics programmes will not be available until the second phase of the survey has been completed, it is not possible at present to estimate the components of variance attributable to T and the interactions of T with other facets in the design. It is, however, important to know whether the survey design, as presently planned, will provide an adequate degree of precision for detecting treatment differences. We, therefore, plan to use a special analysis procedure for making some rough preliminary estimates of the upper bounds of variance components involving T.[5]

3.2.   Analyses along the person and task dimensions of the survey design

The analyses along these dimensions were conducted on the basis of a design that includes six facets: E:CKS, C:K, K, Q:OS, O, S. The 17 distinct sub-areas in the diagram of this design (Figure 4, shown on next page) correspond to the 17 variance components which may be estimated. If a completely crossed six-facet design had been employed, 63 variance components could have been estimated. Because of the nesting in the survey design, a sizeable number of variance components are confounded.

Table I (page 131) presents the values of the 17 variance components and indicates the sources of variation that are confounded in estimating each component. Henceforth we will refer to variance components by the abbreviated designations shown in Table I.

---

[5]   Our strategy for making these estimates includes two steps. Pooled variance components will be estimated on the basis of an analysis of the data collected under the new programme in the canton of Geneva, and the data collected under the traditional programme in the canton of Neuchâtel. (The Neuchâtel data were selected for this analysis because of the similarities between its fifth-grade population and that of Geneva). By adjusting the obtained estimates to take into consideration the confounding of canton and treatment, it will be possible to formulate upper bounds for the variance components involving T.

FIGURE 4 - Diagram for Analysis of the Person and Task Dimensions

(abbreviated designations of variance components)

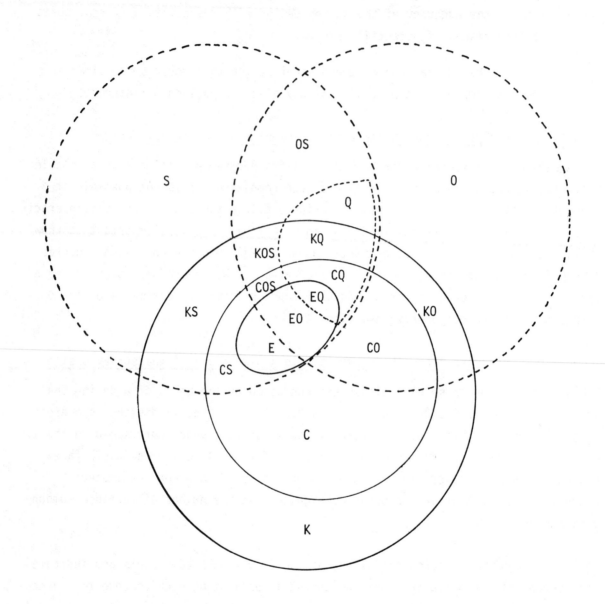

TABLE 1 - Estimates of Variance Components for the Six-Facet Design

Sources of variation		Variance component (X 10^{-5})	Sources of variation confounded with each variance component
Abbreviated Designation	Complete Designation		
E	E:CKS	1368	EC, EK, ES, ECK, ECS, EKS, ECKS
C	C:K	413	CK
K	K	283	-
Q	Q:OS	4321	QO, QS, QOS
O	O	1460	-
S	S	95	-
EQ	(E:CKS)(Q:OS)	12499	ECQ, EKQ, EQO, EQS, ECKQ, ECQO, ECQS, EKQO, EKQS, EQOS, ECKQO, ECKQS, ECQOS, EKQOS, ECKQOS
EO	(E:CKS)O	196	ECO, EKO, EOS, ECKO, ECOS, EKOS, ECKOS
CQ	(C:K)(Q:OS)	589	CKQ, CQO, CQS, CKQO, CKQS, CQOS, CKQOS
CO	(C:K)O	33	CKO
CS	(C:K)S	214	CKS
KQ	K(Q:OS)	246	KQO, KQS, KQOS
KO	KO	38	
KS	OS	25	
OS	OS	0	
COS	(C:K)OS	0	CKOS
KOS	KOS	0	

Since our computer program   for analysis of variance requires an equal number of observations within each cell of the design, it was necessary to base the analysis on minimal cell frequencies (i.e., 2 pupils per series and per class).   The analysis therefore included following number of observations for each facet in the design:

no. of cantons:...................N_k=5

no. of classes per canton:........N_c=15

no. of pupils per series
and per class:.............N_e=2

no. of series:....................N_s=8

no. of objectives:................N_o=2

no. of questions per objective
and per series.............N_q=4

Since the actual number of pupils and classes sampled was considerably larger than the above frequencies, we can consider our estimates of margin of error as upper bounds on the margins of error that would apply in making comparisons based on all the data collected in the survey.

Before conducting the analysis of variance, the raw data were transformed so that each observation (i.e., pupil score on a question) would be expressed on a scale of 0 to 1.   All estimates of variance components, of error variances and of margins of error are expressed in the same metric.

In interpreting margins of error for comparisons along each facet, we considered a margin of error of .05 as the maximum acceptable.   A margin of error of .05 means that the observed difference between two scores would have to exceed approximately .10 in order to conclude, with 95% confidence, that the two scores represent levels of achievement that are in fact different.   The total length of a 95% confidence interval on the difference between two scores is approximately .20 (i.e., 20% of the distance on a scale of 0 to 1). [6]

---

[6]   The above statements assume a confidence interval based on the standard normal distribution (for a 95% confidence interval, Z = 1.96).   A confidence interval based on the Z or t distribution is appropriate when a single comparison of two scores is to be made.   Since one may often wish to make multiple comparisons of scores, it would be useful to develop a confidence interval expression that takes into consideration the lack of independence between the comparisons.

4. DIFFERENTIATION OF CANTONS, CLASSES AND PUPILS

In analysing the person dimension of the design, we estimated the margins of error that exist in making comparisons along each of the hierarchically nested facets of this dimension. In each case, our estimates apply to mean scores across the responses to all questions dealt with by a canton, a class or a pupil. Table 2 (page 135) presents the results of the analysis for each facet.

In conducting these analyses, Q, O and S are facets of instrumentation. Since we wish to generalize over all series that could be constructed by random sampling of questions within each of the domains defined by the two objectives, Q and S are facets of generalization and O is a fixed facet.

We will describe in detail the estimation procedure for differentiation along one facet - cantons. For the other two facets - classes and pupils, the results will be summarized.

4.1. Differentiation of cantons

Our goal is to estimate the margins of error that exist in comparing the mean scores of different cantons. K is the facet of differentiation under consideration. We wish to draw conclusions that pertain to stable canton-specific differences (i.e., differences that would hold up across repeated random sampling of classes and pupils). Thus, C and E are facets of generalization.

The variance of relative errors is estimated by a weighted sum of variance components. By examining Figure 4, it is possible to identify the variance components which constitute relative error variance. The interactions of K (the facet of differentiation) with ECQS (the facets of generalization) correspond to the 11 sub-areas that are found in the intersection of the area of facet K with the union of the areas of facets ECQS. Having identified the 11 variance components of relative error variance, the weight of each component may be determined as follows. Each component is divided by the N's corresponding to the 'effective number' of observations along the facets whose areas contain the sub-area of the component under consideration. The term 'effective number' of observations refers to the number of observations that enter into the mean score whose error variance is being estimated. For example: the sub-area CQ is contained in the areas of facets K, C, Q, O and S; thus V_{cq} is divided by the product of N_k, N_c, N_q, N_o and N_s (however, N_k equals 1 when estimating error for the mean score of one canton). This product represents the number of observations of type CQ (i.e., N_c class means with respect to each of $N_q \times N_o \times N_s$ questions) that enter into the mean score of a canton.

$$Ve\ /NeNc\ +\ Vc/Nc\ =$$
$$(1368/240\ +\ 413/15)\ 10^{-5}\ =\ (5.70\ +\ 27.34)\ 10^{-5}\ =\ 33.24\ (10^{-5})$$
$$+\quad Vkq/NqNoNs\ +\ Vks/Ns\ +\ Vkos/NoNs\ =$$
$$(246/64\ +\ 25/8\ +\ 0)\ 10^{-5}\ =\ (3.84\ +\ 3.13)\ 10^{-5}\ =\ 6.97\ (10^{-5})$$
$$+\quad Veq/NeNcNsNqNo\ +\ Veo/NeNcNsNo\ =\ 6.92\ (10^{-5})$$
$$+\quad Vcq/NcNqNoNs\ +\ Vco/NcNo\ =\ 1.71\ (10^{-5})$$
$$+\quad Vcs/NcNs\ +\ Vcos/NcNoNs\ =\ 1.78\ (10^{-5})$$

Adding up the above components, we obtain an estimate of the relative error variance for the mean score of a canton.

$$\hat{\sigma}^2\ (\delta_k)\ =\ 50.62\ (10^{-5})$$

The corresponding margin of error, ErR, equals   .0318.

Absolute error variance includes all of the above componets, plus the components (found, in Figure 4, outside the area of the facet K) that are specific to the facets of generalization, or to their interaction with the fixed facet O.   Three components are specific to absolute error variance.

$$Vq/NqNoNs\ +\ Vs/Ns\ +\ Vos/NoNs\ =$$
$$(4321/64\ +\ 95/8\ +\ 0)\ =$$
$$(67.52\ +\ 11.88)\ 10^{-5}\ =\ 79.40\ (10^{-5})$$

An estimate of absolute error may now be calculated.

$$\hat{\sigma}^2\ (\Delta_k)\ =\ \hat{\sigma}^2\ (\delta_k)\ +\ 79.40\ (10^{-5})\ =\ 130.02\ (10^{-5})$$

The corresponding margin of error, ErX, equals .0510.

An examination of this analysis leads to the following conclusions.   The estimates of margin of error indicate that the survey design permits an acceptable level of precision for both relative and absolute comparisons of cantons.   The difference between the mean scores of two cantons would have to exceed approximately .06 in order to conclude, with 95% confidence, that the relative universe scores of the cantons are different.   To draw a similar conclusion concerning absolute universe scores, the observed difference would have to exceed approximately .10.

It may be noted that if we wished to generalize over objectives, the margins of error would be higher than those obtained with 0 as a fixed facet.   If 0 is a

TABLE 2 - Differentiation of Cantons, Classes and Pupils

		Differentiation under consideration		
		Mean scores of CANTONS	Mean scores of CLASSES	Mean scores of PUPILS [1]
Partition of the facets of the design	Differentiation facets	K	C,K	E,C,K
	Generalization facets	E,C,Q,S	E,Q,S	Q,S
	Fixed facets	0	0	0
Error variance (x 10^{-5})	Relative	50.62	232.20	1905.76
	Absolute	130.02	311.60	2540.89
Margin of error	Relative	.0318	.0681	.1952
	Absolute	.0510	.0789	.2254

[1] Because of the nesting of E in S, the interactions ES and EOS (which should be included in error variance) are confounded with E and EO (components of the variance of differentiation). Thus, unless ES and EOS can be assumed to be zero, the margins of error for comparisons of pupils are somewhat underestimated.

facet of generalization, the component KO is added to both error variances, and the component O is added to absolute error variance. In this case, ErR = .0373, ErX = .1326.

4.2. Differentiation of classes and pupils

Let us first consider how the facets of the design are partitioned in carrying out the analyses of the facet class and the facet pupil.

In estimating the margins of error for comparisons of mean scores of <u>classes</u>, we wish to generalize over random samples of pupils who could be assigned to classes (i.e., a class corresponds to instruction by a given teacher in a given school setting). E is therefore a facet of generalization. On the other hand, since a class is invariably situated in a single canton, it would not make sense to genralize over cantons. Thus, both C and K are facets of differentiation.

In estimating the margins of error for comparisons of mean scores of <u>pupils</u>, it makes no sense to generalize over classes or over cantons (a pupil is invariably taught in a certain class in a certain canton). Thus, E, C and K are facets of differentiation.

As our analysis proceeds from differentiation of cantons, to differentiation of classes, to differentiation of pupils, there is a successive reduction in the number of facets of generalization. This leads to successive reductions in the number of variance components that enter into our estimates of error variance. However, since there is also a successive reduction in the number of observations on which a mean score is based, the net result is an <u>increase</u> of error variance.

This principle may be illustrated by examining one source of variation, EQ, which contributes to error variance in all three analyses.

When differentiating:	the contribution of EQ to error variance is:
mean scores of CANTONS	$V_{eq}/N_eN_cN_sN_qN_o$ =
a canton is based on (Ne x Nc x Ns) pupils' responses to (Nq x No) questions.	$(12499/1920)\ 10^{-5}$ = $6.51\ (10^{-5})$
mean scores of CLASSES	
a class mean is based on (Ne x Ns) pupils' responses to (Nq x No) questions	$V_{eq}/N_eN_sN_qN_o$ = $(12499/128)\ 10^{-5}$ = $97.65\ (10^{-5})$

When differentiating:	the contribution of EQ to error variance is:
mean scores of PUPILS	
a pupil mean is based on one pupil's responses to (Nq x No) questions	$Veq/NqNo =$ $(12499/8) \ 10^{-5}$ $1562.38 \ (10^{-5})$

The margins of error shown in Table 2 indicate that the present survey design does not permit a sufficient level of precision for comparisons of class scores, and is totally inadequate as far as comparisons of individual pupils are concerned. In the latter case, an observed difference between two pupils' scores would have to exceed approximately .45 (nearly half of the range of the test scale) in order to conclude that there is a significant difference in their absolute levels of mathematics achievement!

In examining the components which enter into the error variance formulas, it is found that the interaction pupil-question (EQ) is the largest source of error variance when making relative comparisons of pupil scores or of class scores. When making absolute comparisons of pupil or class scores, the principal sources of error are both EQ and Q. To increase precision of differentiation along the facet C, it would be necessary to modify the design in one or more of the following ways: (a) increase the number of questions in the test, (b) increase the number of pupils answering each question, (c) increase the homogeneity of the difficulty levels of the questions. To improve precision of differentiation along the facet E, sizeable increases would be needed with respect to points (a) and (c) above.

5. DIFFERENTIATION OF QUESTIONS, OBJECTIVES AND SERIES

In analysing the task dimension of the design, there is a transposition of perspective. Questions, objectives and series now constitute the objects under study, whilst pupils, classes and cantons now serve as the instruments used to assess variations in achievement levels attained for different questions or groups of questions. Estimates of error variance and margins of error were calculated for each task facet Q, O and S. In each case, the estimates apply to mean scores based on the total number of pupils who responded per question, per objective or per series. These mean scores indicate the level of success attained - on the average, throughout the five cantons - by the pupils who dealt with each question, each objective or each series.

Since we wish to draw conclusions about tasks that are generalizable across random

TABLE 3 — <u>Differentiation of Questions, Objectives and Series</u>

		Differentiation under consideration		
		Mean scores of QUESTIONS[1]	Mean scores of OBJECTIVES	Mean scores of SERIES
Partition of the facets of the design	Differentiation facets	Q,O	O	S
	Generalization facets	E,C,S	E,C,Q,S	E,C,Q
	Fixed facets	K	K	K,O
Error variance (x 10^{-5})	Relative	92.93	140.02	570.30
	Absolute	210.41	159.54	576.03
Margin of error	Relative	.0431	.0529	.1068
	Absolute	.0649	.0565	.1073

[1] Because of the nesting of Q in S, the interactions QS and KQS (which should be included in error variance) are confounded with Q and KQ (components of the variance of differentiation). Thus unless QS and KQS can be assumed to be zero, the the margins of error for comparisons of questions are somewhat underestimated.

samples of pupils and classes, E and C are facets of generalization.   Cantons are considered as a fixed facet since all French-speaking Swiss cantons are included in the survey and there is no larger population to which we wish to generalize.

5.1.   Differentiation of questions and objectives

When differentiating questions, it would make no sense to generalize over objectives. Any given question is necessarily nested within a given objective.   On the other hand, series are merely stratified random samples of questions - a question does not necessarily belong to any particular series.   Thus, in estimating margins of error for comparison of questions, the facet O is not included among the facets of generalization, but the facet S is.

When differentiating objectives, it makes sense to generalize over both questions and series (i.e., over all equivalent versions of the test constituted by random sampling of questions representative of each objective).   Thus, in the analysis of objectives, both Q and S are facets of generalization.

The margins of error shown in Table 3 indicate that the survey design permits an acceptable level of precision for both relative and absolute comparisons of object-ives.   With respect to the differentiation of questions, the margin of error is acceptable for relative comparisons, but not for absolute comparisons.   In exam-ining the sources of variation that contribute to absolute error variance, it is found that the component S is responsible for 81% of the difference between rel-ative and absolute error variance.   Thus, to decrease the margin of error for absolute comparisons of questions, it would be necessary to decrease the variation between series of the test.

5.2.   Differentiation of series

If we assume that all future series of the test will be constructed by random sampling of questions representative of each of the two objectives in the present test, Q is a facet of generalization, but O is considered as a fixed facet.

The margins of error for the facet series are considerably larger than those for the facets question and objective.   This is due primarily to the fact that there is a large amount of interquestion variability, and, at the same time, a fairly small number of questions per series.   The variance component Q therefore makes a large contribution to the error variance for series.

We need not, however, be very concerned about the relatively high margin of error for series.   Since series are supposed to be nothing more than random samples of

questions (stratified by objectives), we are not interested in being able to
differentiate series.   For this facet, our major concern is that the variance of
differentiation be very low, relative to the variance of generalization.   This is
in fact the case.   Calculating the variance of differentiation (composed of the
components S, KS, OS and KOS) we obtain a value of 100 (10^{-5}).

6. ADAPTATIONS OF THE SURVEY DESIGN

The analyses reported in the preceding sections provide an illustration of one
application of the principles of generalizability theory: the study of a survey
design already employed in order to determine the degree of precision it permits
with respect to various kinds of comparisons that may be of interest to educational decision-makers.   The analyses reported in this section will illustrate a
second application of the principles of generalizability theory: estimation of
the effects of various adaptations of a survey design.   In this case, the theory
becomes a tool for planning the designs of future surveys in which certain types
of differentiation or generalization are to be optimized.

Two sorts of adaptations of the present design are examined in this section:

i.   increasing sampling along facets of generalization in order to
improve precision of differentiation along a given facet of interest,

ii.   restructuring the design in order to enlarge a universe of
generalization.

6.1.   Effects of increased sampling along facets of generalization

In our previous analyses, unacceptable margins of error were found for both relative and absolute comparisons along three facets of the present design: C, E and S.
When conducting a survey to evaluate educational programmes, comparisons of mean
scores of individual pupils or of equivalent forms of a test is of little or no
interest.   Comparisons of mean scores of classes may, however, be of interest to
certain educational decision-makers.   We will therefore examine the ways in
which the sampling plan of the present design could be adapted to increase
precision of differentiation along the facet class.

As a general rule, precision of differentiation along a facet of a design can be
improved by increased sampling along the corresponding facets of generalization of
the design.   In estimating margins of error for comparisons of classes, it was
found that the components EQ, Q and E all make substantial contributions to error
variance.   This variance could be reduced by increasing the sample of questions

in each series of the test, and by increasing the number of pupils, per class, who receive each test series.   There are, of course, certain practical constraints which need to be taken into consideration when estimating the effects of increased sampling along the facets Q and E.

First, let us consider the constraints with respect to increased sampling along the facet Q.   It will be assumed that, for fifth-grade pupils, a testing session should last no longer than 45 minutes, and, in this amount of time, fifth-graders can answer a maximum of 10 questions of the type we wish to use to evaluate mathematics achievement.   It will be further assumed that a maximum of two testing sessions can be organized for administration of the survey tests.   Given these assumptions, the maximum possible length of each series is 20 questions (10 questions per objective).

The error variances and margins of error for mean scores of classes may now be recalculated using Nq = 10, instead of Nq = 4.   The increase of Nq leads to a reduction of three components of relative error variance (EQ, CQ, KQ), and of one component (Q) that is specific to absolute error variance.   The following values are now obtained for the margins of error: ErR = .0576, ErX = .0640.

These margins of error may be further reduced by increasing the sample of pupils per class who receive each series from Ne = 2 to Ne = 3.   In making this increase, classes having less than 24 pupils will be eliminated from the analysis.   Thus, this increase would be justified only if it can be assumed that achievement patterns do not differ systematically between classes having 24 pupils or more and those having less than 24 pupils.

The increase of Ne leads to a reduction of three components of relative error variance (E, EQ and OE).   When margins of error are recalculated, on the basis of Nq = 10 and Ne = 3, the following values are obtained: ErR = .0494, ErX = .0568.

The results of the above and analyses indicate that in order to attain margins of error that are acceptable for relative comparisons, and nearly acceptable for absolute comparisons, of mean scores of classes, it would be necessary to increase both Nq and Ne to their maximum possible levels.   It is worth noting that in order to make modest reductions in margins of error (from .0681 to .0494 for ErR, and from .0789 to .0568, for ErX), it is necessary to increase the total number of observations per class (Ne x Nq x No x Ns) very substantially (from 128 to 480).

6.2.   Effects of restructuring the survey design; nesting of objectives in series

In the present survey design, the facets O and S are crossed. The same two objectives are included in each of the eight series. Our conclusions about the levels of achievement of pupils, classes and cantons therefore pertain to a universe of generalization which contains only two objectives. If we wished to draw conclusions that pertained to a larger universe of objectives, the survey design would have to be modified in one of several ways.

If we increased the number of objectives but maintained the present (O x S) structure of the design, it would be necessary to increase the length of each series. The effects of this type of increase could be estimated by the same procedure as that used in section 6.1. to estimate the effects of an increase in the number of questions per objective. An alternative approach would be to restructure the design so that O is nested in S. In this case, the total number of objectives can be increased without increasing the length of each series or the number of series.

Let us examine the effects on various margins of error if two objectives are nested in each of the eight series, but all other facets of the design remain unchanged. In this case, our conclusions about levels of achievement of pupils, classes and cantons pertain to a universe of generalization that contains a total of 16 objectives.   The structure of each series remains unchanged (Nq = 4, No = 2), but since both O and Q are nested in S, the total number of questions per objective is reduced from 32 to four.

The nesting of objectives in series means that pupils are now nested in four other facets: CKOS.[7] Four variance components that could be estimated previously (OE, OS, COS, KOS) are confounded in the new design with the components E, O, CO and KO, respectively.   We can estimate the values of these four components of the new design as follows:

$$E' = E + OE = 1564 \qquad CO' = CO + COS = 33$$
$$O' = O + OS = 1460 \qquad KO' = KO + KOS = 38$$

We can now determine the effects on various margins of error of the restructuring of the design (see Figure 5).

---

[7]   Since there are two objectives in each series, pupils are nested in a block of two objectives rather than in each objective. For sake of simplicity in re-estimating variance components, we will treat pupils as fully nested in objectives.   Since the contribution of OE to error variance is in any case quite small, this simplification will have no appreciable effect on the resultant estimates of margins of error.

FIGURE 5 — Restructured Design Giving Better Coverage of Objectives

(abbreviated designations of variance components)

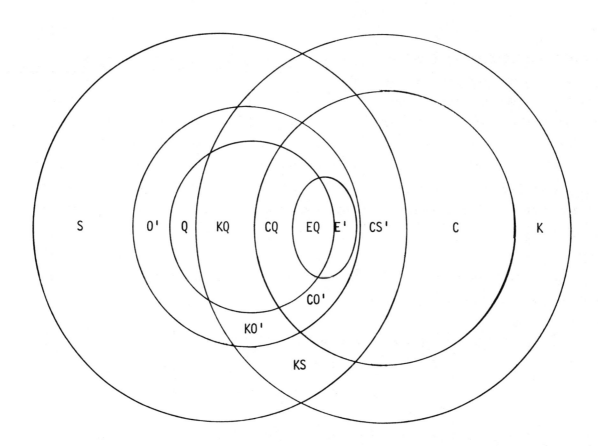

In recalculating the margins of error for comparisons along the facets of the person dimension of the design, the following values are obtained:

For comparing mean scores of: ErR equals: ErX equals:

	ErR	ErX
cantons	.0316	.0509
classes	.0690	.0797
pupils[8]	.1952	.2254

These values differ very little or not at all from those estimated previously. Thus, we may conclude that for making comparisons along person facets, it may be preferable to restructure the design: the nesting of O in S permits generalization to a larger universe of objectives without any appreciable loss of precision. The restructuring does not, however, permit any gain of precision. Thus, if comparisons of class means are to be made, it would be advantageous to restructure the design (for increased generalization with respect objectives), but it would be necessary, in addition, to increase sampling along the facets Q and E (in order to improve precision).

In recalculating margins of error for comparisons along the task facets Q and O, the following values are obtained:

For comparing mean scores of: ErR equals: ErX equals:

	ErR	ErX
questions	.0428	.0649
objectives	.1501	.1567

The nesting of O in S leads to no change in the margins of error for comparisons of questions, but, as is to be expected, there is a substantial increase in the margins of error for comparisons of objectives. This increase is the result of the reduction of the total sample of questions per objective from 32 to four. If a major aim of an educational survey is to compare average levels of achievement for different objectives, the restructured design could not be used unless the sampling of questions per objective could be substantially increased.

*   *   *   *

8   Because of the additional nesting of pupils in objectives, new variance components are confounded. Thus, for reasons analogous to those mentioned in the footnote of Table 2, the margins of error for pupils may be somewhat underestimated.

This paper has attempted to describe and illustrate the applications that can be made of generalizability theory when conducting surveys of educational achievement.   The major uses of the theory may be briefly summarized.

1.   It provides a comprehensive framework for analysing the adequacy of a survey design that has already been employed.

2.   In analysing an existing design, it is possible to identify the sources of variation which make major contributions to different kinds of error of measurement.

3.   Having identified these sources of error and estimated their effects, it becomes possible to plan future survey designs which offer adequate levels of precision for studying the aspects of achievement that are of major interest to educational decision-makers.   It also becomes possible to abandon a survey project in the event that the design needed to attain an adequate level of precision is not feasible for practical reasons.

4.   When conducting a long-term periodic survey, the design of the survey may be progressively refined by carrying out generalizability studies at each successive stage of the survey.

REFERENCES

CARDINET, J., TOURNEUR, Y. and ALLAL, L. (1976). The symmetry of generalizability theory: Applications to educational measurement. Journal of Educational Measurement, 12.

CRONBACH, L.J., GLESER, G.C., NANDA, H. and RAJARATNAM, N. (1972). The Dependability of Behavioral Measurements: Theory of Generalizability for Scores and Profiles. New York: Wiley.

CRONBACH, L.J., RAJARATNAM, N. and GLESER, G.C. (1963). Theory of generalizability: a liberalization of reliability theory. British Journal of Statistical Psychology, 12, 137-163.

MULTIPLE MATRIX SAMPLING

A.N. JAMES

abstract - The main advantages and disadvantages of Multiple Matrix sampling techniques are summarised.

When all items in a pool are used by a sampling scheme the standard error of the mean item score is very low. It is argued that this arises because no account is taken of the 'generic variance' of items. However, if the whole pool is not used the standard error includes a contribution from the 'generic variance' thus leading to safer inferences. Finally the use of the Rasch model in the analysis Multiple Matrix sampling schemes is discussed.

INTRODUCTION

The purpose of this paper is to describe briefly the statistical properties of multiple matrix sampling, and in particular to look at the advantages and explain their nature. The behaviour of the 'Rasch' model under multiple matrix sampling is also examined.

The level of this paper is conceptual rather than analytical: the somewhat tedious arithmetic of the methodology of multiple matrix sampling has been avoided; likewise, the more esoteric forms of mathematical analysis. Reference is made to two publications, Lord and Novick, 1968, "Statistical Theories of Mental Test Scores" and Shoemaker, 1973, "Principles and Procedures of Multiple Matrix Sampling".

WHAT IS MULTIPLE MATRIX SAMPLING?

It is common practice to administer tests to a sample of pupils from a population, which is being studied. There are two main reasons for sampling as opposed to testing the whole population: firstly, the population may be more easily defined than actually located, secondly, the expense of administering a test to all pupils may outweigh the value of the information which is gained over that obtained from a sample.

A test may be viewed as a 'population' of items since all are administered: thus common practice can be represented as the administration of a population of items to a sample of pupils.   The objective of such a procedure is to estimate the average test score (on the population of items) of the population of pupils.

The asymmetry of this sampling design suggests that we might equally sample the items: this is the basis for multiple matrix sampling.

In multiple matrix sampling the items are sampled (at random without replacement) and formed into subtests and each subtest is administered to a (different) sub-sample of pupils.   The objective is to estimate the average score, on the complete population of items, of the population of pupils.

In justification of this approach, it is worth considering multiple matrix sampling in the light of general test theory.   Inferences can only be drawn about a pupil's response to a test if something is known about its items.   In particular the items must 'measure' that quality which is being investigated in the pupil; if they did not then they would not be included in the test.   It follows that every item in a test must be a measure of 'the same thing'.   This is not to say that the items must be identical in the responses they provoke, but that there is a common quality in these responses, and, this is the quality being measured.   Shoemaker rightly emphasises the necessity for a rigorous screening and testing of items.   A clear consequence of the necessary qualitative homogeneity of items in a test is that a valid inference can be drawn from a sample of items, and this will not differ in kind from that drawn from the whole test or population.

Item sampling imposes no restrictions additional to those required in the constr-uction of the traditional test items.   However, if the items in the tests are to be stratified as, for example, in a test of 'general ability' which contains verbal and non-verbal items, then the different strata of items should be treated as separate populations.   This is because items in a population should be homogeneous. Each pupil can then be presented with distinct samples from each item population.

Finally in this section we should draw a distinction between the technology of multiple matrix sampling and the underlying science.   Shoemaker concentrates heavily on the technology: much of this is concerned with equating multiple matrix sampling outcomes to classical test theory.   In the author's view this is unnec-essarily restrictive to the application of the principles to a wider field.

ADVANTAGES AND DISADVANTAGES

The main advantages of multiple matrix sampling are:-

Reduced standard error of estimate: In general terms it is almost always possible to reduce the standard errors of a group estimate by a suitable design of
sampling scheme.   However, in all but special cases such a reduction in standard error will be of little more than technical, rather than substantive, importance.   What is true is that sampling of items is unlikely to increase the
standard error.

Reduced testing time: A consequence of reducing the number of items attempted
by each pupil (by suitable sampling) is that testing time is thereby reduced.
This gives considerable advantages to the test administrator; if, as in many
projects, many tests are to be administered, the testing programme can be arranged
so as to fit the time available.

Larger item populations: When the population of items is very large, say 200-
300, then clearly item sampling is the only feasible procedure - such a large
population is essentially an Item Bank.

The technology of multiple matrix sampling requires that an estimate is made of the
score that a population of pupils would achieve if they had responded to the whole
bank (Shoemaker).   Lord and Novick emphasise that the objective is the estimation
of average item score, i.e., $\left(\dfrac{\text{estimated Bank score}}{\text{number of items in Bank}}\right)$.

This seems philosophically to be the more preferable, as it removes from consideration the discrete number of items regarded as the population (i.e. test) appropriate for the quality to be measured.

Parallel tests: The principle of item homogeneity implies that samples of items
are in essence parallel tests.   This consequence will be used in Section 4.
Shoemaker points out that in certain circumstances the sampling of items may have
advantages over 'matched item tests'.

Disadvantages

Sampling and administration Problems: The technology, as currently developed,
requires random samples of pupils and items within their populations.   Stratification, by age, sex and school type for example, within the population is not
currently catered for.   There is, of course, no prohibition to defining different

strata as different populations. However, the technical problems of sampling are accordingly increased. In addition, despite reduced testing time, there may be administrative penalties in distributing the item samples (i.e. different subtests) at random among pupils.

Item context effect: It is a basic assumption of item sampling that the pupil responds to the sample in the same way as he would if the sample were embedded in the whole test. Shoemaker reports that the evidence is that they do: he also points out that this restriction implies careful item selection in compiling the initial 'test' population.

Individual measurements: The technology of multiple matrix sampling has yet to be developed to allow estimation of individual test scores. The method is essentially one of group measurement. The latent trait models, discussed briefly in the section on the Rasch model, can be adapted for individual measurement through the administration of samples of items from a calibrated pool.

THE NATURE OF THE STATISTICAL PROPERTIES

In this section the nature of the standard error of the estimate is explored. Heavy reliance is placed on Lord and Novick (Chapter 11) which gives an excellent account of the statistical properties of multiple matrix sampling.

Problems of Inference: In an analysis of the problems of drawing inferences from item responses, it is helpful to distinguish two levels of inference.

Level 1 - At this level the raw data (item responses) are manipulated to give an estimation of some parameter of the appropriate population, for example, the mean item response, together with a measure of the estimate's precision; typically its standard error. Such a procedure is conditional on the actual data: that is, the estimate and its standard error are dependent on the statistical relationships among the data.

Level 2 - The next stage is to use the parameter estimate in order to infer some 'quality' of the population which the parameter is intended to measure. For example, the mean item score of a mathematics test may be used to draw inferences about the 'numeracy' quality of a population. Such an inference is less concerned with the statistical aspects of the data than with their 'validity' (in the psychometric sense) and 'content'.

It is not always clear which level of inference is to be used: for example, it might be sufficient to compare two groups of pupils, both tested with the same instrument, at the lower level because: "We are only interested in their response to a test".   However, if the pupil's 'quality' or underlying 'trait' which manifested the test response is being considered then clearly the higher level of inference is necessary because it would not be certain that both groups are responding on an identical trait.   A consequence is that the precision, with which such a comparison is made, is inevitably reduced.

A further difficulty arises with certain response models, for example, the 'Rasch' model.   In these cases the 'trait' is specified by the model and the scaled value of this trait is the parameter being estimated.   Thus it appears that inferences are being made at level 2; it is, however, clear that it is a level 1 inference.   The question "whether the 'trait' which actually manifests the response is different from the one which is intended?" is simply not asked.

Generic Variance and Item Sampling

In the classical analysis of item response the concept of 'generic' variance is introduced.   'Generic' variance measures the difference of the 'true' trait from the actual trait: it is thus a measure of the imprecision resulting from the higher level inference.   Lord and Novick point out that generic variance can be estimated by analysis of parallel tests.   Now the structure of an item bank implies that random sampling of items effectively generates parallel tests.   Thus certain multiple matrix sampling procedures will have built into them a contribution from generic variance.   This is an advantage over the fixed test procedure because higher level inferences can be drawn from the data without having to resort to formal parallel tests.   The above argument is examined in more detail below by means of an example.

An example: The table below shows the standard errors in mean item responses of a population of items under a variety of multiple matrix sampling schemes.   The parameters of the example are as follows.

Variance of pupil's mean item response	=	0.02
Variance of item facility	=	0.05
Mean item facility	=	0.50
Number of pupils per subtest group, N	=	700

The general procedure is that M (Column 2) groups of pupils are administered samples of n (column 1) items drawn without replacement from a population of $\bar{n}$ items. $\bar{n}$ takes the values of 36, Case 1 (column 3), 50, Case 2 (column 4) and 100, Case 3 (column 5). It will be noted that the total number of item responses, nMN is constant, i.e., the amount of information gathered is identical for each scheme.

n	M	Case 1 $\bar{n} = 36$	Case 2 $\bar{n} = 50$	Case 3 $\bar{n} = 100$
1	36	0.00281	0.02011	0.03009
2	18	0.00291	0.02013	0.03010
3	12	0.00301	0.02015	0.03012
4	9	0.00311	0.02016	0.03013
6	6	0.00329	0.02019	0.03015
9	4	0.00355	0.02024	0.03019
12	3	0.00379	0.02029	0.03022
18	2	0.00423	0.02039	0.03029
36	1	0.00534	0.02067	0.03051

In Case 1 all the items in the pool are used and the final row of the table represents the case of a single fixed test.

The standard error of the mean item response from a design which requires 36 groups of 700 pupils each to respond to one item is just over half that of the design where 700 pupils respond to all 36 items. Cases 2 and 3 show the effect of increasing the size of the pool. The effect of the sample design is apparent but not so marked as in Case 1; however, the standard error increases sharply when the pool size is different from the total number of items used.

The formulae from which the table is derived are reproduced from Lord and Novick in Appendix A.

The variation in standard error is related to both sample design and the effect of pool size.

Sample design: In the example each item is administered to exactly the same number of pupils - 700: because sampling of both items and pupils is random, and, because in a valid pool there is no context effect, the information about each item has equivalent value whether it has come from the same 700 pupils or different samples of 700 pupils. It follows that the sample design will be most efficient if the number of pupils can be maximised: this is achieved by administering one item to each of 36 random samples of 700 pupils.

The effect of pool size: In Cases 2 and 3 (in the table), the number of items used in the survey is less than the total number in the pool. Since the objective is to estimate the mean item score of all the items in the pool, then the measure of precision (standard error) of this estimate must take into account the variation among those items from which the survey items are sampled: the greater the variability among the items the less precise (higher standard error) will be the estimate of the mean item score. The variation among the items comprises two components. The first of these is the variation in item facility; this is shown in the formula (2) in Appendix A. The second is the generic variance already referred to: although not explicitly evaluated in the calculation of the standard error, the practical analysis of any such survey must implicitly include the generic variance because each sample of items is essentially a parallel test.

If all the items in the pool are used in the survey, then the standard error of the estimate of mean item score contains no contribution from either the sampling variation or the generic variance. This is because the objective is to measure mean item score of the pool, not the underlying trait, and all the items are used.

The consequential reduction in standard error is demonstrated in Case 1 of the example and in Formula (1) in Appendix A. It is concluded that if all items are used in the survey then inferences about mean item score are necessarily at the first level. If not all of the items are used then any inference, at best, will be at the higher level. The reason for the qualification is that if all the test items match the trait exactly then inference from a partially used pool will remain less precise than those from a fully used bank. A practical way around this difficulty is discussed in the next section.

MULTIPLE MATRIX SAMPLING AND THE RASCH MODEL

It is instructive to ask what happens if the population of items, instead of being constructed along classical lines, comprised items calibrated according to the Rasch model. It should be emphasised that such a calibration imposes no formal modifications to item content and construction. The Rasch model is just a different way of interpreting the item data.

The item 'difficulties' are pre-calibrated to some value on an (hypothetical) trait, and hence can be viewed as fixed: that is each item will have a known 'difficulty' value.   Item responses are adjusted by these constants in order to estimate each pupil's ability.   It follows that the only contributions to the standard error of the estimate of the population ability (average item score) are the variations in ability in the population and the error variance of the response. This leads to results similar to Case 1 in the previous section.   That is, the correct strategy is to maximise the number of pupils in the sample and this strategy, unlike the results for classical test theory, is independent of the size of the pool.   This is because responses on a trait are being sampled, not the items themselves; the 'pool' therefore is effectively infinite.

A further consequence of Rasch scaling is that the prohibition on stratification (section 3) is removed.   This follows from the sample independence of the item calibration.

It was pointed out previously that inferences drawn from the parameter estimates of models of this kind, i.e., latent trait models, are at the first level.   This is because the model requires the specification of a particular trait and this specificity necessarily excludes the concept of generic variance.   Nevertheless, the practical investigator has to contemplate the possibility that his items do not measure exactly the trait for which they were designed, and, more importantly, to moderate his inferences accordingly.   Fortunately there appears to be a simple operational solution to this problem.   It was remarked that generic variance can be measured by parallel tests.   A fortiori, with Rasch scaled items, (because in a sense every item is a parallel test) the pupil's ability estimates will contain as an error component a contribution from the generic variance.   Thus if a sufficiently large number of items are sampled from the pool and distributed among pupils then the standard error of the estimate should reflect the generic variance. Furthermore, each pupil can respond to more than one item: the variation among the estimates of ability (from each item) will contain a major contribution from the generic variance and can be used to estimate it.

The main advantage in the use of the Rasch model lies in the pre-calibration of the item statistics.   Hence the standard error of the estimate will, in general, be lower than that derived from classical test theory.   However, the standard error may well be under-estimated unless some allowance is made for the contribution of generic variance.   Perhaps the value of the Rasch model is that it allows the experimenter to be explicit about his analysis.   In classical analysis the item statistics are not independent of the population being measured and hence their sampling variance must contribute to the standard error of the estimate. The lower precision that this implies is not necessarily a disadvantage because the 'item variance' includes 'generic variance' and thus prevents the appearance of spurious precision.

Appendix B gives the derivation of some approximate formulae on which this section is based.

MULTIPLE MATRIX SAMPLING - ITEM BANKS - CONCLUSION

In this paper it is argued that the principles of multiple matrix sampling give useful results. They demonstrate, even under the very general assumption of classical test theory, that sampling of items loses nothing to the common practice of fixed tests. This, in essence, is the validation of an item bank.

The more spectacular gains of multiple matrix sampling are clearly dependent on the level of inference with which the experimenter is concerned. If a latent trait response model is used the results of multiple matrix sampling theory hold; in particular a method is suggested for estimating 'generic' variance.

A P P E N D I X   A

STANDARD ERRORS IN MULTIPLE MATRIX SAMPLING

The following formulae are taken from Lord and Novick, Chapter 11.

$n, \bar{n}, N, M,$ are as defined in section 4

σ_z^2 is the variance in mean item score over pupils

σ_π^2 is the variance of mean item facility

$\bar{z}$ is the mean item score of all items

If we ensure that all items from the pool, or list, are used so that $M = \bar{n}/n$ then:

$$(\text{Standard Error})^2 = \frac{1}{N.\bar{n}.(\bar{n} - 1)} \left[\bar{n}(n-1)\sigma_z^2 + (\bar{n}-n)\{\bar{z}(1-\bar{z}) - \sigma_\pi^2\} \right] \quad (1)$$

If we sample from a pool leaving some items unused, i.e. $nM < \bar{n}$, then a derivation of Lord and Novick's formula 11.12.3. for infinite pupil population gives:

$$(\text{Standard Error})^2 = \frac{1}{n.N.M(\bar{n}-1)} \left[\bar{n}(n-1)\sigma_z^2 + N(\bar{n}-nM)\sigma_\pi^2 + (\bar{n}-n)\{\bar{z}(1-\bar{z}) - \sigma_\pi^2\} \right] \quad (2)$$

The term in curly brackets in both formulae represent the binomial error in sampling from a mixed population of items. Referring to Appendix B, the similarity in form of the expressions is obvious. The contribution of the 'generic' variance is given by the second term in equation 2.

A P P E N D I X   B

THE RASCH MODEL

The logistic form of the Rasch model can be written:-

$$P_{ij} = \frac{\exp(\beta_j - \delta_i)}{1 + \exp(\beta_j - \delta_i)} \tag{1}$$

where P_{ij} is the probability of a correct response of a pupil with ability β_j to an item with difficulty parameter δ_i. β and δ are measures of some (specified) latent trait.

P_{ij} is also the 'average' response of a pupil to an item.

Using Taylors theorem we can readily approximate (1) to give

$$P_{ij} = \frac{1}{4} \{\beta_j - \delta_i + 2\} \tag{2}$$

whence we can write conceptionally a pupil's actual response:

$$r_{ij} = \frac{1}{4} \{\beta_j - \delta_i + 2\} + \varepsilon_{ij}$$

where ε_{ij} is an error term.

Suppose we select n items from a pool then we would use the following equation to estimate β_j.

$$r_{\cdot j} = \frac{1}{4} \{\beta_j - \frac{\Sigma \delta_i}{n} + 2\} + \sum_i \varepsilon_{ij} / n$$

Again a sample of N pupils would provide the estimating equation

$$r_{\cdot\cdot} = \frac{1}{4} \{\frac{\sum_j \beta_j}{N} - \frac{\Sigma \delta_i}{n} + 2\} + \sum_j \sum_i \varepsilon_{ij} / n.N$$

The variance of the statistic $r_{..}$ which is the average item response for the group is:

$$\text{Var } r_{..} \quad = \quad \frac{1}{16} \left\{ \frac{\text{Var } \beta}{N} \right\} \quad + \quad \frac{\text{Var } \varepsilon}{N.n}$$

where the ε_{ij} are assumed to be identically distributed over all ij and the δ_i's are known constants. Var β is the population variance in ability.

Finally suppose there are M such samples (random without replacement), then the variance of $\frac{\Sigma r_{..}}{M}$ is

$$\text{Var } \frac{\Sigma r_{..}}{M} \quad = \quad \frac{1}{16} \left(\frac{\text{Var } \beta}{M.N} \right) \quad + \quad \frac{\text{Var } \varepsilon}{M.N.n} \qquad (3)$$

If we keep the number of item responses $MNn = K$ constant then we can write (3)

$$\text{Var } \frac{\Sigma r_{..}}{M} \quad = \quad \frac{n.\text{Var } \beta}{16.K} \quad + \quad \frac{\text{Var } \varepsilon}{K}$$

whence the larger the value of n the larger the variance of the estimated mean item response.

A RATIONALE FOR DECISION-MAKING IN THE CONTEXT OF CRITERION-REFERENCED MEASUREMENT

I. WEDMAN

Abstract   -   This paper deals with decision-making in the context of criterion-referenced measurement. In terms of Bayesian statistics, a rationale for reaching a decision on whether or not a person should be 'advanced' or 'retained', given his observed score, is discussed.   The main characteristic of the procedure presented here is that it simultaneously takes into account the determination of a person's true level of functioning and the incorporation of such an estimate into a specified utility structure. After presenting the procedure a numerical example is given.

INTRODUCTION [1,2]

Today we can look back to more than a decade of a vast amount of activity in the field of criterion-referenced measurement (C.R.M.).   For a survey of the C.R.M. movement see, for example, works by Brennan (1974); Harris, Alkin and Popham (Eds.), (1974); Hambleton, Swaminathan, Algina, and Coulson (1975); Millman (1974); Wedman (1973).   Furthermore, there is no sign of decreasing interest in the field.

One very 'hot' issue in C.R.M. since the beginning of the movement has been the problem of how to determine the cut-off level on which to base the decision whether or not a certain person should be 'advanced' or 'retained', given his observed score. The present paper is addressed to this problem.   Specifically, our purpose is to deal with criterion-referenced tests (C.R.T.) from a decision-theoretic point of view and to present a rationale for treating the data from C.R.T.'s in order to reach a decision whether or not a person should be 'advanced' or 'retained', given his observed score.

1   The author is grateful to Dr. William E. Coffman, Dr. Melvin R. Novick, Dennis DeKeyrel and Diane Kutzko for valuable support and comments during the work with this paper. The responsibility of the ideas presented, however, falls completely on the author.

2   This study has been made possible by financial support from The Swedish Council for Social Science Research and Iowa Testing Programs, University of Iowa, Iowa City, U.S.A.

CRITERION-REFERENCED TESTS AND DECISION-MAKING

Criterion-referenced tests (C.R.T.) are supposed to give information as to whether or not a person should be 'advanced' or 'retained', given his or her observed score. Clearly, this implies that C.R.T.'s should be looked upon from a decision-theoretic point of view. This has very convincingly been argued by e.g. Hambleton and Novick (1973) in an article that was a fresh addition to the somewhat 'loose' discussions that so far had characterized research in this field.

Three characteristics signify the decision-oriented view in this context. One is to determine the true level of functioning of each testee. A second feature is to 'choose' a utility structure that reflects the decision to be made (given an estimate of a certain person's true level of functioning). A final characteristic is to decide upon a rule that takes into account both of the above features. In the next section these features will be elaborated upon in some detail.

THREE DECISION-MAKING APPROACHES

Briefly stated, three different ways of making decisions based on data from C.R.T.'s can be used.

The Intuitive Approach

The first approach is simply to use the observed score as an estimate of the true level of functioning and to decide whether this value is above or below a predetermined cut-off level, making the decision accordingly. This is the most common procedure used. Depending on the context in which it is used, this approach may also be fairly accurate. That is, if the test used consists of a fairly large number of items randomly chosen from a well-defined domain of items, and if the decision to be made is not too important, then the above approach may very well be used. However, if only a small number of items can be administered and the decision process is to be taken seriously, then the above procedure may be inaccurate. Two things should be said here. First, when the number of items is small, which often is the case in the context of C.R.M., the chance component may heavily influence the observed score, i.e., may lead to very imprecise measures. This is definitely not a new finding but, nevertheless, is sometimes overlooked. From the formula due to Kelly (1927), it follows that as the reliability decreases, lesser weight should be given to the observed score and more weight be given to the population mean, i.e.,

$$R(T_i | X_i) = \rho_{xx} X_i + (1 - \rho_{xx}) \mu_x \qquad (1)$$

where $R(T_i|X_i)$ = the regression of true score given observed score, ρ_{xx} = the reliability, and μ_x = the population mean.

Another limitation with the procedure mentioned above has to do with how the cut-off level is set.   For a long time this has perhaps been one of the most difficult problems in the field of C.R.M.   Several procedures have been suggested (see. e.g. Millman, 1973 and Neskavskas, 1976 for a review) but no procedure seems to 'stand out' as the best one, and often a very arbitrary cut-off limit is set; for instance, that 80% of the items must be answered correctly.   Without going into detail it certainly can be said that many of the suggested procedures for setting cut-off scores represent fairly superficial 'solutions' to a very important problem (see, however, de Klerk (1975) for an interesting procedure).

A Bayesian Approach Based on a Predetermined Cut-off Level

One very promising way of overcoming some of the difficulties inherent in the 'intuitive' approach is represented by a Bayesian approach discussed by Hambleton and Novick (1973); Novick, Lewis and Jackson (1973); Lewis, Wang and Novick (1975); and illustrated by Millman (1974) and Swaminathan, Hambleton and Algina (1975) (see also Novick and Jackson, 1974).

The problem that is addressed in these works is to determine a person's true level of functioning and to apply this information in a decision-theoretic context.   This is done first by incorporating prior/collateral information (i.e. information external to the test) into sample information (i.e. information obtained from the test).   The result of this is a so-called posterior distribution for each individual respresenting his true level of functioning.   Subsequently, this information is 'combined' with a predetermined cut-off level to obtain the probability of success associated with 'advancing' a person, given his observed score.   For a detailed account of how this is accomplished, the reader is referred to Millman (1974) and Swaminathan et al., (1975), who give a step-by-step procedure based primarily on the works of Novick et al., (1973) and Lewis et al., (1975).

By incorporating prior/collateral information, the Bayesian approach, so to speak, strengthens the information given by the test.   Interestingly enough, the procedure for doing this is, in form, very similar to the procedure due to Kelly although carried out quite differently.   The weight given to the prior information in the Bayesian procedure has the effect of regressing the observed score to the group mean. In other words, the weights given to the sample and prior information correspond to the reliability concept in Kelly's formula.

One practical effect of using a Bayesian procedure in the context of C.R.M. is that the number of items can be kept fairly small, a feature clearly illustrated by Novick and Lewis (1974), which hence facilitates the implementation of criterion-referenced systems. As to the cut-off problem, however, the Bayesian approach discussed above carries the same limitation as does the 'intuitive' approach. The Bayesian procedure mentioned above presupposes a predetermined cut-off level and the arbitrariness of that level will consequently also influence the decision to be made.

Clearly, then, what is needed is a procedure that at the same time takes into account the determination of the true level of functioning as well as the cut-off aspect of a C.R.M. procedure. A method for doing this has recently been discussed by Wedman and DeKeyrel (1976).

A Bayesian Approach Based on Expected Utilities

The unique characteristic of this third approach is the way it handles the problem of setting a cut-off level and how it combines this with a determination of the true level of functioning. The starting point in this procedure is to determine the true level of functioning in the same way as has been discussed above. The final result of this step is a posterior distribution of the true level of functioning for each examinee. The next step is to obtain utility functions reflecting the evaluator's values of different degrees of the true level of functioning for an 'advance' and a 'retain' decision respectively. Finally, these two pieces of information are combined and expected utilities for the two decisions are obtained. Figure 1 shows the situation at hand for a certain examinee.

Figure 1 shows that the posterior distribution for individual i is located in the middle of the scale. Furthermore, it displays two hypothetical utility functions for an 'advance' and a 'retain' decision respectively. By multiplying the posterior distribution by the utility function for, say, an 'advance' decision, the expected utility for 'advancing' this person is obtained - similarly for the expected utility for a 'retain' decision. A decision based on the higher of these expected utilities is finally made to 'advance' or retain' a certain examinee.

The different steps involved in this last procedure will be elaborated in the next section followed by a numerical example.

FIGURE 1 - <u>Utility Functions for an 'Advance' and a 'Retain' Decision Respectively, and a Posterior Distribution for a Certain Examinee (Ficticious)</u>

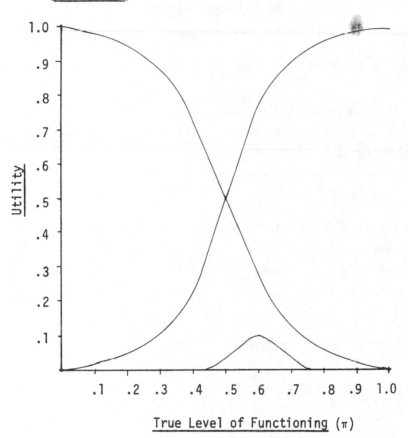

OUTLINE OF A FULL DECISION-MAKING PROCEDURE

The procedure briefly mentioned above and which will be discussed in more detail here is an example of what can be called a full Bayesian procedure.   Its main charact- eristic is that it simultaneously takes into account the problem of determining the true level of functioning and the decision situation in which this value is to be placed.

Basically the following steps signify the Bayesian procedure dealt with here.

    i.   Choose a statistical model to describe the parameter and the data at hand (normal, binomial, etc.).

    ii.   Determine the posterior distribution of the parameter for each person using a Bayes' theorem by accounting for sample as well as prior information.

iii.   Determine the utility functions that reflect the values of the parameter as to an 'advance' and a 'retain' decision respectively.

iv.   Combine (i.e., multiply together) (i) and (iii) and calculate the
expected utility for both decisions.

v.   Make the decision that corresponds to the largest expected utility.

While each of these steps merits detailed discussion, we will keep the discussion
within a reasonable scope by concentrating on the main characteristics involved and
referring to supplementary works wherever possible.

The Model

In a C.R.T. it seems reasonable to assume that X_i, i.e., the observed score for
individual i is a binomial random variable with parameters (n_i and π_i), where n_i is
the number of observations and π_i is the true proportion correct score.   Here we
will use a transformation of π namely,

$$\gamma = \sin^{-1} \sqrt{\pi} \qquad (2)$$

and on the 'observed side' use the transformation rule due to Anscombe (1948; ref.
Novick et al., 1973).

$$g_i = \sin^{-1}\sqrt{(x_i + 3/8) / (n_i + 3/4)} \qquad (3)$$

These transformations have "the effect of simplifying the likelihood function so it
can be more easily approximated by a normal likelihood with known variance" (Novick
et al., 1973, p.21).   Without going into further detail here about these transformations and the mathematics underlying them, it may suffice to say that the end
result of the Bayesian procedure based on these transformations will be a normal
posterior distribution for each examinee in the γ - metric, i.e. a normal
distribution representing the true level of functioning for each examinee.

The Posterior Distribution

The distribution referred to at the end of the last paragraph is obtained through
Bayes' theorem by incorporating prior as well as sample information.   A step-by-
step procedure for doing this has been illustrated by Millman (1974) and Swaminathan
et al., (1975).   It is sufficient to note here that this posterior distribution is
approximately normal distributed in the γ-metric.

Utility Functions for 'Advance' and 'Retain' Decisions

Having determined the posterior distribution for each examinee, the next step, figuratively speaking, is to come up with utility functions reflecting the evaluator's values as to different degrees of the parameter π for an 'advance' and a 'retain' decision.   In a practical situation, of course, this valuation should be carried out without knowledge of the actual school data to hand.   This step is crucial in the procedure discussed in this paper and must be dealt with seriously.

A procedure for accomplishing this task was suggested by Lindley and Novick (1975) in the context of the selection of applicants.   Their procedure has recently been developed by Wedman and DeKeyrel (1976) to fit the situation in C.R.M.   Basically the procedure amounts to putting oneself into a 'gambling' situation where one has to select one of two individuals, given that one of these will obtain a certain outcome for sure, should he be selected, while the other may, if selected, obtain a better or worse result.   The task for the evaluator is to state the probability of the second person obtaining the better result, whilst the evaluator remains neutral as to the merits of either 'applicant'.

To give a concrete example, suppose that you are to select one of two applicants. You know for sure that if you accept, say, A, he will obtain the result π_n in the following course.   Person B, on the other hand, may obtain π_{n+1} (a better result), should he be selected, but he may also obtain π_{n-1} (a worse result).   Your task now is to state the probability for π_{n+1} to occur (against π_{n-1} to occur) where you are indifferent between selecting A or B.   Based on several such gambling situations, where π_{n-1}, π and π_{n+1} assume different values, the utilities for the different states (i.e., π's) can be determined according to the following formula:

$$u_n = p_n (u_{n+1}) + (1 - p_n) (u_{n-1}) \qquad (4)$$

where $\underline{u}$ signifies the utility and $\underline{p}$ the probability.   From this formula it follows that to determine the utilities for, say, $\underline{n}$ different 'states', $\underline{n}$ gambles have to be taken.   In order to explore the consistency of the utility estimates, however, more gambles than are necessary for a mathematical point of view must be taken, or as Lindley and Novick (1975) put it:

> "If this [to take just $\underline{n}$ gambles] is all that the subject is asked to do,
> then the most important aspect of decision-making by maximizing expected
> utility is not exploited at all. We refer here to the principle of co-
> herence. This has been discussed elsewhere, (Lindley, 1971), but the

basic result is that maximization of expected utility is the only way to achieve coherence; that is, to prevent losing money for sure" (p. 11).

In a somewhat loose meaning, what is obtained by 'overspecifying' the gambles is to make sure that the probabilities stated are consistently given, in about the same way as the responses in a paried comparison situation are examined as to their consistency. In other words, the overspecification of the gambles allows for a kind of reliability control.

This control is perhaps accomplished most easily by a least-square technique. Suppose we want to estimate the utilities for nine different 'states' (i.e., values for the parameter of interest). Furthermore, let us assume that the overspecification amounts to taking 15 gambles (about the nine 'states'). The reliability control might then be as follows. The first nine gambles are used for calculating the utility for each of the nine different 'states'. Then, using all the 15 gambles and estimating the same nine values from a least-square point of view, the consistency in the given probabilities is checked. Large deviations mean that the evaluator has been inconsistent and should go through the process again until a better agreement has been obtained.

Before continuing, two more points must be mentioned with respect to the estimation of the utilities. First, it is to be noted that the estimation of utilities must be made both for the 'advance' and the 'retain' situation (as Figure 1 shows). Note here that corresponding values of the parameter need not have utilities that are each other's complement (i.e., they do not necessarily have to sum to 1.0).

Furthermore, by having to come up with two utility functions for the same decision situation there is the added problem of coherence. This is due to the fact that for each situation the utilities have been estimated only in relation to each other. To make sure that they also are coherent 'across' the two decisions situations dealt with here, similar gambling tasks as were referred to above have to be taken but where a 'state' within an 'advance' decision is compared with a 'state' within a 'retain' decision. A simple procedure for dealing with this situation is discussed by Wedman and DeKeyrel (1976).

Given that coherent estimates of the utilities have been obtained, the next step is to try to represent them by a function. It is to be noted, however, that before a function is fitted to the obtained utilities, the latter have to be transformed into the γ-metric, i.e., into the same metric as the true level of functioning is expressed. Should a normal ogive give a good fit, the next step of calculating the expected utilities becomes very simple (see e.g., Lindley and Novick, 1975). If that is not the case, some other function must be used.

In case a normal ogive does not give a good fit of the estimated utilities, Wedman and DeKeyrel (1976) suggest a 'linear combination approach'. i.e., to combine the different linear functions that can be fitted between the different points of the parameter used in the above gambling approach.   At present this approach seems to be satisfactory for most criterion-referenced situations we have encountered.

Determining the Expected Utilities

As has been pointed out earlier (Figure 1), the expected utility for an 'advance' ('retain') decision is obtained by multiplying the posterior distribution by the utility function for 'advancing' (or 'retaining') a student.   This amounts to saying that the probabilities for being at certain 'intervals' on the parameter of interest are multiplied by the corresponding utilities and then the products are added.   The result of this step is an expected utility for each decision, 'advance' and 'retain'.

Making a Decision

In consequence of the last step, the decision is finally made that corresponds to the largest expected utility.   Note again that these two expected utilities do not have to add to 1.0.   This happens only when the two utility functions are 'mirror images' to each other.

A NUMERICAL EXAMPLE

To illustrate the foregoing discussion a numerical example based on ficticious data will be presented in this section.   The data consist of four hypothetical dist- ributions of observed scores from a 10-item test administered to 20 students.   The first three distributions are symmetrical and identical except for their points of location.   The fourth distribution is negatively skewed and 'centered' at the upper part of the scale.   Furthermore, four different sets of utilities and their corresponding utility functions based on the 'linear combination approach' mentioned above have been used.

The data used in this example may or may not be realistic.   The reader is, however, reminded that the prime aim of this presentation is to give an illustration of how the suggested procedure 'works'.   For this purpose we think the data are valid. For a more elaborate illustration, the work by Wedman and DeKeyrel (1976) is recommended.

TABLE 1 - Means and Standard Deviations in the Gamma (γ) Metric for Different Test Scores and Different Amounts of Prior Information (t = 6, 12, 18, 24)

Distri-bution	Test Score	Freq.	Prior Information							
			t = 6		t = 12		t = 18		t = 24	
			Mean	S.D.	Mean	S.D.	Mean	S.D.	Mean	S.D.
I	4	3	.81	.10	.83	.09	.84	.08	.84	.08
	5	4	.84	.10	.85	.09	.86	.08	.86	.08
	6	6	.88	.10	.88	.09	.88	.08	.88	.08
	7	4	.92	.10	.91	.09	.90	.08	.90	.08
	8	3	.96	.10	.94	.09	.93	.08	.92	.08
	9	0								
	10	0								
II	4	0								
	5	3	.90	.10	.92	.09	.93	.09	.94	.08
	6	4	.94	.10	.95	.09	.96	.08	.96	.08
	7	6	.98	.10	.98	.09	.98	.08	.98	.08
	8	4	1.02	.10	1.01	.09	1.00	.08	1.00	.08
	9	3	1.07	.10	1.04	.09	1.03	.08	1.02	.08
	10	0								
III	4	0								
	5	0								
	6	3	1.00	.11	1.03	.10	1.04	.09	1.05	.08
	7	4	1.05	.11	1.06	.09	1.07	.09	1.07	.08
	8	6	1.09	.10	1.09	.09	1.09	.09	1.10	.08
	9	4	1.14	.11	1.13	.09	1.13	.09	1.12	.08
	10	3	1.24	.11	1.21	.10	1.19	.09	1.18	.09
IV	4	0								
	5	1	.98	.11	1.01	.10	1.03	.09	1.04	.09
	6	1	1.02	.11	1.04	.10	1.06	.09	1.07	.08
	7	3	1.06	.11	1.07	.09	1.08	.09	1.09	.08
	8	6	1.10	.10	1.11	.09	1.11	.09	1.11	.08
	9	6	1.16	.10	1.15	.09	1.14	.09	1.14	.08
	10	3	1.25	.11	1.22	.10	1.21	.09	1.19	.09

Table 1 shows the mean and standard deviation of the posterior distribution for each individual under different amounts of prior information (t). Two things can be observed here. First, we can see how the regression effect increases as the amount of prior information increases. This is due to the fact that as the amount of prior information increases, less weight is given to the observed score and more weight to the group mean (compare Kelly's formula). Second, the standard deviations within each category of prior information are almost identical. This is a result of the variance stabilizing transformation formula used.

In Table 2 the utilities used in this example are given. The different utility curves that can be linearly fitted to these values are displayed in Figure 2, based on the earlier mentioned 'linear combination approach' (Wedman and DeKeyrel, 1976).

TABLE 2 - <u>Sets of Utility Values. All Values Represent the Utility for</u> <u>Advancing a Person Given His True Level of Functioning</u>

True level of functioning		U_1	U_2	U_3	U_4
π	γ				
.00	.0000	.0000	.0000	.0000	.0000
.10	.3218	.0400	.0333	.0286	.1000
.20	.4636	.0800	.0667	.0571	.2000
.30	.5796	.1200	.1000	.0857	.3000
.40	.6847	.1600	.1333	.1143	.4000
.50	.7854	.2000	.1667	.1429	.5000
.60	.8861	.5000	.2000	.1714	.6000
.70	.9912	.8000	.5000	.2000	.7000
.80	1.1071	.8667	.8000	.5000	.8000
.90	1.2490	.9333	.9000	.8000	.9000
1.00	1.5708	1.0000	1.0000	1.0000	1.0000

FIGURE 2 - <u>Utility Functions for an 'Advance' Decision</u>

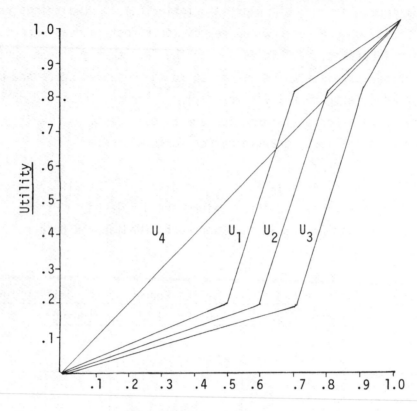

<u>True Level of Functioning (π)</u>

As can be seen in Figure 2 the utility functions are quite different in form.   The fourth curve (U_4) can be looked upon as an extreme curve in the context of C.R.M., contrasted with the commonly used 'threshold curve' (not displayed).   The sharp increments of the curves are meant to represent (but in more realistic terms) the 'all-or-none' problem in C.R.M.   Note that only values and curves for an 'advance' decision are reported.   Corresponding values and curves for the 'retain' situation <u>for the sake of illustration</u> can be obtained by simply taking the complement values and the 'mirror images' of the displayed values and curves respectively.

Based upon the posterior distributions in Table 1 and the utility curves in Figure 2, finally, the expected utilities for an 'advance' decision are given in Table 3.

TABLE 3 — Expected Utilities for Advancing a Person Given His Test Score for Different Utility Functions and Different Amounts of Prior Information

Distri-bution	Test Score	Freq.	t = 6				t = 12				t = 18				t = 24			
			U_1	U_2	U_3	U_4	U_1	U_2	U_3	U_4	U_1	U_2	U_3	U_4	U_1	U_2	U_3	U_4
I	4	3	.35	.21	.15	.52	.37	.22	.16	.54	.39	.22	.16	.55	.40	.22	.16	.56
	5	4	.42	.24	.17	.56	.43	.24	.17	.57	.44	.24	.17	.57	.44	.24	.17	.58
	6	6	.49	.29	.19	.59	.49	.28	.18	.59	.49	.27	.18	.59	.49	.27	.18	.59
	7	4	.58	.35	.21	.63	.56	.33	.20	.62	.55	.31	.19	.62	.54	.30	.19	.61
	8	3	.66	.43	.25	.66	.63	.38	.22	.65	.61	.36	.21	.64	.59	.34	.20	.63
	9	0																
	10	0																
II	4	0																
	5	3	.55	.33	.20	.62	.59	.36	.21	.63	.62	.37	.21	.64	.64	.38	.22	.65
	6	4	.63	.39	.23	.65	.66	.41	.23	.66	.67	.42	.23	.67	.68	.42	.23	.67
	7	6	.70	.47	.27	.68	.71	.47	.27	.69	.72	.47	.26	.69	.73	.47	.26	.69
	8	4	.77	.56	.33	.72	.77	.54	.31	.71	.77	.53	.29	.71	.77	.52	.29	.71
	9	3	.83	.65	.41	.76	.81	.61	.37	.74	.81	.59	.34	.73	.80	.58	.33	.73
	10	0																
III	4	0																
	5	0																
	6	3	.74	.53	.32	.71	.79	.58	.34	.73	.81	.61	.36	.74	.82	.62	.37	.75
	7	4	.80	.61	.38	.74	.83	.64	.40	.75	.84	.66	.41	.76	.85	.67	.42	.77
	8	6	.85	.69	.46	.78	.86	.71	.46	.78	.86	.71	.47	.78	.87	.72	.47	.79
	9	4	.88	.77	.56	.82	.88	.77	.54	.81	.88	.77	.54	.81	.88	.77	.53	.81
	10	3	.92	.87	.72	.88	.91	.85	.68	.86	.91	.84	.65	.85	.90	.83	.63	.84
IV	4	0																
	5	1	.70	.48	.28	.68	.76	.54	.32	.71	.80	.58	.35	.73	.82	.61	.37	.74
	6	1	.76	.56	.34	.72	.81	.61	.37	.74	.83	.64	.39	.75	.84	.66	.41	.76
	7	3	.82	.64	.40	.75	.84	.67	.43	.77	.86	.69	.44	.77	.86	.71	.45	.78
	8	6	.86	.72	.49	.79	.87	.73	.49	.79	.87	.74	.50	.80	.88	.75	.50	.80
	9	6	.89	.79	.58	.83	.89	.79	.57	.82	.89	.79	.57	.82	.89	.79	.56	.82
	10	3	.92	.87	.74	.88	.91	.86	.70	.87	.91	.85	.68	.86	.91	.84	.66	.85

In this table, the combined effects of prior information, the group to which a certain individual belongs, and the utilities for the parameter of interest, are illustrated. Take for instance the first value that appears in Table 3, i.e., the expected utility for 'advancing' a person belonging to the first distribution (I) with an observed score of 4 and with the amount of prior information equal to t = 6. The expected utility for 'advancing' him/her is .35. This value is derived by integrating the product of the corresponding posterior distribution (.81;.10) obtainable from Table 1 and the utility function U_1 depicted in Figure 2.

As to the prior information we can see that as this amount increased the expected utility (EU) increases for values below the group mean and the reverse for values above the group mean. This is due to the same regression phenomenon dealt with earlier (see e.g., Table 1). Furthermore, we may note the great 'impact' of the utility function used. Finally, we may observe that even though the test score for two individuals may be the same and that the utility function is the same, the decision made may be different, depending on which group the individuals belong to. Here again, the regression phenomenon plays an important part.

Due to the interactive characteristic of the variables involved in Table 3, it is somewhat complicated to convey all of its information. However, let us look at two cases and examine what can be inferred. In doing this, let us also assume that the utility functions for a 'retain' decision are the 'mirror images' of those displayed in Figure 2. This amounts to saying that each EU in Table 3 has a complement which is simply (1-EU$_A$; where 'A' denotes 'advance').

   i. Let us first take an observed score of 5. The EU$_A$ for this score, given the first score distribution, the utility function U_1, and the amount of prior information t = 6, is .42, i.e. EU$_A$ (5|I,U_1, t = 6) = .42. If we assume that the corresponding utility function for a 'retain' decision is U_1's 'mirror image' ($\bar{U}_1$), the expected utility for a 'retain' decision is .58 (1-.42), i.e., EU$_R$(5|I, $\bar{U}_1$, t = 6) = .58. The decision would consequently be 'retain'. Should, however, our conditions be (5|I, U_4, t = 6) and (5|I, $\bar{U}_4$, t = 6), respectively, then the opposite decision would be made - likewise if the conditions are (5|II, U_1, t = 6) and (5|II, $\bar{U}_1$, t = 6). However, if the conditions are (5|II, U2, t = 24) and (5|II, $\bar{U}_1$, t = 24), then we would accept the person as his EU$_A$ = .38 and his EU$_R$ = .36.

   ii. Now let us look at a test score of 8. If that score belongs to a person within the first distribution he would be accepted under, for example, the following conditions (8|I, U_1, t = 6) and (8|I, $\bar{U}_1$, t = 6);

but not, for example, under the following conditions $(8 \mid I, U_2, t = 6)$ and $(8 \mid I, \bar{U_2}, t = 6)$. However, should this test score belong to a person within the third distribution he would also be accepted under the second circumstance, i.e., $EU_A (8 \mid III, U_2, t = 6) = .69$ and $EU_R(8 \mid III, \bar{U_2}, t = 6) = .31$.

Before ending this section we want to encourage the reader to closely examine these tables for himself/herself to obtain a clear understanding of their information. By so doing we think that the sometimes intricate aspects of a decision-making process will be clarified and the value of the procedure discussed here illuminated.

DISCUSSIONS

By definition criterion-referenced measurements almost always involve a decision component. Hence, the teacher or evaluator making use of such tests has to decide whether a student, given his test score, should be 'advanced' (to the next sequence of instruction) or 'retained'. One critical step in this undertaking has been the determination of the cut-off level.

The procedure discussed in this paper makes, interestingly enough, the concept of a single cut-off level superfluous. Rather one compares expected utilities and chooses the larger. It is also to be noted that the procedure for doing this is systematic in its character and certainly somewhat more complicated than a more intuitive approach. This we believe is a necessary price to pay in order to implement a rational decision-theoretic procedure.

Besides, the seeming complexity of the suggested procedure is more artificial than real. Actually, all the steps involved can very simply be carried out by using an interactive data terminal. A programme for handling the requisite data (CADA) is available from Iowa Testing Programs in Iowa City, U.S.A. But even without a computer it is quite possible to handle the procedure using published Tables (Isaacs, Christ, Novick & Jackson, 1974; Wang, 1973). Therefore, practical arguments of this kind are not reasons for rejecting the procedure discussed in this paper.

There may be, however, sound reasons for investigations, from a psychological standpoint (aside from a mathematical point of view), into the possibilities of eliciting from students estimates of prior information and the effects of using different approximation procedures. The same might also be said as to the utility functions.

Such investigations should provide evidence as to the practicality of the Bayesian procedure described here and lead to a more rational and systematic application of a decision-making strategy to test data than we sometimes encounter today.

REFERENCES

BRENNAN, R.L. (1974). Psychometric methods for criterion-referenced tests. Final report. Department of Education. SUNY at Stony Brook. Stony Brook, New York.

de KLERK, LEN.F.W. (1975). On the establishment of passing standards for criterion-references tests. Tijdschrift vor Psychologie, 4/5, 215-222.

HAMBLETON, R.K. and NOVICK, M.R. (1973). Toward an integration of theory and method for criterion-referenced tests. Journal of Educational Measurement, 10, 159-170.

HAMBLETON, R.K., SWAMINATHAN, H., ALGINA, J. and COULSON, D. (1975). Criterion-referenced testing and measurement: a review of technical issues and developments. An invited symposium presented at the annual meeting of the American Educational Research Association. Washington, D.C. April 1975.

HARRIS, C.W., ALKIN, M.C. and POPHAM, W.J. (Eds.) (1974). Problems in criterion-referenced measurement. Los Angeles: Center for the Study of Evaluation.

ISAACS, G.L., CHRIST, D.E., NOVICK, M.R. and JACKSON, P.H. (1974). Tables for Bayesian statisticians. Iowa City, Iowa: The University of Iowa.

KELLY, T.L. (1927). Interpretation of educational measurements. Younkers on Hudson, New York: World Book.

LEWIS, C., WANG, MING-MEI. and NOVICK, M.R. (1975). Marginal distributions for the estimation of proportions in m groups. Psychometrika, 40(1) 63-75.

LINDLEY, D.V. and NOVICK, M.R. (1975). Assessing utility functions with application to education. University of Iowa, Iowa City, Iowa 1975 (paper).

MESKAUSKES, J.A. (1976). Evaluation models for criterion-referenced testing: views regarding mastery and standard-setting. Review of Educational Research. 46, 133-158.

MILLMAN, J. (1973). Passing scores and test lengths for domain-referenced measures. Review of Educational Research. 43, 205-216.

MILLMAN, J. (1974). Criterion-referenced measurement. In: W.J. POPHAM (Ed.): Evaluation in education: current applications. Berkeley, California: McCutchan Publishing Company.

NOVICK, M.R. and JACKSON, P.H. (1974). Statistical methods for educational and psychological research. New York: McGraw Hill.

NOVICK, M.R. and LEWIS, C. (1974). Prescribing test length for criterion-referenced measurement. In: HARRIS, C.W., ALKIN, M.C. and POPHAM, W.J. (Eds.): Problems in criterion-referenced measurement. Los Angeles: Center for the Study of Evaluation.

NOVICK, M.R., LEWIS, C. and JACKSON, P.H. (1973). The estimation of proportions in m groups. Psychometrika, 38(1), 19-46.

SWAMINATHAN, H., HAMBLETON, R.K. and ALGINA, J.A. (1975). Bayesian decision-theoretic procedure for use with criterion-referenced tests. Journal of Educational Measurement, 12, 87-98.

WANG, MING-MEI. (1973). Tables of constants for the posterior marginal estimates of proportions in m groups. ACT Technical Bulletin. No.14. Iowa City, Iowa: The American College Testing Program.

WEDMAN, I. (1973). Theoretical problems in construction of criterion-referenced tests. Educational Reports, Umeå. No.3.

WEDMAN, I. and DeKEYREL (1976). Allocating individuals to mastery states based on expected utilities. The University of Iowa, Iowa City, Iowa (in press).

THE RASCH MODEL - AN OPERATIONAL ITEM BANK

A.S. WILLMOTT

Abstract - This paper described the philosophy behind
work which is being carried out within the
Examinations and Tests Research Unit of the
National Foundation for Educational Research
and which is funded by the Schools Council
for Curriculum and Examinations.

THE RASCH MODEL

"It is only by establishing objectivity that we can ever achieve a quantitative grasp of mental abilities or ever construct a science of
mental development" (Wright, 1968); and to do so requires first that
the characteristics of the items in a test must somehow be made independent of the distribution of attainment in the group who are given the
test, and, secondly, that the test should give estimates of attainment
which are independent of the particular set of items which comprise the
test.   The first of these requirements begs for an 'item calibration'
which is 'person-free', the second for 'person measurement' which is
'item free'."   (Willmott and Fowles, 1974)

The desire for objectivity in measurement is the key to the benefits which accrue
from the use of the Rasch Model for Item analysis, and, indeed, the model has
objectivity as its very heart.   A measurement which is objective, in the sense of
the quotation above, may be reported without reference to the particular instrument
or to the particular group of people measured by the instrument.   The interaction
of a person with test material (test items) yields conventionally a test score which
is often simply the number of correct answers to the test items.   This 'observation' is clearly not a 'measurement' in the sense discussed above, since different
sets of test items would yield different test scores.   The Rasch Model attempts to
translate a crude observation into meaningful measurement.   (Rasch, 1960, 1961,
1966).

Two principles are extremely important here, however, since they relate directly to the very nature of measurement.   First, the measuring instrument used must be relevant to the attribute being measured and, secondly the measurement of a continuous attribute - such as attainment in a subject area - can never be precise. Bearing these principles in mind, the Rasch Model may be stated simply as follows:

i.   When a person encounters an item, a single outcome is recorded (i.e., pass/fail) and this outcome depends only on (a) a person parameter which is constant for all items attempted by that person and (b) an item parameter which is constant for all persons attempting that item.

ii.   The person parameter is measuring the 'same thing' as the item parameter and both parameters are expressed on the same scale.

iii.   All the items in a test evoke responses from people on the same trait - (all the items must measure the same thing).

A MATHEMATICAL STATEMENT OF THE MODEL   (Taken from Willmott and Fowles, 1974)

The model has two parameters, i.e., an item parameter δ_i associated with each item i, and a person parameter β_v associated with each person v.   These parameters determine probabilistically the outcome of the encounter between person v and item i. The basic statement of the model describes the probability of a response X_{vi} by person v to item i and is of the following form;

$$Pr\left[X_{vi} = 1 \middle| \beta_v, \delta_i\right] = Pr\left[X_{vi}\right]$$

$$= \frac{\exp\lambda_{vi}}{1+\exp\lambda_{vi}}$$

(1)

where an observation x_{vi} is recorded as '1' if correct, and zero otherwise, and where

$$\lambda_{vi} = \beta_v - \delta_i$$

(2)

(N.B.:   Any symmetric function λ of β and δ could be used; $\lambda_{vi} = \beta_v \delta_i$ for example may be found in the literature.   Wright currently uses form 2).   It is seen that the probability of a correct response increases with the attainment of a person (β_ν) and decreases with the difficulty of the item (δ_i).

Thus, if '0' is recorded for an incorrect answer:

$$Pr\left[X_{\nu i} = 0\right] = 1 - Pr\left[X_{\nu i} = 1\right]$$

and therefore

$$Pr\left[X_{\nu i} = 0 \middle| \beta_\nu, \delta_i\right] = 1 - \frac{\exp\lambda_{\nu i}}{1 + \exp\lambda_{\nu i}}$$

$$= \frac{1}{1 + \exp\lambda_{\nu i}}$$

(3)

Combining (1), (2) and (3)

$$Pr\left[X_{\nu i} \middle| \beta_\nu, \delta_i\right] = \frac{\exp\left[X_{\nu i}(\beta_\nu - \delta_i)\right]}{1 + \exp(\beta_\nu - \delta_i)}$$

(4)

In the special case where $\beta_\nu = \delta_i$

then $\lambda_{\nu i} = 0$ from (2)

and $Pr\left[X_{\nu i} = 1 \middle| \beta_\nu, \delta_i\right] = 0.5$ from (1)

Thus there is a 50 per cent chance of success for person ν with attainment β_ν attempting item i of difficulty δ_i when $\beta_\nu = \delta_i$. As seen, this probability increases or decreases depending upon the positive or negative distance of $\lambda_{\nu i}$ from zero, i.e., according to the difference between β_ν and δ_i.

DOES IT WORK?

It is usually the case with a mathematical model that it is formulated in order to fit the data to be analysed. In the case of the Rasch Model, the benefits of objectivity are such that since the three statements above are a necessary and sufficient condition for objectivity (Rasch, 1968), the task may be taken as finding data which will fit the model. Before this approach is followed up, however, it is worth noting that the model is saying that, in any testing situation, the item characteristic curves should be roughly parallel. If they are not then, since the curves must cross at some point, depending on the ability of the testee so item A will be harder or easier than item B. This, clearly, would not be objective measurement.

The claims of objectivity are appealing and it is relevant to consider how test items may interact with the model and may be seen to 'fit' the model, or not. From statement 1(b) above, the idea of a stable item parameter, which remains constant for all people answering that item, is seen. To test 'fit' to the model, therefore, the responses to the same set of items of groups of people of different ability may be noted. Since the model allows for the standard errors of the estimates of β and δ to be obtained (see Appendix A for the development of the parameter estimation procedures, together with their standard errors) the various estimates of δ may be compared for statistical equivalence. This question of fit is discussed more fully by Willmott and Fowles (1974) but it is important to note the symmetry of the model: just as items may be fitted to the model, so too may people and this point will be taken up at a later stage herein.

THE ORIGINS OF THE BIOLOGY ITEM BANK (B.I.B.)

In order to test the Rasch Model in operation, a series of tests were constructed and administered to school pupils in their fifth year of secondary education (i.e., aged 16+). The subject matter was biology and the intention was to establish a Biology Item Bank (i.e., B.I.B.). The pretesting design was set up with a series of 16 overlapping tests constructed such that they formed a 'cartwheel'; each test consisted of half the items from the preceeding test in the wheel and half the items from the following test in the wheel. The items were short-answer and multiple-choice in nature, and were all objectively scored (i.e., 0/1). B.I.B. is more fully described by Duckworth and Hoste (1976).

The analysis of the B.I.B. design led to the basis of the current thinking on item bank procedures and to the problem of the consideration of the 'error' of the fit of the data to the model in large scale designs. In the analysis of the cartwheel, the 16 individual tests were tested for fit to the model, and any items which were not appearing to fit were dropped at that stage. Test 01 in the B.I.B. was then analysed alongside Test 02 in the B.I.B. and the common test items (i.e., half of each test) used:

i.   to test the stability of the trait being assessed by each of the tests and to reject items which did not appear to yield responses from the testees on the same trait   and

ii.   to estimate the linking parameter between the two tests.

The linking (or chaining) parameter is simply the overall shift in estimated ability of the testees from the two tests and must be obtained in order to relate all the estimated item parameters to the same origin.   This procedure was repeated for Tests 02 and 03 in the B.I.B. and so on up to Tests 15 and 16 in the B.I.B.   When the cartwheel had been completed in this manner, the closure of the wheel was attempted by the analysis of Test 16 and 01 in the B.I.B.   At this stage it was found that the estimate of the linking parameter was statistically within the error tolerance, although numerically non-zero.   Thus linking had been 'satisfactory' statistically, but the items in Test 01 in the B.I.B. had two sets of item statistics which were inconsistent (one set obtained from the initial analysis of Test 01 with Test 02 and one obtained from the final analysis of Test 01 with Test 16).   The way this problem was overcome will be reported in due course, but involved the equivalent of a least squares solution to the problem.   Nevertheless, the problems associated with the 'error' in the linking process indicated that better testing designs could be adopted.

THE DEVELOPMENT OF THE BIOLOGY ITEM BANK

The original B.I.B. analyses were carried out in 1973 and, at that time, the items rejected as 'not fitting the model' were discarded for later investigation.   Out of a total of 336 items pretested, over 200 were accepted into the final bank.   In 1974 a test of biology was required for use, and the opportunity was taken to construct this test from the bank of 200 satisfactory items.   Given to a group of sixteen-year-old pupils studying biology, it was reassuring to note that the bank values of the item calibrations were recovered very well indeed: stability over a period of one year seemed to have been achieved.

A year later, in 1975/76, three more tests, with overlapping items between themselves, and between themselves and the item bank, were pretested in schools with a view to broadening the content and the relevance of the bank.

The bank had never been used for purposes other than research and it was part of the aim of the project to involve practising teachers fully in a small-scale trial operation of the bank.   At that stage the work paused for a while and the ideas behind the use of any item bank were looked at.

SOME USES FOR ITEM BANKS IN BRITIAN

The public examination system at 16+ in Britain currently consists of eight boards examining for the General Certificate of Education (G.C.E.) examination and of fourteen boards examining for the Certificate of Secondary Education (C.S.E.) examination.   In the C.S.E. examinations in particular, there has been a steady increase in the number of teachers who are willing and able to prepare their own courses, to teach their own courses and to examine their own courses, subject only to the continued approval of their examining boards as far as their course is concerned and to the moderation of their final grades by representatives of their examining board.   This approach to examining - known as the Mode III approach - means that a number of teachers of, say, biology may have courses which differ only slightly in content but which require assessments to be made on a common subject grade scale.   An item bank, properly established, could help to play a part here, but a far more immediate use would be to allow teachers using the Mode III approach to have access to suitable material for in-course assessment.   Not all teachers would need to use all the material in the bank, since, if the object- ivity referred to above was attained, this would ensure that scores on tests consisting of different sets of items, each drawn from the bank, could be related with confidence.   Further, teachers involved in preparing candidates for the traditional external examination syllabus - as laid down by the examining board - could also benefit from using the bank for making in-course assessments.   With the item bank calibrated in terms of public examination grades, immediate feedback would be available to every teacher drawing tests from the bank and making educat- ional assessments on the standing of his pupils.   In the extreme case, the item bank could well be used to check grading standards between the various examining boards and, implicity, between one examination system and another (i.e. C.S.E. and G.C.E.), since the two separate scales are operationally related.   These latter uses would depend, however, on considerable background work being carried out in order to establish a viable and valid item bank.

However, by far the most important contribution to the critical thinking on the subject of item banking in the British context was published as long ago as 1969 by Wood and Skurnik.   This book, which should be considerably more prominent in the literature than it is, serves both as an example of procedures which may be adopted and problems which may be met in the field, as well as providing a philo- sphical basis for discussion.   The use of an item bank to ensure that grades are only awarded at a comparable level, and not just to check whether subject grades already awarded are at a comparable level from board to board, is discussed in detail and, indeed, the book is subtitled "A method for producing school-based examinations and nationally comparable grades".   This is the ideal to which the development of item banks may progress in Britain, but the acceptance of the content of such banks, by all concerned, is a critical prerequisite. There are, of course, other uses for item banks which are applicable other than in the British context in particular, as the title of this workshop states directly. It is within this framework that the move towards an item banking system will be discussed.

PRINCIPLES BEHIND THE ITEM BANKING SYSTEM

Within the Examinations and Tests Research Unit (ETRU) of the N.F.E.R. it was agreed to develop a comprehensive Item Banking System (IBS) to enable the full benefits of the objective measurement implied by the Rasch Model to be realised. The I.B.S. has been designed to allow for a flexible use of the items in the bank and the emphasis has been placed on the statistical characteristics of item and test analysis, rather than on a complicated system of item storage and retrieval.

The main principles on which the system has been developed are:

(a) The Statistics should be Sample-Free

The use of the Rasch Model, leading to the estimation of sample-free statistics, is taken as the heart of the I.B.S. As a consequence, from the complete bank different tests may be drawn and may yield test scores which are able to be interpreted on the common bank dimension (or trait). This allows for flexibility of use and a meaningful interpretation of results as well as a thorough investigation of the nature of both items and people at any time that the data are collected.

(b) The Bank should be able to be Extended

When tests are drawn from the bank, new items may be included and may be calibrated alongside the bank items. Any new items surviving the tests of fit (see below) will be added to the bank on a tentative basis and made available to other bank users as required. Until a sufficiently wide data base on such items has been collected, however, their use will be restricted as far as tests drawn from the bank are concerned.

(c) There should be Item-Fit at each stage

Whenever data are collected and analysed, the fit of the data to the model will be investigated and levels of acceptable criteria will be specified. This will be true at both the test calibration and the linking stages. Whenever new items fail to meet the criteria, an item quality code will be attached to each item in order to indicate the degree of the lack of fit. At the stage of constructing tests from the bank these item quality codes will be borne in mind, since although

a few items of poor quality will not upset the objective nature of the final measurements (and may be included specifically for reasons of validity), a large number
of such items could cause considerable measurement problems.

(d) There Should be a Person-Fit: Diagnostic Testing

When measurement is carried out with bank items of known quality, those to whom the
test has been given may be fitted to the model in order to look for those testees
who are yielding item response patterns which are significantly different from what
is expected.   Such a procedure will allow for diagnostic results to be obtained
on individuals who might be suffering from learning difficulties of many kinds or
who may be finding the material too easy.   This aspect of the use of item banks
has yet to be explored in any detail but, potentially, the area is an extremely
important one.

(e) The Bank Statistics should be Updated

At each stage when the bank is used, the extra data collected will be used to up-
date the statistics of the item used.   This procedure will only be carried out
with data from testees whose responses appear to fit the Rasch Model, since the
items are known to scale correctly.   In this manner the 'breadth' of the bank
items in terms of background information will grow with its use.

(f) There should be indications of the Relevance of Items in the Bank

Allied with the updating procedures, it is necessary to consider the relevance of
an item to a given group of people to be tested.   Not all items which fit the
model may be expected to work equally well at every level of ability or, put
another way, different items of the same apparent level of difficulty will have
different levels of optimum efficiency in terms of ability levels.   The appropriate level for each item will be indicated.

(g) The Content of the Bank should be wide ranging

Since the I.B.S. is designed to handle operational banks in the context of British
Examinations at 16+, the system will allow for a wide range of content to be
covered by the items in the bank.   Strictly speaking this is not a facility of
the I.B.S. itself but more a way in which it will be used.

(h) The Bank will be Tied to National Standards

It is hoped that, in the fullness of time, the scale of measurement of the bank
will be related directly to the public examination grade scales at 16+, in order

that the most use may be made of the bank's resources.   This will take some time
to attain and is a long term aim.

(i)   The Bank Items should be able to be Removed

The I.B.S. will allow for items which are felt by subject experts not to be relevant at any time to their subject, to be removed from the bank.

(j)   Access to the Bank should be Centrally Based

The I.B.S. is designed to hold only a reference number and a minimum amount of data
relevant to each item, with the items themselves being held in card index files.
Access to the bank will be initiated centrally and will reflect the requests of
teachers, and other users, for tests based on a given balance of subject matter.

In the fullness of time other factors will undoubtedly become important but these
are the main issues which form a basis for the operation of the Item Banking System.

THE ISSUE OF VALIDITY

In all that has been said, one essential prerequisite for constructing an item bank
and for its continued efficient use is that of validity.   If items with specific
subject content are presented to individuals who have not been prepared for that
subject content, then the response to the items is, in some sense, 'undefined' -
if not actually a random event.   This factor may be a problem in some contexts,
but not in others.   In the context of B.I.B., and examinations at 16+, the problem is minimised since most pupils are prepared by most teachers to cover most of
the subject content of any test which the teacher would draw from the bank.   At
the present time, even a general test drawn to represent the content of an item
bank would not be likely to uncover any particular problems of validity.

The issue may be faced, however, on a wider front when it comes to national monitoring, since the objectives of such a study are usually broader and not tied
specifically to a given set of subject material.   If a bank of established items
is used in a national survey, then a test of item-fit within the monitoring
instrument(s) will yield useful results.   If all seems well with the items, then
person fit may be investigated and further analyses conducted to yield the appropriate national figures.   If, however, some items appear not to fit the model (in
the context of the monitoring work), then some kind of 'sifting' process becomes
necessary in order to detect the source of the lack of fit: it cannot, by
definition, be the bank items, if the bank has been properly constructed.   A comb-

ination of person-fit and item-fit will probably uncover some inconsistency in the way the pupils in the monitoring study approached the subject concerned, perhaps on a school basis.

Clearly, the existence of an established, but organically renewable, bank of subject-based items of known quality creates an environment where meaningful measurements of attainment may be made; in the context of the use of any such bank, however, the issue of validity will always be central.   For an item bank to be able to be used in national monitoring studies, it is argued that a well-defined bank needs to be contructed <u>outside</u> the monitoring study itself, in order that the item indices are rendered stable and accurate in relation to each other.   In the period in which the bank would be established, the validity problem would be overcome by trying out items only on pupils who were prepared in the subject.   This procedure would ensure that, before the all important work started, a 'reference instrument' - i.e. the set of items in the bank - existed against which to test the national population in an agreed manner.   If an attempt is made to establish a bank as part of the monitoring exercise itself, then it is more likely that stable item calibrations would not be achieved.   Given the established bank, any lack of fit of data collected in the context of a national study could be investigated as outlined above and the cause for apparent changes in the level of item parameters, one to another, could be investigated; without an established bank it would be far more difficult to establish a connection between any lack of fit of the data collected and any particular feature of the sample used for the national monitoring study.

IN CONCLUSION

It is important to note that all this investigation could not be carried out without the aid of an explicit model.   The Rasch Model, seen to be the most simple kind of model necessary and sufficient to allow for objective measurement (the Rasch Model may be seen, not suprisingly, with hindsight, to be the analysis of variance model in disguise - James, 1973), allows for many aspects of investigation to be executed which would not have been possible without considerable extra effort otherwise.   Nevertheless, although the use of objective measurements brings with it a substantial increase in the effectiveness of rendering meaningful educational measurements, the data used are only those used in the more conventional test and item-analysis procedures; for parameter estimation to take place, only the number of people answering each item correctly, and the number of items each person answers correctly, are needed.

Thus, the assumptions behind the conventional testing procedures are brought into the open.   In the context of B.I.B., most of the items 'dropped' from the analysis at the item fit stage would have not passed scrutiny when looked at with more conventional item analytic methods; this was not true of all items, however.

The Item Banking System is still in its very early days and has yet to be used operationally.   The principles of approach, as discussed above, are intended to lead to the development of a useful resource which may be used at a number of levels as time goes by.   Ultimately, however, it will be up to those constructing the items themselves to make the whole process meaningful.   The statistical experience and computational technology will provide no answers without an educational consideration of the purpose of the bank, the bank content, the ways in which the items in the bank are used and the careful interpretation of the results produced by tests drawn from the bank.

It is, perhaps, best to leave the last word to Wood and Skurnik whose thoughts are as true today as they were in 1969:

"Item banking is an examining technique for the future, and perhaps the time is not yet ripe in Great Britain to adopt it lock, stock and barrel.   However, it ought not to be dismissed as an 'excellent academic exercise for psychometricians'.   We believe we found enough evidence to demonstrate that the idea has practical utility and that it can be made to work.   It remains for others to decide how to invest their resources to gain maximum returns."   (Wood and Skurnik, 1969)

A P P E N D I X   A

(Taken from Willmott & Fowles, 1974)

1. The Data

The data matrix $\left[X_{\nu i}\right]$ of item/person encounter outcomes may be summed across rows and down columns to give two marginal totals.

Summing over the entries for person ν gives $X_{\nu .}$, that person's total score on the test, i.e. for a k-item test

$$X_{\nu .} = \sum_{i=1}^{k} X_{\nu i} \tag{5}$$

Summing over the entries for an item i gives $X_{.i}$, the number of people getting item i right, i.e. for N people

$$X_{.i} = \sum_{\nu=1}^{N} X_{\nu i}$$

2. Estimation of Parameters β and δ by the Method of Maximum Likelihood

The aim is to derive two sets of parameter estimates. The first set estimates each of the item parameters δ_i; the other set estimates each of the person parameters β_ν. The derived values will be those that together give the best fit to the likelihood function.

The likelihood of function ℓ is obtained by taking the product of Equation (4) over all persons (N) and all items (k), i.e.

$$\ell = \prod_{\nu=1}^{N} \prod_{i=1}^{k} \frac{\exp\left[X_{\nu i}\,(\beta_\nu - \delta_i)\right]}{1+\exp\,(\beta_\nu - \delta_i)} \tag{6}$$

The numerator of this expression becomes

$$\exp\left[\sum_{\nu=1}^{N} \sum_{i=1}^{N} X_{\nu i}\,(\beta_\nu - \delta_i)\right]$$

or

$$\exp\left[\sum_{\nu=1}^{N} X_{\nu.}\beta_{\nu} - \sum_{i=1}^{k} X_{.i}\delta_{i}\right]$$

The original matrix entries $(X_{\nu i})$ do not therefore appear in either the numerator or the denominator.   They have been summarized and replaced by the marginal totals $X_{\nu.}$ and $X_{.i}$.

$$\therefore \ell = \frac{\exp\left[\sum_{\nu=1}^{N} X_{\nu.}\beta_{\nu} - \sum_{i=1}^{k} X_{.i}\delta_{i}\right]}{\prod_{\nu=1}^{N}\prod_{i=1}^{k}\left[1+\exp(\beta_{\nu} - \delta_{i})\right]}$$

The log likelihood, L, is therefore

$$L = \sum_{\nu=1}^{N} X_{\nu.}\beta_{\nu} - \sum_{i=1}^{k} X_{.i}\delta_{i} - \sum_{\nu=1}^{N}\sum_{i=1}^{k} \log\left[1+\exp(\beta_{\nu} - \delta_{i})\right]$$

In order to differentiate the log likelihood, it is necessary to include a La Grange multiplier α as L is a symmetric function of β and δ,

Thus $$L = \sum_{\nu=1}^{N} X_{\nu.}\beta_{\nu} - \sum_{i=1}^{k} X_{.i}\delta_{i} - \sum_{\nu=1}^{N}\sum_{i=1}^{k} \log\left[1+\exp(\beta_{\nu} - \delta_{i})\right] + \alpha\sum_{i=1}^{k}\delta_{i}$$

Differentiating L with respect to β_{μ} and δ_{j} now gives

$$\frac{\partial L}{\partial\beta_{\mu}} = X_{\mu.} - \sum_{i=1}^{k}\frac{\exp\left[\beta_{\mu} - \delta_{i}\right]}{1+\exp\left[\beta_{\mu} - \delta_{i}\right]}$$

$$= X_{\mu.} - \sum_{i=1}^{k} Pr\left[X_{\mu i}\right]$$

(7)

and similarly,

$$\frac{\partial L}{\partial \delta_j} = X._j + \sum_{\nu=1}^{N} Pr\left[X_{\nu j}\right] + \alpha$$

(8)

Summing Equation (7) over all items and Equation (8) over all people must give the same total; hence $\alpha = 0$.

In order to be able to solve explicitly for the item and score group parameters, it is first necessary to 'locate' one of the scales. For convenience, and without loss of generality, the sum of the item difficulties is taken to be zero: equivalently, the mean item difficulty may be considered to be zero.

It is now seen that the model does not differentiate between two persons whose total score on the test is the same. The only place the data occur in the above estimating equations is as the marginal totals $X_{\nu.}$ and $X._j$. At this point therefore, the sample is 'reduced' to (k-1) groups on the basis of total score and 'person μ' is replaced by 'score group r'. (Persons with a score of 0 or k are excluded.)

Hence, putting the first derivative to zero and writing $X_{\mu i}$ as X_{ri} gives

$$r = \sum_{i=1}^{k} Pr\left[X_{ri}\right] \quad \text{from (7), and writing } X_{\mu.} \text{ as r.}$$

(9)

Similarly, if S_i is the number of people correctly answering item i, then from (8)

$$S_i = \sum_{r=1}^{k-1} n_r Pr\left[X_{ri}\right]$$

(10)

where n_r is the number of people in the rth score group.

The parameter estimation strategy is to find the values of the item and person parameters to jointly satisfy (9) and (10). The computational techniques will not be laboured here but the procedure is to start from an initial estimate of the set of the item parameters and score group parameters.   These estimates are used as starting values in an iterative process which has been found to converge rapidly in practice (about five iterations are required for a reasonably accurate solution).

3. The Standard Errors of β and δ

The required standard errors are found by noting that the negative reciprocal of the second derivative of the likelihood function (with respect to each of the two parameters in turn) gives the asymptotic variance estimates of β and δ.   From (7),

$$\frac{\partial L}{\partial \beta_\mu} = X_{\mu \cdot} - \sum_{i=1}^{k} Pr\left[X_{\mu i}\right]$$

$$\therefore \quad \frac{\partial^2 L}{\partial \beta_\mu^2} = - \sum_{i=1}^{k} \left[Pr(X_{\mu i})\right] \left[1 - Pr(X_{\mu i})\right]$$

i.e. Variance of β_μ =
$$\frac{1}{\sum_{i=1}^{k} \left[Pr(X_{\mu i})\right] \left[1 - Pr(X_{\mu i})\right]}$$

Similarly, from (8)
$$\frac{\partial L}{\partial \delta_j} = - X_{\cdot j} + \sum_{v=1}^{N} Pr\left[X_{vj}\right]$$

$$\therefore \quad \frac{\partial^2 L}{\partial \delta_j^2} = - \sum_{v=1}^{N} \left[Pr(X_{vj})\right] \left[1 - Pr(X_{vj})\right]$$

i.e. Variance of δ_j =
$$\frac{1}{\sum_{v=1}^{N} \left[Pr(X_{vj})\right] \left[1 - Pr(X_{vj})\right]}$$

REFERENCES

DUCKWORTH, D. and HOSTE, H.R. (1976).   Question Banking: an approach through biology.   To be published in the Schools Council Examinations Bulletin 35. Evans/Methuen Educational.

JAMES, A.N. (1973).   From Rasch to classical test theory.   Paper delivered at a seminar on sample-free item analysis at the National Foundation for Educational Research, Slough, in March 1973 (unpublished).

RASCH, G. (1960).   Probablistic Models for some Intelligence and Attainment Tests. Copenhagen: Danish Institute for Educational Research.

RASCH, G. (1961).   'On General Laws and the Meaning of Measurement in Psychology'. In: Proceeding of the Fourth Berkeley Symposium on Mathematical Statistics and Probability.   Berkeley: University of California Press, IV, 321-334.

RASCH, G. (1966).   'An item analysis which takes individual differences into account', Brit. J. Math. Stat. Psychol., 19, part 1, 49-57.

RASCH, G. (1968).   'A Mathematical Theory of Objectivity and its Consequences for Model Construction.'   Paper delivered at European Meeting on Statistics, Econometrics and Management Science,   Amsterdam, September 1968.

WILLMOTT, A.S. and FOWLES, D.E. (1974).   The Objective Interpretation of Test Performance: the Rasch Model Applied.   Slough: National Foundation for Educational Research.

WOOD, R. and SKURNIK, L.S. (1969).   Item Banking.   Slough: National Foundation for Educational Research.

WRIGHT, B.D. (1968).   'Sample-free test calibration and person measurement', Proceedings of the 1967 Invitational Conference on Testing Problems.   Princeton: E.T.S.

SOME ELEMENTARY CONSIDERATIONS ON CROSS-CULTURAL COMPARISONS OF SCHOOL-ACHIEVEMENT

H. SCHEIBLECHNER

Abstract - The problem of comparing the school achievement of pupils who are subject to different
curricula is investigated.   The 'specific
objectivity' or 'samplefreeness' of the comparison procedure is considered to be the
crucial requirement.   That is, no pupil should
be disadvantaged or favoured by the comparison
procedure solely on the basis of the curriculum
to which he is exposed.   The curriculum deter-
mines the universe from which the test items of
the pupil are sampled.   Sufficient conditions
for specifically objective ordinal comparisons
are derived.   It is shown that conjoint measurement models, bi-order models, linear probabilistic models and conditional inference models
are special cases of the ordinal model.   Some
generalizations of the conditional models and
some procedures for specifically objective comparisons of populations are indicated.

PRELIMINARIES: POPULATIONS OF PUPILS, ITEM UNIVERSES AND COMPARISONS

A collection of schoolchildren who are exposed to the same curriculum for some
subject (e.g. mathematics) is called an s-population.   The curriculum is an
educational programme which specifies the learning goals or objectives of instruction.   The objectives may range from rather abstract guiding principles (e.g.,
the ability to handle formal structures) to more precisely defined qualifications or
behavioural dispositions (e.g. the ability to perform the four basic arithmetic
operations with two digit numbers) and rather specific operationalized learning
goals (e.g. transform inches to metres; Heyner 1974).   The learning objectives
define a universe of items which may be used to evaluate the achievement of a
pupil from the s-population.   This universe is characterized by its content and
the formal construction principles of admissible test items.   It is called a
c-universe (content construction-universe).   The c-universe may contain subsets of
items (objectives) which are psychologically different with respect to ability and
learning processes involved (e.g. mathematics as composed of arithmetic and geometry

in traditional instruction). Psychologically homogeneous subsets of a c-universe are called <u>c(a)-universes</u> (content-ability-universes). Curricula, which agree with respect to learning objectives, differ with respect to the method of instruction and thus give rise to different c(a)-partitions of the same c-universe. The relations between concepts are illustrated in Figure 1.

FIGURE 1 - <u>Analytical Steps in the Definition of Populations of Pupils and Universes of Items</u>

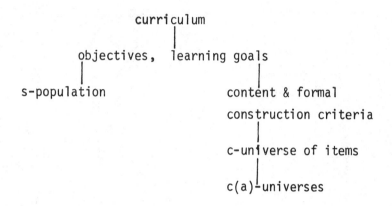

Comparisons between pupils belonging to different s-populations are called '<u>cross-cultural</u>'. The necessity for cross-cultural comparisons does arise, e.g., if pupils from different s-populations have to be selected for further education or if the effectiveness of different 'school systems' has to be evaluated. <u>Comparisons in the narrow sense</u> refer to differences between objects (pupils or items) on a common comparison dimension. <u>Comparisons in the wide sense</u> refer to common aspects of (psychologically) different processes (e.g., degree of correctness or time needed for the solution of an item obtained by psychologically different algorithms). Comparison procedures for single individuals will be considered first, since the feasibility of <u>individual comparisons</u> implies the feasibility of <u>group comparisons</u>, whereas the reverse is not in general true. Then some short remarks on group comparisons will be added.

Let P_1, P_2, P_3 represent three s-populations and I_1, I_2, I_3 stand for the c-universes defined by their curricula for some subject of instruction (e.g., elementary arithmetic in the third year of primary education). Then it is in general not possible to assign each test item to each pupil since the admissible test items depend on his curriculum. The hatched area of the left diagram in Figure 2 represents the individual and item combinations for which empirical observations

194

are obtainable.

FIGURE 2 - OBSERVABLE (ADMISSIBLE) PUPIL AND ITEM COMBINATIONS (A) AND THEORETICAL RELATIONS BETWEEN SUBSETS OF OBSERVATIONS FROM DIFFERENT S-POPULATIONS AND C-UNIVERSES (B)

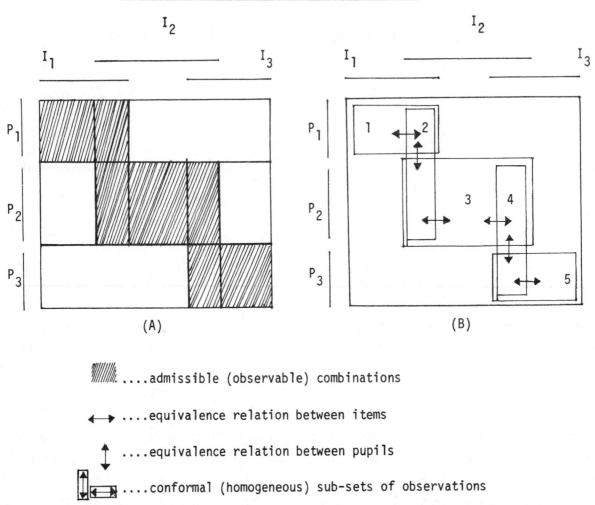

(A)   (B)

▨....admissible (observable) combinations

↔ ....equivalence relation between items

↕ ....equivalence relation between pupils

....conformal (homogeneous) sub-sets of observations

Without loss of generality the s-populations have been assumed not to intersect in Figure 2. If individuals exist who belong to more than one s-population (e.g., "bilinguals" educated in more than one school system), they appear as a separate s-population whose c-universe is the union of the c-universes of the corresponding s-populations.

If pupils are to be compared who belong to different c-populations, then by definition the test items have to be sampled (selected) from different c-universes. Then it is necessary to require from the comparison procedure that no pupil should be disadvantaged or favoured a priori solely on the basis of the c-universe from which his test items are selected.   No systematic or biasing effect should result from an appropriate comparison procedure by the selection of test items from different c-universes (provided that the items are admissible for the pupil), even when the c-universes differ in difficulty and the pupils derive different benefits from their curricula.

Students of the Rasch-models will recognize that the above requirement is just another wording of the principle of specific objectivity.   Students of the theory of generalizability (Cronbach et al., 1972) probably will agree with the principle but will notice that it is difficult to realize the principle within the framework of the theory of generalizability, because by the definition of the problem, the "facet" of items (c-universes) is "nested" within the facet of pupils (s-populations). Differences between c-universes with respect to distributions of item difficulties would distort comparisons unless these differences are removed by some restricted sampling procedure.   At first glance there may be a seeming contradiction between the principle of specific objectivity and the Bayesian or decision theoretic approach (Wedman, 1976).   However, differences between s-populations with respect to distributions of individuals abilities would be reflected by specifically objective measurement procedures.   Furthermore specific objectivity does not preclude the use of additional information (utilities, prior distributions), provided that such information is available.

CONNECTEDNESS: A GENERAL, NECESSARY CONDITION

A basic, necessary condition for cross-cultural comparisons is the connectedness-condition:

CC: The graph of intersection of the c-universes must be connected (connectedness of c-universes).

The points of the graph of intersections represent the s-populations.   Two points are joined by an edge (line) iff (if and only if) the intersection of the c-universes of the corresponding s-populations is not empty.   The construction of the graph of intersections is shown in Figure 3 for the three s-populations of Figure 2.

FIGURE 3 - CONSTRUCTION OF THE GRAPH OF INTERSECTIONS OF C-UNIVERSES

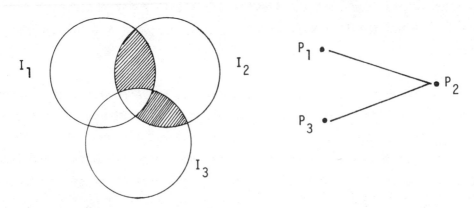

Intersections of c-universes   Graph of intersections

.....nonempty intersections of c-universes

CC requires the graph of intersections to be connected, that is, any two points either must be joined directly by an _edge_ or there must exist an uninterrupted sequence of edges (a path) establishing an indirect connection. There may exist more than one path between two points of the graph. In terms of the c-universes the connectedness requires that any pair of universes must be linked together either directly or indirectly by non-empty intersections.

If we establish the graph of intersections for, say, mathematical instruction in different grades of classical secondary education in Austria, we probably find non-empty intersections between adjacent grades, that is, the grades graph is connected. In a similar graph for different school systems at a single (low) level of age, adjacent school systems again may be joined by an edge. In this event it follows that the _combined graph_ for grades and school systems is connected. The combination of graphs opens the possibility of comparisons between individuals of quite distinct s-populations who differ widely with respect to age, school system, geographical region,... and whose c-universes have no items in common and only bear a remote resemblance.

Indirect linkages between s-populations give rise to _mediated comparisons_ which are performed by means of intervening s-populations (or c-universes). If two s-populations are connected by more than one path in the graph of intersections, then it is natural to require mediated comparisons to be consistent, that is, comparisons accomplished along different mediating links must not contradict each other. But otherwise, comparisons must be independent of the path of the comparison, i.e., of the intervening s-populations which mediated the comparison.   The path-independence of comparisons is equivalent to the transitivity of comparisons (Rasch, 1961): it places at our disposal a powerful tool for testing comparison procedures, provided that links are not too rare between s-populations.

If the condition CC is not empirically valid, then the gap between s-populations can be bridged over under certain circumstances by parametric models, e.g., the linear logistic model (Cox, 1970; Scheiblechner, 1972a; Fischer, 1974).   The bridging is possible e.g., if the items of different c-universes are composed of overlapping sets of 'building blocks' by different 'rules of combination'.

A SPECIFICALLY OBJECTIVE, ORDINAL MODEL

For most situations of practical or theoretical interest comparisons at an ordinal level of measurement are sufficient (c.f., Lord & Novick, 1968, p.215).   A simple ordinal model will be suggested which, first, serves as a common base for a variety of quite different and more complicated models and, second, exhibits the most attractive ideal of specific objectivity at a very elementary level.

The following conditions refer to the sets of observations obtained from the combinations of s-populations and c-universes as illustrated in the right diagram of Figure 2.   We suppose that to each admissible combination of a pupil v and item i corresponds a response variate x_{vi}, which can be weakly ordered across items within each pupil and across pupils within each item.   That is, we only assume that it is possible to compare (rank order) the performances of a given pupil at different items and of different pupils given an item.

> O1:   Within each set of observations the rank orders of pupils given the items of the c-universe must be strictly monotonically related (more precisely: $x_{vi} \geq x_{wi}$ iff $x_{vj} \geq x_{wj}$, provided that the pupil - item combinations are admissible; strict monotonicity or independence of items).

> O2:   Within each set of observations the rank orders of items given the pupils of the s-population must be strictly monotonically related (more precisely: $x_{vi} > x_{vj}$ iff $x_{wi} \geq x_{wj}$, provided that the pupil - item combinations are admissible;   strict monotonicity or independence of pupils).

O1 requires that if pupil v performs at least as well as pupil w on item i, the same must be true for all other items j; O2 requires that if the performance of pupil v is at least as good on item i as on item j, the same must be true for all other pupils w. That is, the rows (O2) and the columns (O1) of the matrix of observations must be strictly monotonically related. A data matrix satisfying O1 and O2 is given in Figure 4 (Blair, O'Connor & Pollatsek, 1970, p.19).

FIGURE 4 — DATA MATRIX SATISFYING STRICT MONOTONICITY (O1 AND O2), BUT VIOLATING CANCELLATION (⟶...AT LEAST AS LARGE AS, SEE THE PARAGRAPH AFTER NEXT FOR EXPLANATION)

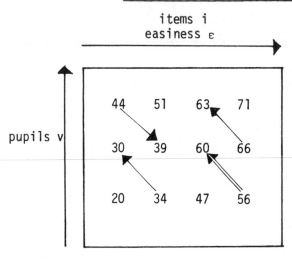

items i
easiness ε

pupils v

x_{vi}.....response variate, an ordinal measure of performance of pupil v on item i (e.g., degree of correctness, probability or speed of solution)

ability θ

If O1 and O2 are empirically valid, then it is possible to arrange the rows and the columns of the matrix such that the entries increase from the left to the right and from the bottom to the top of the matrix. The arrangement of columns corresponds to a rank order of increasing easiness of items and the arrangement of rows is a rank order of increasing ability of pupils. Stated otherwise, the monotonicity conditions imply the existence of functions θ (ability) on the set of individuals, ε (easiness) on the set of items and f on the product set of individuals and items such that

$$x_{vi} = f(\theta_v, \varepsilon_i)$$

and f is strictly monotone (increasing) in θ and ε.

It is a trivial but theoretically important consequence of 01 that the rank order of pupils is _independent_ of the item used to perform the ranking (since all items yield the same rank order of pupils).   Likewise, by 02, the rank order of items is independent of the pupil.   These statements, however, just define the _specific objectivity of ordinal comparisons._   The horizontal double arrows in the right diagram of Figure 2 represent the monotonicity of the rank orders of pupils at different items and the vertical double arrows indicate the monotonicity of the rank orders of items given the pupils.   The monotonicity thus turns out to be the required equivalence relation (between items or pupils) for the specific objectivity of an ordinal model.   Universes of items or data sets satisfying conditions 01 and 02 (or the conditions of any other specifically objective model) will be called "conformal" (c.f., Rasch, 1960; "conformal" and "conformity" are better names than "homogeneous" and "homogeneity" since the latter may be confused with constant easiness or constant discriminating power and the like).   If all subsets of observations linking c-universes and s-populations are conformal, then it is a further consequence of the ordinal model that all pupils (the union of the s-populations) can be arranged on a single, common ordinal scale (and the items as well).   The rank orders are transitive or path-independent.   Conformal rank orders establish comparisons in the narrow sense, since they involve a single comparison dimension.   They can claim general validity with respect to a well specified class of comparison situations within which they are invariant.

If the items belonging to the intersection of two s-universes are ranked differently for the pupils of the two s-populations (that is, 02 is violated), then comparisons between the s-populations depend systematically on the items which are included in and excluded from the comparison.   These comparisons depend on the _specific selection_ of items on which they are based (they are not 'sample free') and can not be generalized to some broader class of comparison situations.   They were called comparisons in the wide sense in the first section of the present paper and are useful to the extent that a specific selection of items is dictated by theoretical or practical reasons.

We just have shown that (strict) monotonicity is sufficient for the specific objectivity of ordinal comparisons.   Hence it follows that all models which include the conditions 01 and 02 are specifically objective in the sense of the ordinal model.   We shortly shall see that the most common measurement models are special cases of the ordinal model which include stronger axioms in addition to the conditions of the ordinal model.

TWO GENERALIZATIONS OF THE ORDINAL MODEL[1]

As is well known from empirical practice, <u>strict deterministic monotonicity</u> tends to be violated frequently (but usually not seriously) if pupils of high (low) ability are exposed to items of low (high) difficulty (the upper right and lower left corner of the hypothetical data matrix in Figure 4, whereas it tends to hold quite well if the difficulty level of the items is a tolerable match with the ability level of the pupils. Hence, the empirical range of the ordinal model can be greatly enhanced if the deterministic monotonicity is replaced by <u>probabilistic monotonicity</u> or is <u>restricted to appropriately defined subsets</u> (samples) of items or pupils.

It is easy to relax the conditions O1 and O2 in a probabilistic manner. Let P_{vi} (or $P_{vi}(c)$) the probability that pupil v solves item i correctly, if the response variate is dichotomous, or the probability that pupil v attains or surpasses the criterion of performance c at item i (where c eventually may depend on i), if the response variate is polychotomous (e.g. ordered categories), discrete (e.g., number of errors) or continuous (e.g. time for solution). Probabilistic monotonicity then simply requires:

$$PO1: \quad P_{vi} \geqslant P_{wi} \quad iff \quad P_{vj} \geqslant P_{wj} \quad \underline{\text{(probabilistic monotonicity of items)}}$$

$$PO2: \quad P_{vi} \geqslant P_{vj} \quad iff \quad P_{wi} \geqslant P_{wj} \quad \underline{\text{(probabilistic monotonicity of pupils)}}.$$

The probabilistic generalization becomes really fruitful only when the probabilities are fixed by a more specific model. Special models will be given in a later section. The analysis of variance model for repeated measurement designs may serve as a well known illustrative example of a model satisfying probabilistic monotonicity, provided that no pupil-item interaction is present or that it can be removed by a strictly monotone transformation of the response variate.

Another weakening of strict deterministic monotonicity is to restrict it to appropriately defined subsets of items or pupils. The essence of this weakening is to require strict monotonicity only for those situations where differences (between pupils or items) can be reliably detected. One way to make small differences become more apparent is to summarize them over an appropriately selected set of several instances. To this end we define individual scoring functions for all

---

1. This section may be skipped without loss of continuity.

subsets of items of a c-universe which meet given substantial and formal demands. Similarly item scoring functions are defined for all admissible subsets of pupils from an s-population. A scoring function gives a summary measure of performance for a set of items given the responses of an individual or for a set of individuals given their responses to an item. The most common scoring functions are (weighted) raw score functions. Let $x_{v|S} = \sum_{i \in S} x_{vi}$, the total achievement of pupil v on the subset S of items; and similarly let $x_{T|i} = \sum_{v \in T} x_{vi}$, the score of item i given the subset T of pupils. The strict deterministic monotonicity of single items or individuals then is replaced by the strict deterministic monotonicity of subsets of items or individuals:

S01: $x_{v|S} \geqslant x_{w|S}$ iff $x_{v|S'} \geqslant x_{w|S'}$ for appropriately defined individual scoring functions $x_{v|S}$ and adequately composed subsets S and S' of items (monotonicity or independence of item subsets).

S02: $x_{T|i} \geqslant x_{T|j}$ iff $x_{T'|i} \geqslant x_{T'|j}$ for appropriately defined item scoring functions $x_{T|i}$ and adequately selected samples T and T' of pupils (monotonicity or independence of subsets of pupils).

An item subset may be considered to be adequately composed if it contains a sufficient total number of items and sufficient numbers of items of each of several given types of items and if it has sufficient discriminating power (for the pair of pupils under consideration). Adequately selected samples of pupils similarly may be defined to contain sufficient numbers of pupils of appropriate levels of ability such that the items to be compared can be reliably ordered. The important aspect of S02 is that the rank of items must not depend on the descriptive properties of the sample of pupils (proportion of sexes, social classes,...) other than those determining the discriminative power of the sample (relative to the items to be compared). In particular, the rank order of items must be independent of the proportion of pupils from two s-populations if the items belong to the intersection of their c-universes.

The strict monotonicity of item subsets is a true generalization of the strict monotonicity of single items since the former only requires weak monotonicity of single items. A pair (i,j) of items is weakly monotone (or compatible) iff $x_{vi} > x_{wi}$ implies not ($x_{vj} < x_{wj}$). That is, the pupils are ordered in the same way by both items or they are not discriminated by one or both items, but strict orders never contradict each other. The weak monotonicity allows for the inclusion of items of varying response formats and discriminating power into the same item universe, since the discriminating power of the item subsets can be controlled and regulated by their construction. If the c-universe is restructured such that the item subsets take the position of the original items (and samples of pupils replace the individual pupils), then the strict monotonicity of subsets of items (or pupils) is formally equivalent to the strict monotonicity of items.

For completeness we add that more complicated scoring rules than the raw score function are conceivable.   For example, it may be considered satisfactory if an examinee answers correctly at least once to a given type of items in which case incorrect responses given previously to the same type of questions are ignored. However, the raw score function is the simplest scoring rule and has the most compelling formal consequences.   Finally we mention that it is of course possible to combine the probabilistic generalization of monotonicity and the generalization to subsets of items or pupils.

ADDITIVE CONJOINT MEASUREMENT

In addition to the comparisons within rows and columns which must be available for the ordinal model conjoint measurement requires comparisons across all individual and item combinations.   That is, it is assumed that it is possible to compare the performance of pupil v on item i with the performance of pupil w on item j and to weakly order them.   If monotonicity (01 and 02) holds and the pupils are arranged in order of increasing ability and the items in order of increasing easiness, as in the sample matrix of Figure 4, then the entries of the matrix necessarily must increase from the lower left to the upper right of the matrix. What remains to be settled is the rank order of the entries when we move along the direction of the main diagonal of the matrix.   This is done by the (double) cancellation axiom (or the weaker Thomsen condition, Orth, 1974, p.60).

DC: If $x_{vi} \geq x_{wj}$ and $x_{uj} \geq x_{vk}$, then $x_{ui} \geq x_{wk}$ (<u>double cancellation</u>; c.f. e.g. Coombs, Dawes & Tversky, 1970, p.26).

The meaning of the axiom is illustrated best with the aid of a diagram (Figure 5).

FIGURE 5 - THE DOUBLE CANCELLATION AXIOM

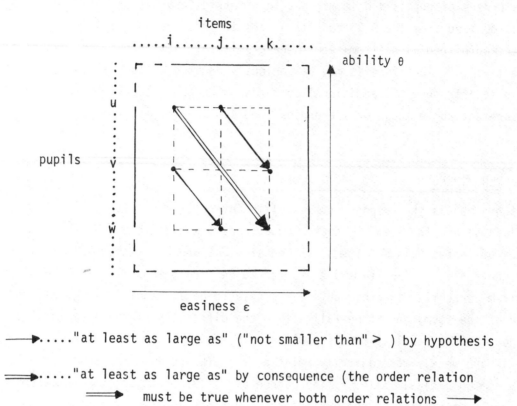

----▶....."at least as large as" ("not smaller than" >) by hypothesis

====▶....."at least as large as" by consequence (the order relation
 ====▶ must be true whenever both order relations ----▶
 are true).

If the conditions 01, 02 and DC hold, then there exist functions θ, ε , and γ
defined on the sets of pupils, items and their product set, respectively, such that

$$\gamma \left(x_{vi} \right) = \theta_v + \varepsilon_i$$

and γ is strictly monotone in x. That is, the response variate x can be <u>strictly
monotonically transformed</u> such that it can be regarded as the <u>sum of two factors</u>,
the ability of the pupils and the easiness of the items. Furthermore, if it is
assumed that the two factors are sufficiently dense (<u>solvability</u>, c.f. e.g.,
Coombs, Dawes and Tversky, 1970, p.27), then it follows that the scales θ and ε are
<u>unique up to positive linear transformations</u> ("interval scales" with a common unit).

If, however, the sets of pupils and items are finite, then it is possible to find
additive representations which are not linearly related. Likewise, if some rows
or columns are arbitrarily removed from or added to a given data matrix (without

violating D C), then the resulting scales θ and ε are not in general linearly related.   Thus, by O1 and O2, conjoint measurement yields specifically objective rank orders of pupils and items, but the "metric information" (the order of inter-vals) derived from the D C condition does in practice depend on the specific selection of pupils or items and therefore is not 'samplefree' or 'specifically objective'.   Therefore it may be seriously doubted whether it is really worth while to introduce the additional comparisons and conditions required for conjoint measurement above those of the ordinal model.

BI-ORDER MODELS

In these models the response (variate) is interpreted as a comparison between the individual and the item.   These comparisons are used to establish a common rank order of individuals and items.   The simplest and best known example is the Guttman scale.   The items are assumed to be dichotomous.   If the pupil solves an item correctly, then his ability is said to be at least as large as the diffic-ulty of the item, and if he fails, then the difficulty of the item is said to be larger than the ability of the pupil.   If the rows and the columns of the data matrix are weakly monotonically related, then the pupils and items can be arranged on a common ordinal scale.   The degree of differentiation (the number of distin-guishable positions) of the ordinal scale depends on the selection of items and pupils, but otherwise the rank order is unaffected by the sample.   As an example, dichotomize artificially the response variate of the matrix in Figure 4 by setting to 1 all entries above an arbitrary cutting score c and setting to 0 all entries below c.   The resulting zero-one matrix satisfies Guttman's model indep-endently of the cutting score c.

If the response variate is trichotomous, three outcomes of a comparison between an item and a pupil are distinguished: +1, if the ability of the pupil surpasses the difficulty of the item by at least an amount c, 0, if the ability and the diffic-ulty differ by less than c, and -1, if the difficulty is larger than the ability by at least the amount c.   If the rows and the columns are weakly monotonically related, then the pupils (rows) can be arranged in order of increasing ability and the items (columns) in order of increasing easiness, such that each row from left to right and each column from bottom to top consists of an uninterrupted sequence of -1, followed by an uninterrupted sequence of 0 and an uninterrupted sequence of +1; one or two subsequences may be empty for some of the rows or columns.   The resulting pattern of entries is called a 'bi-semi-order' and is illustrated in Figure 6.

FIGURE 6 -   BI-SEMI-ORDER OF ABILITIES AND DIFFICULTIES

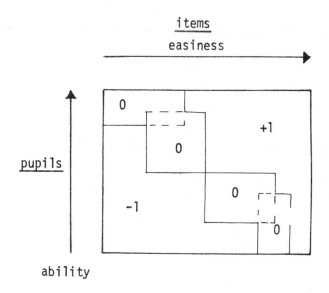

The dependence properties of the bi-semi-order from the specific selection of pupils and items out of conformal sets of pupils and items are similar to those of the Guttman scale: that is, the 'grain' of the ordinal scale is affected by the sample, but strict orders can not be reversed.   As an example, trichotomize artificially the response variate of the matrix in Figure 4 by setting to 0 all entries contained in a symmetric interval of width 2c around the mean (= 48, 42) or median (= 49), and setting to +1 and -1, respectively, the entries above and below the middle interval.   The resulting matrix satisfies the bi-semi-order conditions independently of the width 2c of the middle interval.

LINEAR PROBABILISTIC MODELS

We now suppose that to each (admissible) pupil-item combination corresponds a probability P_{vi} (instead of the deterministic response variate x_{vi} considered so far). P_{vi} (or $P_{vi}(c)$) is the probability that pupil v solves item i correctly, if the response variate is dichotomous, or the probability that pupil v attains or surpasses the criterion of performance c at item i, if the response variate is ordered polychotomously (e.g., successive categories), discretely (e.g., number of errors) or continuously (e.g., time for solution).   If it is possible to construct scales θ and ϵ such that for all v and i

$$P_{vi} = F(\theta_v + \epsilon_i)$$

where $F(x)$ increases strictly monotonically from $F(-\infty) = 0$ to $F(\infty) = 1$ and $F(-x)$ $= 1 - F(x)$, then the probabilities are said to satisfy a <u>linear probabilistic model</u> (David, 1969), p.14). $F(x)$ is the cumulative distribution function (cdf) of a random variable symmetrically distributed about zero. $F(x)$ is called an <u>item-characteristic</u> function or item characteristic curve (Lord & Novick, 1968, p.358) and most commonly has been chosen to be the normal ogive (Lord & Novick, 1968, p.366), or the cdf of a logistic (Rasch) or uniform (Lazersfeld) distribution.

If the probabilities P_{vi} of a linear model contained in the interval $1/2 \pm c$ (for $0 < c < 1/2$) are set equal to 0 and the larger and smaller probabilities are set equal to +1 and -1, respectively, then the resulting matrix satisfies the conditions of a bi-semi-order independent of the value of c (Tack, 1974,1975).   The probabilities of a linear model also satisfy the conditions of additive conjoint measurement (with $F^{-1}(P)$, the inverse function of the cdf, as the required strictly monotone transormation of P).   Therefore, the order relations between the probabilities of a linear model provide the same specifically objective ordinal information as the more elementary models do.   If, however, the probabilities are numerically known and the cdf of the model is given, then even 'metric' information about the distances between pupils and items can be deduced from the linear model, which is independent of the sample upon which it is based.   This is best seen from the fact that the item parameters can be eliminated from comparisons between pupils (abilities) and the ability of pupils can be eliminated from comparisons between items.   The latter is shown below:

$$P_{vi} = F(\theta_v + \varepsilon_i)$$
$$\underline{P_{vj} = F(\theta_v + \varepsilon_j)}$$
$$F^{-1}(P_{vi}) = \theta_v + \varepsilon_i$$
$$F^{-1}(P_{vj}) = \theta_v + \varepsilon_j$$
$$\overline{F^{-1}(P_{vi}) - F^{-1}(P_{vj}) = \varepsilon_i - \varepsilon_j}$$

where the last line is the difference between the easiness of item i and item j and is independent of the ability parameter of the pupil; $F^{-1}(P)$, the inverse of the cdf, exists, because $F(x)$ is strictly monotone.   Thus linear probabilistic models are basically sufficient to provide metric information about pupils which is independent of the sample of items and vice versa.

CONDITIONAL INFERENCE MODELS

A psychometric measurement model is called a conditional inference model if the conditional likelihood of the observations given sufficient statistics for a set of parameters does not depend on that set of parameters. Andersen (1973, p.74) has shown, that in order for that independence property to hold, the item characteristic must be of the form

$$f(x|\theta, \varepsilon) = c^{-1}(\theta, \varepsilon) \exp(\alpha(x,\theta) + \delta(x,\varepsilon))$$

where α, δ and c are suitable functions (and exp(x) stands for e^x). The simplest and best known example is Rasch's dichotomous logistic model, where $\alpha(x,\theta)_k = x\theta$, $\delta(x, \varepsilon) = x\varepsilon$ and $o^{-1}(\theta,\varepsilon) = [1 + \exp(\theta+\varepsilon)]^{-1}$ and the 'raw score' $T_v = \sum_{i=1}^{k} X_{vi}$ is the (minimal) sufficient statistic for the individual parameter θ_v, which is the same function of the random variates X_{v_1}, X_{v_2},........,X_{vk} for all values of ε_1, ε_2,........,ε_k. The (minimal) sufficient statistic for the item parameter ε_i is $S_i = \sum_{v=1}^{n} X_{vi}$, whose form is independent of θ_1, θ_2,........,θ_n.

As can be seen from the general formula given above, the conditional inference models are special cases of the linear probabilistic models. The reason for the statistical superiority of the special cases is a somewhat intricate parameter estimation and model evaluation problem which tends to invalidate statistical inference from two-parameter models and was first described by Neyman & Scott (1948). In their terminology the observations of a psychometric experiment are only 'partially consistent' as a consequence of which the maximum likelihood estimates of parameters are not in general consistent (that is the estimates do not converge asymptotically towards the true value of the parameter even if the size of the sample is increased without limit). From the inconsistency it follows that the estimate of a pupil's ability does in general depend on the sample of items on which it is based and vice versa. Therefore, in contrast to the specific objectivity requirement, estimates of pupils' abilities based on different samples of items can in general not be compared. This however obviates the solution of the problem introduced at the outset of the present paper, namely to compare the attainment of pupils belonging to different s-populations and for whom the items therefore necessarily have to be sampled from different c-universes. The consistency problem can be solved by the method of 'modified maximum likelihood equations' suggested by Neyman and Scott (1948). The conditional inference procedures (Andersen, 1973, p.9), which are available for models of the form given above, are special cases of the method of Neyman & Scott in which the distortive effect of the sample is eliminated by means of the <u>elimination of nuisance parameters</u> through their sufficient statistics (c.f., the definition of conditional inference models given above). The most widely used conditional inference models are listed below. The reader's attention is drawn to the models for discrete and continuous variates, which are no less interesting formally and psychologically than the dichotomous and polychotomous models, but which have received much less consideration in the psychological literature.

<u>Dichotomous model</u>   (Rasch, 1960)

$$p(x_{vi}) = \exp\left[(\theta_v + \epsilon_i)\, x_{vi}\right] \Big/ \left[1 + \exp(\theta_v + \epsilon_i)\right]$$

$x_{vi}\ldots = 1$ for positive, $=0$ for negative response

$$\sum_{i}^{k} \epsilon_i = 0$$

<u>Polychotomous model</u>   (Rasch, 1961)

$$p(x_{vi}) = \prod_{h=1}^{m} \exp\left[(\theta_v^{(h)} + \epsilon_i^{(h)})\, x_{vi}^{(h)}\right] \Big/ \sum_{h=1}^{m} \exp(\theta_v^{(h)} + \epsilon_i^{(h)})$$

$x_{vi}\ldots = (x_{vi}^{(1)}, x_{vi}^{(2)},\ldots,x_{vi}^{(m)})$ where exactly one of the components is
                                      1 and the rest are 0

$\epsilon_i^{(m)} = 0$ for all i   (selection vector)

$\sum_{1} \epsilon_i^{(h)} = 0$ for all h

<u>Polychotomous, one dimensional model</u> (Rasch; Andersen, 1973, p.185, 186)

$$p(x_{vi}) = \prod_{h=1}^{m} \exp\left[(\theta_v \Psi(h) + \epsilon_i \phi(h) + \tau(h))\, x_{vi}^{(h)}\right] \Big/ \sum_{h=1}^{m} \exp(\theta_v \Psi(h) + \epsilon_i \phi(h) + \tau(h))$$

$\Psi(1) = \phi(1) = 1$ $\Psi, \phi\ldots$scoring functions

$\Psi(m) = \phi(m) = \tau(m) = 0$ $\tau\ldots$structure function

$\sum_v \theta_v = 0$ $\sum_i \epsilon_i = 0$

Poisson model (Rasch, 1960)

$$p(x_{vi}) = \exp(-\xi_v \sigma_i)(\xi_v \sigma_i)^{x_{vi}} \big/ x_{vi}!$$

$$x_{vi} \ldots = 0,1,2,\ldots(\text{number of errors})$$

$$\sigma_1 = 1$$

Exponential model (Scheiblechner, 1976, in preparation)

$$p(x_{vi}) = (\theta_v + \varepsilon_i) \exp\left[-(\theta_v + \varepsilon_i) x_{vi}\right]$$

$$x_{vi} \ldots > 0 \quad (\text{solution time})$$

$$\varepsilon_1 = 1$$

Gamma distribution model (Rasch, 1960): "almost specifically objective"

$$p(x_{vi}) = (\xi_v \sigma_i) \exp(-\xi_v \sigma_i x_{vi}) (\xi_v \sigma_i x_{vi})^{N-1} \big/ (N-1)!$$

$$x_{vi} \ldots > 0 \quad (\text{solution time})$$

$$N \ldots \text{degrees of freedom}$$

$$\sigma_1 = 1$$

In these formulas $p(x_{vi})$ is the probability density of the observation x_{vi} and θ_v and ε_i are usually interpreted as ability and easiness parameters, whereas ξ_v ($=1/\theta_v$ or $-\theta_v$) and σ_i ($=1/\varepsilon_i$ or $-\varepsilon_i$) are inability and difficulty parameters. The last model is not specifically objective in the strict sense of the word, but it approaches specific objectivity if the parameters are restricted to an appropriate range. Various other models have been suggested, which are specifically objective with respect to some but not all of their aspects (e.g., Kempf, 1973).

The first five models have been generalized to include linear decompositions of the individual and item parameters (Rasch, 1965; Cox, 1970; Scheiblechner, 1971, 1972a, 1972b; Fischer, 1974; Kempf, 1974; Scheiblechner, 1976). Thus the overall difficulty of an item can be considered as the sum of the difficulties of all sources of difficulty (factors, components) which are contained in the item, the ability of the pupil may be conceived as the sum of the beneficial effects of the facilitating treatments he has received and finally all sorts of pupil-item inter- actions may be added.   Therefore the linear generalisations of the models are very valuable tools for the analysis of the psychological 'microstructure' of the task solution process (c.f., Cardinet and Tourneur in the present volume; Fischer, 1973; Spada, 1976).   Formally the linear generalizations can be represented by

$$\theta_v + \varepsilon_i = \sum_{\ell=1}^{m1} a_{v\ell}\alpha_\ell + \sum_{\ell=1}^{m2} b_{i\ell}\beta_\ell + \sum_{\ell=1}^{m3} c_{vi\ell}\gamma_\ell + d$$

where the coefficients $a_{v\ell}$ describe the treatment structure of the pupils, $b_{i\ell}$ the task structure of the items, $c_{vi\ell}$ the structure of the effects relevant for specific pupil-item combinations and d is a normalization constant.   As an example of a pupil-item interaction think of two s-populations P_1 and P_2, which have the same c-universe, but a relatively larger proportion of time is spent for the training of the subset I_1 of items in P_1 whereas the curriculum of P_2 places relat- ively more weight on the training of the subset I_2 of items.   Thus the pupils of P_1 would appear to be superior, if items of I_1 are presented, or (what amounts to the same thing) the items of I_1 would appear easier if presented to pupils of P_1, whereas the reverse would hold for the P_2-I_2 combination.   The interaction can be accounted for by the addition of a facilitating effect γ_1 to all P_1-I_1 pupil-item combinations and γ_2 to all P_2-I_2 pupil-item combinations.   The example is summ- arized in Figure 7.

FIGURE 7 - The Representation of Pupil-Item Interactions in Linear Generaliz- ations of Conditional Inference Models (population P_1 has received additional training for items I_1 and population P_2 for items I_2; γ_1, γ_2 facilitating effects of additional training)

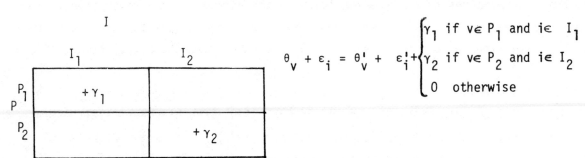

$$\theta_v + \varepsilon_i = \theta'_v + \varepsilon'_i + \begin{cases} \gamma_1 & \text{if } v \in P_1 \text{ and } i \in I_1 \\ \gamma_2 & \text{if } v \in P_2 \text{ and } i \in I_2 \\ 0 & \text{otherwise} \end{cases}$$

SPECIFICALLY OBJECTIVE COMPARISONS BETWEEN POPULATIONS

If school-systems, curricula or pedagogical objectives of some sort are to be compared, then comparisons via (specifically objective) measurements on individual pupils may become uneconomic or unnecessarily technically involved (c.f., Cardinet and Tourneur, and James in the present volume). Although group comparisons are always feasible whenever individual comparisons can be performed, the population rather than individuals are of primary concern in these investigations. As an 'outgrowth' of his measurement models Rasch (1965) developed a theory of specifically objective comparisons between populations, which is closer to conventional measurement theoretic, statistical and experimental principles than his individual models. As a simple example the one-way (or multifactorial) analysis of variance with the usual assumptions (normality, homogeneity of variances, stochastic independence) is a specifically objective model for the comparison of populations.

The basic assumption of the population or distributional models is the homogeneity of populations assumption. All individuals within population v are assumed to be characterized by the same parameter θ_v, which therefore now represents a population parameter. Observations from different individuals of the same population are considered to constitute independent replications of an experiment or to be drawn from the same probability distribution (in contrast to the individual models where no replications are available). The theoretical probability density therefore can be empirically estimated by sample distributions. The homogeneity of a population can be tested by comparing the distribution of several samples from the population by means of multinomial tests or the Chi-square test for independence in contingency tables. As an example let us compare two s-populations. The attainment of the pupils can appear to be different because;

      a.   there exist 'real' or 'true' differences in performance of the s-populations e.g., caused by the curricula,   or

      b.   because the test performance does not only depend on the curriculum but also on the sex, social class, home environment and other attributes of the pupils and the s-population differ with respect to these variables.

The principle of specific objectivity requires that the s-populations are stratified into subpopulations according to these and other potentially important external variables and to continue the stratification process until;

      a.   each sub-population can be shown to meet the homogeneity requirement, and

      b.   the distributions in the subpopulations can be shown to constitute a

one-parameter exponential family of probability densities (that is the distributions differ only with respect to a single parameter θ_v).

This procedure is a statistical counterpart to the well known experimental principle
of isolated variation.   If more than one variate (item) is observed in each population, then the variates must depend on the same population parameter and must be
locally stochastically independent - the latter condition being an essential part
of Lazarsfeld's latent class and latent structure definition.

Specifically objective comparisons between populations can be performed by means of
the probability densities given at the end of the previous section.   Since the
individuals of a population provide us with independent replications, it is possible
to perform the comparison by means of a single item (variate).   The probability
density functions can then be simplified by eliminating the parameters referring to
items.   Examples for the use of the dichotomous model can be found in Cox (1970).
The one dimensional polychotomous model (third in the list) is the most likely
candidate for applications in distributional comparisons.   The ordered 'categories'
of the model could correspond, for example, to the raw scores of an attainment test,
in which case the model describes the raw score distribution of a population.
The attainment test needs not necessarily to be specifically objective at an individual level for that sort of application.   The one dimensional polychotomous
model includes as special cases the Poisson and the exponential model (fourth and
fifth in the list) and the normal distribution, (Rasch, 1965), i.e.,

$$(1 / \sqrt{2\pi}\sigma)\exp \left[- \frac{1}{2}\left(\frac{x-\mu}{\sigma} \right)^2 \right] = \exp \left[- \frac{x^2}{2\sigma^2} + \frac{x\mu}{\sigma^2} - \frac{\mu^2}{2\sigma^2} - \ln(\sqrt{2\pi}\sigma) \right]$$

where $\mu = \theta$, $\Psi(x) = x/\sigma^2$, $\tau(x) = -x^2/2\sigma^2$ and

$$c^{-1}(\theta) = \exp \left[- \frac{\theta^2}{2\sigma^2} - \ln(\sqrt{2\pi}\sigma) \right] \qquad \text{(a normalization constant,}$$

which makes the area under the density equal to 1).

If more than one normally distributed variable is observed for each population, then

$\mu = \theta + \epsilon$, $\Psi(x)$ and $\tau(x)$ remain as before,

$\gamma(x) = \Psi(x)$ (as in all examples Rasch gives) and

$$c^{-1}(\theta, \epsilon) = \exp \left[- \frac{(\theta + \epsilon)^2}{2\sigma^2} - \ln(\sqrt{2\pi}\,\sigma) \right]$$

In order to apply the one dimensional polychotomous model the functions Ψ and τ (and γ if necessary) either have to be known in advance - as they are, if the family of distributions is known - or have to be estimated numerically. They can not be estimated in a specifically objective manner (i.e. by conditional inference methods), which is the largest crux of the models in practical applications. In case of the normal model it does not essentially matter whether the variance σ^2 is known in advance, since the familiar estimator is unbiased and distributed independently of the sample mean (c.f., e.g. Mood and Graybill, 1963, p.178 and 228). Therefore the traditional statistical methods, which are based on the normal model and the homogeneity of variances and appropriate stochastic independence assumptions, are specifically objective distributional models.

Rasch (1965) also comments on <u>bivariate comparisons</u> between populations. Suppose we want to compare two s-populations with respect to achievement in mathematics as composed of arithmetic (variable x, measured on a ten point scale, say) and geometry (variable y, rated on a 20 point scale, say). The bivariate probability density then must be of the form

$$p(x',y') = \exp(\theta_v \Psi(x',y') + \tau(x',y'))\bigg/ \sum_x \sum_y \exp(\theta_v \Psi(x,y) + \tau(x,y))$$

in order to achieve specifically objective, one dimensional comparisons. Since the bivariate distribution can be decomposed into marginal and conditional distributions by means of the relations

$$p(x,y) = g(x|y)\, h(y) = d(y|x)\, e(x)$$

and the conditional distributions completely determine all other distributions, Rasch requires the <u>specific objectivity for the comparison of conditional distributions</u>. This postulate leads to the following distributional assumptions:

$$p(x',y') = \exp(\theta_v \Psi(x')\, \phi(y') + \gamma(x') + \tau(y'))\bigg/ \sum_x \sum_y \exp(\theta_v \Psi(x)\, \phi(y) + \gamma(x) + \tau(y))$$

$$p(x'|y') = \exp(\theta_v \Psi(x')\, \phi(y') + \gamma(x'))\bigg/ \sum_x \exp(\theta_v \Psi(x)\, \phi(y') + \gamma(x))$$

$$p(y'|x') = \exp(\theta_v\, \Psi(x')\, \phi(y') + \tau(y')\,) \Big/ \sum_y \exp(\theta_v\, \Psi(x')\phi(y) + \tau(y))$$

where

$$\Sigma\Psi(x) = \Sigma\gamma(x) = \Sigma\phi(y) = \Sigma\tau(y) = 0$$

Thus both variables must depend on a common population parameter, but their 'metric' ($\Psi(x)$, $\gamma(y)$) may differ.

REFERENCES

ANDERSEN, E.G. (1973). Conditional inference and models for measuring. Copenhagen: Mentalhygiejnisk Forlag.

BLAIR, C.W., O'CONNOR, M.F., POLLATSEK, A.W. (1970). Workbook for mathematical psychology. New Jersey: Prentice-Hall.

CARDINET, J., TOURNEUR, Y. (1976). Structure et mesure des objectifs educatifs dans les surveys periodiques. Present volume.

COOMBS, C.H., DAWES, R.M., TVERSKY, A. (1970). Mathematical psychology. New Jersey: Prentice-Hall.

COX, D.R. (1970). The analysis of binary data. London: Methuen.

CRONBACH, L., GLESER, G., NANDA, H., RAJARATNAM, N. (1972). The dependability of behavioral measurements: Theory of generalizability for scores and profiles. New York: Wiley.

DAVID, H.A. (1969). The method of paired comparisons. Griffin's statistical monographs and courses. London.

FISCHER, G.H. (1973). The linear logistic test model as an instrument in educational research. Acta Psychologica 37, 359-374.

FISCHER, G.H. (1974). Einfuhrung in die Theorie psychologischer Tests. Huber, Bern.

HEYNER, W. (1974). Handlungsstrategie fur den Aufbau einer Itembank zu den Volkshochschul-Zertifikatscurricula. Frankfurt: Deutscher Volkshochschulverband,

JAMES, A.N. (1976). Multiple matrix sampling. Present volume.

KEMPF, W.F. (1973). Beschreibung abhangiger Beobachtungsreihen mit Hilfe des Testmodells von Rasch. Kiel: IPN.

KEMPF, W.F. (1974). Ein probabilistisches Modell zur Messung sozialer Normen. In: KEMPF, W.F. (Ed.) Probabilistische Modelle in der Sozialpsychologie. Huber, Bern.

LORD, F.M., NOVICK, M.R. (1968). Statistical theories of mental test scores. Massachusetts: Addison-Wesley.

MOOD, A.M., GRAYBILL, F.A. (1963). Introduction to the theory of statistics. New York: Mc Graw-Hill.

NEYMAN, J., SCOTT, M.L. (1948). Consistent estimates based on partially consistent observations. Econometrika 16, 1-32.

ORTH, B. (1974). Einfuhrung in die Theorie des Messens. Kohlhammer Standards Psychologie. Stuttgart.

RASCH, G. (1960). Probabilistic models for some intelligence and attainment tests. Danmarks paedagogiske Institut. Copenhagen.

RASCH, G. (1961). On general laws and the meaning of measurement in psychology. Proc. Fourth Berkeley Symp. on Math. Stat. and Prob. 5, 321-333.

RASCH, G. (1965). Unveroffentlichtes Vorlesungsmanuskript. Verfa t von Stene, J., Ubersetzt von Repp, B.

SCHEIBLECHNER, H. (1971). The separation of individual and system-influences on behaviour in social contexts. Acta Psychologica 35, 442.

SCHEIBLECHNER, H. (1972)a. Das Lernen und Losen komplexer Denkaufgaben. Zeitschrift fur angewandte Psychologie 19, 3. 476.

SCHEIBLECHNER, H. (1972)b. Personality and system influences on behaviour in groups. Acta Psychologica 36, 322.

SCHEIBLECHNER, H. (1976)a. Specifically objective stochastic latency mechanisms. In preparation.

SCHEIBLECHNER, H. (1976)b. The linear exponential model. In preparation.

SPADA, H. (1976). Modelle des Denkens und Lernens. Huber, Bern.

TACK, W. (1975) Mess-Systeme fur Bi-Ordnungen. In: TACK, W. (Ed.) Bericht uber den 29. Kongre der Deutschen Gesellschaft fur Psychologie in Salsburg 1974. Bank I. Hogrefe, Gottingen, 326-328.

DEVELOPMENTS IN ITEM BANKING

Bruce Choppin

Abstract - Item banks can be used to develop effective
and efficient systems of tests and examinations for the purposes of assessing the achievement of individual students, of monitoring
changes in the curriculum and for evaluating
other educational innovations.   Full expl-
oitation of the advantages inherent in the
item bank concept depends on the adoption of
an explicit model of test-taking behaviour,
such as that proposed by Rasch.   Three diverse
applications of item-banking, based on this
measurement model, are presented.

WHAT ARE ITEM BANKS?

The term item bank should be understood to mean a collection of test items organised
and catalogued in a similar way to books in a library, but also with calibrated data
on their measurement characteristics.   This means that when a test is constructed
from a sub-set of items taken from the bank, these calibrations can be used to
determine the psychometric properties of the test.   In addition scores from two
tests made up of separate items from the bank can be interpreted one in terms of the
other, since both are based on the same set of item calibrations.   So far most of
the item banks that have been constructed have been of the multiple-choice type, and
most have been concerned with the measurement of school attainment, although the
item banking concept need not be restricted in either of these ways.   Item banks
provide the test constructor, whether he be an individual teacher or a member of a
National Examination Board, with access to a very wide range of items.   From these
he may select any one of an astronomical number of alternative groups to use as a
test with specifiable psychometric characteristics.   Since the basis of item calibration is common to all the possible groups, the scores produced may be translated
to a common psychometric scale and hence interpreted almost as though the tests were
parallel.

It should be noted that the above definition of item banks would exclude mere coll-
ections of items which have been assembled as an aid to the sharing of creative

ideas between examiners in different institutions.   The term 'item pool' would be used for any such collection if it lacked the necessary psychometric calibration to permit the use described in the foregoing paragraph.

The chief virtue of a complete item banking system is its flexibility.   In theory at least it enables people who wish to make measures of achievement to have access to a wide range of well documented testing materials to cover a whole variety of sit-uations.   Though it is in many ways rather more complicated to operate than would be a set of standardised tests, it offers several advantages.   When one has a large pool of test items upon which to draw, test security is not the same problem as it sometimes is in a standardised testing situation.   Furthermore, teachers can 'design' their own test and yet have the results readily related back to some larger reference framework.   This should improve the quality of classroom testing and also help teachers to appreciate the value to them of sound educational measurement.

In fact I see applications of item banking in three separate fields; fields which are certainly not mutually exclusive.   Firstly I see them being extremely valuable to teachers who want to design their own high quality assessment instruments, but who do not have the time or the skill to develop an achievement test from the beginning.   Many teachers could undoubtedly make good use of a well organised item bank, and because of the time it would save one might hope that not only the testing but also the teaching would improve.

Secondly, item banks may prove to be especially well adapted for meeting the needs of criterion referenced evaluation as mastery-learning strategies become more and more widely used in education.   When item results rather than test scores become the focus, then an item-based measurement resource would seem to be the natural answer.

Thirdly, more than half the countries of the world are only now beginning to develop large school systems which can offer something like universal education to their young citizens.   In these countries where financial resources and psychometric expertise are both in very short supply the need is for cheap but comprehensive systems of educational assessment, and I believe that item banks can provide this. An area that is still to be explored is the extent to which item banks may be effect-ively shared by different countries and different educational systems, but there seems good reason to suppose that this can be done.   Such a facility would be important in regions such as Latin America or East Africa where language barriers are not insuperable.

Within Europe the language question cannot be ignored, and it is as yet too early to say whether test materials may be freely translated from one language to another without their psychometric properties being substantially altered.

More has been written about the potential advantages of item banking systems than about the practical results of introducing them. Wood and Skurnik (1969) in their influential book on item banking describe in detail how it could serve the British desire to have both national and school-based assessment of secondary school pupils. Scriven (1967), in an article which has had a major impact on the theory and practise of curriculum evaluation, explains how item banks could completely change procedures for both formative and summative evaluation, providing, at the same time, for continuous assessment of student progress. The difficulty in implementing these ideas until very recently has been the lack of an adequate methodology for handling measurements based on responses to individual items. This paper describes such a methodology.

ORGANISATION AND CALIBRATION OF AN ITEM BANK

Just how should an item bank be organised and what data should be stored together with the items. It is usual of course, even in otherwise unstructured item pools to record some information as to what each item is supposed to measure. Here perhaps we can distinguish two quite different types of item banks. In one, each item essentially measures some different aspect of achievement. Each is perhaps concerned with some criterion task, performance of which would demonstrate mastery of a particular objective. Such items are intended to be used and interpreted individually. The other sort of bank will contain substantial numbers of items which purport to measure the same dimension and this dimension is probably quite generally defined as being for instance 'Achievement in Geometry' or 'Knowledge of German Vocabulary' or 'Understanding Scientific Principles'. In these circumstances it is expected that groups of items will be extracted from the bank and used to form an ad hoc test to provide more or less precise measurement for the trait in question. The bank must contain information as to what each item is supposed to measure, but this in itself is not enough. If results on an item are to be interpreted then one needs to know how difficult the item is and to what extent it discriminates between people of different ability. Unfortunately, conventional measures of item difficulty and discrimination are 'sample-bound', which is to say. they are extremely dependent on the nature of the sample of people who provide the data. One way round this problem is to try out test items on a wide variety of different types of people, and to store the results for each group of people together with the description of each group for future use. This approach has been used in the past for a wide variety of standardised tests, but it is basically not very satisfactory. There are problems in adequately defining the groups of

people for whom norms are calculated and also problems in identifying a particular
testee as a member of a particular group.

Gulliksen (1950) hinted at a different approach to the problem:

> "A significant contribution to item analysis theory would be the
> discovery of item parameters that remained relatively stable as
> the item analysis group changed; or the discovery of a law
> relating the changes in item parameters to changes in the group."

Much recent psychometric research has concentrated on the identification of item
parameters with this property.

An important characteristic of an item bank is that, just as with a money bank,
different units deposited and withdrawn from the bank may be related to one another
by means of a well-defined currency.   Normal methods of test analysis do not
provide this property.   A test score is normally interpretable only in terms of
the particular content of the test.   Scores on two different tests cannot normally
be compared directly, but only through the device of transforming to percentiles of
the normal distribution or something similar - and this results in the interpretation
of one individual's score being dependent on who is included in the sample for the
norming of the test.

Such sample dependence is very limiting for measurement.   It would be intolerable
if to compare the lengths of various pieces of string one had to measure all of them
with the same ruler.   Intolerable also if the length we found for a particular
piece of string was dependent upon which other pieces of string had been measured.
This, however, is the situation we face with traditional forms of test analysis.

In the search for 'sample-free' test parameters it was soon realised that any model
for item response would need to be probablistic rather than deterministic if it was
to adequately represent reality.   Earlier work on test taking behaviour has shown
conclusively that, without taking a vast number of other factors into account, a
simple model will only be able to estimate the probability that a particular
individual will correctly respond to a particular test item, and not definitely to
predict whether or not he will succeed.

Of the various possible stochastic models for describing test taking behaviour, we
will here consider only one family with particularly simple measurement characteristics.   This is the one now being used in a number of different item banking
projects, and it is the Rasch model described by Dr. Willmott in his paper.

The basic theme underlying this model is that 'difficulty' of an item should be defined in a special way.   One result is that if you, or I, or anyone else, be confronted with two test items of different levels of difficulty then our probability of responding correctly to the one of greatest difficulty is always less than our probability of responding correctly to the other.   Further, since difficulty is defined in terms dependent of whether you, or I, or anyone else, faced the items, the 'relative difficulty' of the two items is preserved.   The first part seems no more than common sense, but the second is slightly more difficult.   If item 'A' is easier than item 'B' for me then it must be so for you too and for everyone else. Similarly if you have a greater probability than I of responding correctly to item 'A' then you will also have a better chance at item 'B' or indeed any other item in the set.   Any group of items scaled by the Rasch model can be ordered with regard to their difficulty independent of which people will be exposed to them, and conversely any group of people whose abilities are assessed with the Rasch model can be ordered according to their probability of responding directly to a particular item without regard to which item is used.

A convenient way of summarising the behaviour of a test item is the 'item characteristic curve' (ICC).   This plots, for a single item, the probability of a person responding correctly to the item for persons of different ability.   In general the probability is low (near zero) for people of low ability, and high (near one) for people of high ability.   The slope of the curve at its central point gives some indication of the item's discriminating power.   The order relationship of 'relative difficulty' within the Rasch scheme means that the ICC's for a set of items take on a quasi-parallel form as shown in Figure 1.   The curves do not cross.

Now this is the theory behind the model and it does not exactly match what one finds in real life and with actual test data.   Firstly, it clearly does not hold for groups of items measuring different subjects.   If item 'A' concerns 'Euclidean Geometry', and item 'B' - 'knowledge of Spanish Vocabulary', then it is easy to identify types of people for which either one but not the other item is easy.   In addition one cannot usually mix items which allow the answer to be guessed with those which do not, as this offends the relative difficulty rule for persons of different abilities.

FIGURE 1 - <u>Item Characteristic Curves According to the Rasch Model</u>

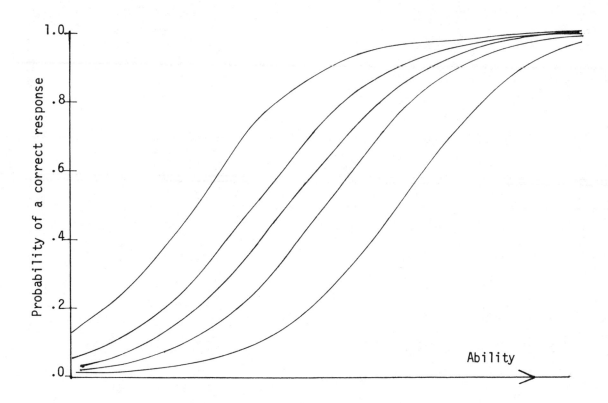

Nevertheless the model has proved to be robust enough to scale large numbers of test items in particular subject areas. It seeks to describe the outcome of a person confronting a set of test items in terms of parameters for the difficulties of each of the items involved and a parameter for the relevant ability of the person. Both ability and difficulty are measured in the same units - the 'wit' is frequently used. Biology test items are calibrated in biology wits; chemistry items in chemistry wits. The calibrated difficulty of an item is a stable property of the item, assumed to be unaffected by the nature of the people who attempt it. An individual will have a certain amount of ability in biology (measured in biology wits); and ability in chemistry (measured in chemistry wits) and so on. A person with ability 60 wits in biology would have a 50% chance of answering correctly a biology item of difficulty of 60 wits. For an item of 55 wits his chance of success would rise to 75%; for an item of 50 wits 90% and so on. The probability of success for various abilities attempting an item of 60 wits is shown by the item characteristics curve in Figure 2.

FIGURE   2   -   The Item Characteristic Curve for an Item of Difficulty 60 Wits

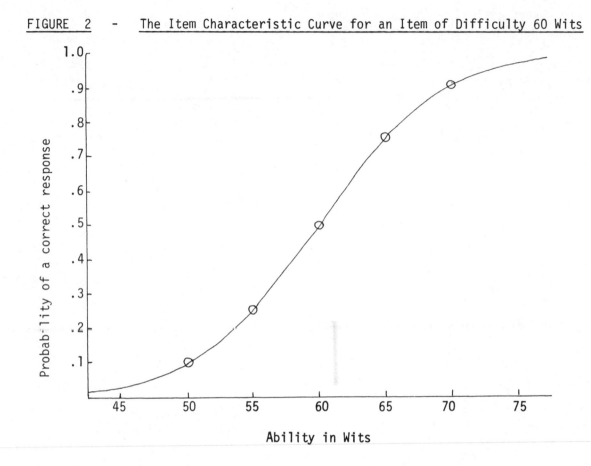

Ability in Wits

In an item banking context it is necessary once a pool of scalable items have been constructed to perform a calibration; that is to estimate the parameters of difficulty for each item.   For this a certain amount of trial data is required, but it should be noted that it is never necessary to have a sample of students attempt all the items.

Once a calibration of the items has been carried out, it is comparatively simple to calibrate the whole range of possible test scores which could be obtained on any sub-set of items withdrawn from the pool to make a test.   This leads to straight-forward estimates of ability for individuals that have the desired characteristics mentioned earlier.

When item data is stored in the bank ready for use it would be necessary to include the difficulty calibration, along with information regarding the item content, directions for administration, for scoring etc.   There is, in theory, no other psychometric data to be included, since topic and difficulty level are the only information needed to interpret test results.   It is, however, rather too early to say whether or not such an idealistic approach will suffice in practice.   Rasch-

scaled item banks are neither norm-referenced nor criterion-referenced, but fall neatly between the two concepts. For a strictly hierarchical subject or for measurement along a single clearly defined dimension, the distinction is not important. For more complex subjects (e.g. Mathematics treated as a whole) discrepancies from the model do appear whenever performance on particular objectives is compared. Research into this matter is continuing, and it appears that for diagnostic use a secondary analysis of test results to locate discrepancies and measure the residuals may be appropriate.

Another unresolved problem concerns the scope of the item bank. Should one have the single bank for mathematics, with one scaling scheme for items in arithmetic, geometry, algebra, analysis etc.? Does it make sense to talk of someone's mathematical ability, or must it be broken down into these sub-areas in order to be meaningful? Here there are still disagreements, but it is not difficult, for the time being, to organise and calibrate a mathematics item bank in two ways. If it turns out that the results of both are essentially the same then the more complex one (of separately scaling each sub-set of questions) can be dropped. As far as possible, it seems desirable to stick to the notion that mathematics items have fixed difficulty levels (in mathematics wits) whether they concern algebra, arithmetic or geometry. If it proves that a particular individual performs much worse on the algebra items than he does for example in geometry, it seems permissible to deduce that his mathematical ability is slanted away from algebra towards geometry. This may be a better way of proceeding than to have entirely different estimates of ability (in algebra wits and in geometry wits) that cannot be directly compared.

I shall now briefly describe three different applications of Rasch-scaled Item Banking. I have selected them not because they are the best in the field or even because they are generally representative. They are here because I feel I know each of them well enough to describe them to you and each illustrates a different type of application of the basic banking concept.

APPLICATION 1

The first example is a piece of exploratory research. This piece of work used the science item bank created by the International Association for Educational Achievement (or IEA for short) for their cross-national study of achievement in science. The main report of the study appeared in 1973 (Comber and Keeves) but the work I shall now describe is an extension using children from the English school system.

For this application the IEA science item bank was divided into three main areas:
Biology, Chemistry and Physics.   Each of these contains items covering a wide
range of ability with at one end some items suitable for children in primary schools
and at the other some appropriate for those preparing to enter university.   Four
tests were constructed with items drawn from the bank.   Each contained sub-tests
in biology, chemistry and physics, but for simplicity I will only refer to the
biology results here.   Test A was intended for ten year old students who in
England are mostly to be found in Grade 5.   Test B was regarded as suitable for
those in the early years of secondary education while Test C was intended for those
in the twelfth grade.   In addition, a particularly difficulty Test D was created
to be administered to those pre-university students who had specialised in the study
of biology.   Each item in these tests had already been calibrated as members of
the total item bank (biology sub-section), and this enabled calibration of the scores
on each of these new tests in terms of ability.

Figure 3 shows the results of the set of calibrations.   It gives equivalenced
scales across the tests as an aid to the interpretation of the scores.   They can
be read in either of two ways.   First, one may say that a student with 45 wits of
ability in biology would be expected to attain a score of seven on Test A or a score
of five on Test B, and so on.   Alternatively, one can argue that a score of ten
on Test A is evidence of an ability of 50 wits whereas a score of ten on Test C
suggests an ability of 57 wits.   A good deal of information about the tests can be
discerned from Figure 3.   Notice, for instance, that the tests are of varying
length; Test A has 13 items, Test B has 19, Test C has 16 and Test D has 40.
This does not cause problems for the analysis, and it is clear how the extra
precision in measurement is obtained when the number of items is increased.   Note
also, how much more imprecise are the measurements made towards the ends.   On a 13
item test such as Test A, although there are 14 possible scores, it is only possible
to make 12 estimates of ability.   For somebody who scored 13 (that is; all
responses were correct), all we can say is that their ability is probably greater
than 59 wits.   Without additional information, it is not possible to put an upper
limit to the ability estimate.   Similarly, somebody who scored zero on Test A
probably has an ability of less than 28 wits.   How much less we do not know.
Finally, note the very considerable degree of overlap that exists between these
different scales even though, for example the items in Test B were substantially
more difficult than the items in Test A.

The appropriate tests were given to random samples of English school children aged
ten (Test A), in Grades 8, 9 and 10 (Test B), and Grade 12 (Test C).   Some members
of the last sample who were specialising in biology were also given Test D.

FIGURE 3 - Calibration in Wits for Four IEA Biology Tests

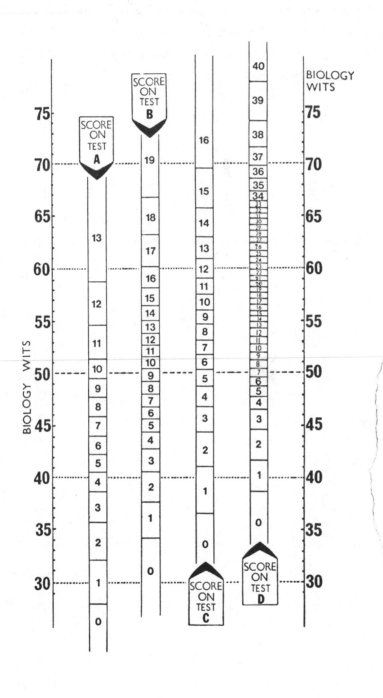

Scores on the test were then converted into wits and frequency distributions for ability were calculated.   They are shown in Figure 4.   The areas under the curves for Grades 5, 8 and 9 are the same since virtually 100% of the children attend school for these Grade levels.   However, at the time the data were collected, Grade 10 was not compulsory in England and some 30% of the 16 year old children were no longer at school.   The smaller area under the curve for Grade 10 reflects this. Similarly for Grade 12 the proportion of children still in school was very much lower.

FIGURE 4   -   Frequency Distributions for Ability in Biology

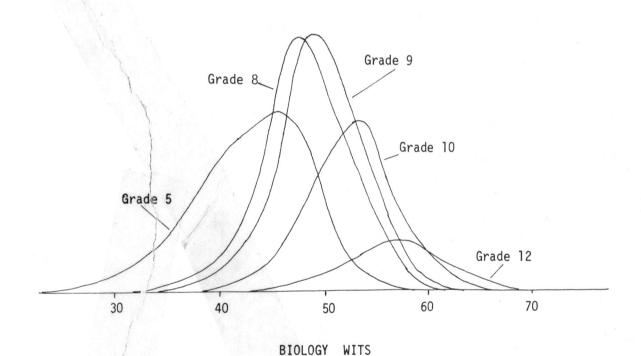

BIOLOGY WITS

The information contained in these related distributions has not yet been fully digested. The spread of achievement in Grade 5 (which, for most children, is before any formal instruction in science begins) is clearly greater than that occurring in Grade 8 and 9, (when all the children have received about the same basic instruction in biology). By Grade 12, when specialisation and a plethora of elective courses lead again to great variation in the amount of exposure to biological ideas and thinking, the spread of achievement is again very high. Further, the growth in achievement from Grade 8 to 9 and 9 to 10 appears remarkedly consistent especially if one remembers it is, by and large, the less able part of Grade 10 that had dropped out of school before testing took place. The annual increase in achievement appears to be between one and two wits, and indeed the growth in achievement from Grade 5 to Grade 8 also appears to support this. The biologists with whom I have discussed these results so far find less than two wits a startingly small improvement for something more than 100 hours of classroom study. A typical student with a probability of 0.50 of responding correctly to a typical item at the beginning of the year, finds this probability increased to only 0.57 at the end.

Of course this is only an average figure. There will no doubt be some specific parts of the curriculum where mastery is achieved and the 0.5 might grow to 0.9 but this implies that there will be many more areas where growth is non-existent. The total amount of learning appears small.

APPLICATION 2

My next example concerns the use of item banks in curriculum evaluation along the lines proposed by Scriven in the article already cited. Some nine years ago a School Reform was initiated in Israel. This involved the gradual establishment throughout the country of a system of comprehensive middle schools to cater for Grades 7, 8 and 9. The old system of eight years elementary and four years high school was to be progressively replaced by a three tier system - six years, three years and three years. Although a major purpose of this reform was to bring about a greater degree of mixing of pupils from different social groups, the opportunity was also taken to modernise the curricula for the middle grades.

As part of the Goverment's plans for monitoring the effects of these changes it was decided to administer achievement tests to a large sample of pupils both in the middle schools and in a control sample of unreformed elementary schools as they completed each school year. This was repeated at the end of the 6th, 7th, 8th and 9th grades. The longitudinal study involved testing in a variety of school subjects, but here I will only report to you some of the results for mathematics.

A large pool of test items for these grades was compiled: partly from existing tests and examinations, partly by the writers of the new curricula and partly by the team in charge of the monitoring.   It was realised early that, although in the sixth grade all the students had followed the traditional curriculum, by the end of the seventh grade the new mathematics was sufficiently different from the traditional approach, that use of the same achievement tests for both groups would be inappropriate.   The picture was further complicated by the fact that two similar, but competing, new mathematics curricula had been introduced in the seventh grade, and students of both appeared with sufficient frequency in the sample to warrant a separate analysis.   While at Grade 7 these curricula were similar enough to permit the use of single achievement test it was considered imperative at Grade 8 to have separate tests for the two groups.   During Grade 9 a major split of the pupils into academic and vocational streams occurs and it was also thought necessary to have separate achievement tests for each stream.   A large number of mathematics tests had therefore to be constructed from the item pool.   At each grade level all the tests used contained some items in common (items which were not considered to be particularly associated with any one curriculum).   Furthermore, each of the tests at the seventh, eighth and ninth grades contained some items that had been used in the preceding year.   In this way it was possible to obtain a complete calibration of the items in the bank (several hundred items were involved). This led to a stable and precisely estimated scale of mathematics achievement in wits, and it was possible to estimate for each child where he stood on this scale at the conclusion of each school year.

When the results are summarised one obtains the average achievement of sampled students studying under each regime as presented in Figure 5 .   It is clear that neither new mathematics programme is producing results strikingly better than those of the traditional curriculum, and also that 'New Mathematics A' is a comparative failure, especially in Grades 7 and 8.   You will note, of course, the considerable differences between the three groups when the Grade 6 testing took place.   This results from the fact that the introduction of middle schools into particular regions of the country was a matter of political expediency rather than random choice. The first middle schools to be established were generally clustered in areas of low educational achievement apart from a group in a somewhat privileged area around Jerusalem.   (The proponents of 'curriculum A' were given to the Jerusalem schools for trials of their programme).   This accounts for the substantial differences between the groups that one finds at the beginning of the study.   It is a fact of life that educational innovations are rarely tried out on random samples of the population, and the strength of this methodological approach to monitoring is that it appears to handle differences in initial ability and subsequent curriculum content without recourse to the rather dubious procedures of covariance analysis.

FIGURE 5 — Average Achievement at the End of the School Year for Groups of Pupils Studying Three Different Curricula

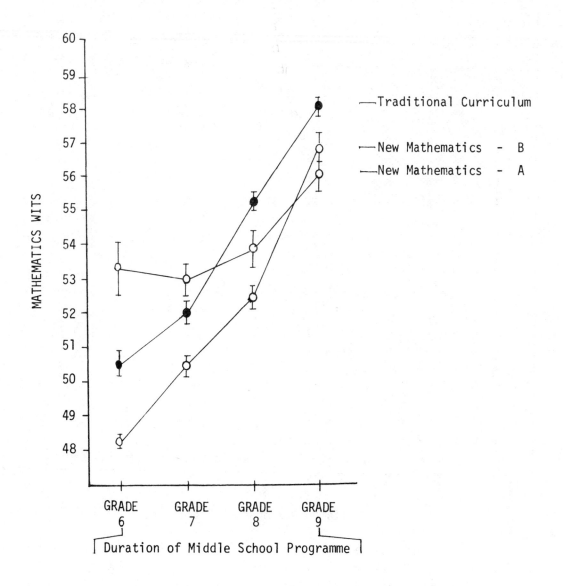

FIGURE   6   -   Relative Difficulty of Items for Pupils of Two New Mathematics
                Curricula

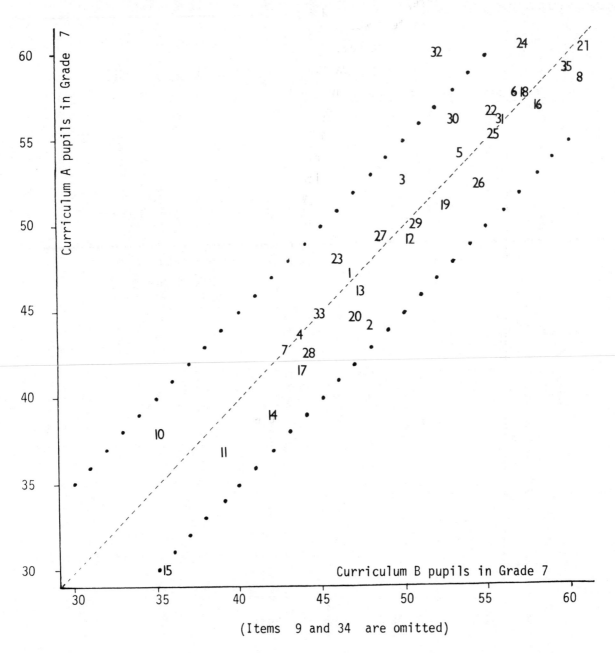

(Items   9 and 34   are omitted)

These results, while somewhat discouraging for the proponents of 'curriculum A', are only the beginning.   It was important to discover which components of the curriculum lead to such massive discrepancies in learning during Grade 7.   At the end of Grade 7 the same mathematics test was given to both 'curriculum A' and 'curriculum B' students.   Figure 6 displays the calibration of the items in this test calculated separately for the two types of students.   This graph is of the 'relative difficulty' of items for the two groups and automatically discounts differences in the student's ability.   It is apparent that, for instance, item 32 is very considerably more difficult for 'curriculum A' students that it is for those of 'curriculum B'.   This in fact was not suprising since it was a simple question in 'Cartesian Co-ordinate Geometry' that 'curriculum B' taught during the seventh grade but which was not introduced by 'curriculum A' until the beginning of the eighth.   The other discrepancies were rather harder to explain.   'Curriculum A' students appeared to find questions involving computation relatively easy, but found great difficulty with questions dealing with graphical representation, algebraic forms and numeric problems requiring algebraic solutions.   This work is still continuing.   The Grade 8 results reveal that the main deficiencies of the students of 'curriculum A' are concerned with problems requiring comprehension and analysis as opposed to Bloom's categories of knowledge and elementary application. It is hypothesised that this stems from a failure in 'curriculum A' to communicate some basic concepts in the early months of the course.   This approach to considering the specific effects of particular curricula appears fruitful.

APPLICATION 3

My last example is in a rather different category in that the project is still at an early stage of implementation, and I have no results of any sort to report.   The scheme being introduced by the Indonesian Ministry of Education will develop a system of item banks for the comprehensive assessment of secondary school performance, the monitoring of changes in curriculum, and the selection of students for higher education.   Although implementation is now restricted to Mathematics, the Sciences and 'Bahasa Indonesia' (the national language), it is intended eventually to extend the concept to all examinable subjects of the secondary curriculum.

Figure 7 gives an outline of the activity within the project.   Three distinct cycles can be identified.   The first concerns the design and building of the bank (involving item writing, trials, etc.), and leading to a series of calibration exercises.   The next and simplest cycle concerns the generation of tests with specific characteristics, and the feedback to the bank of test results to be used

FIGURE 7 — Projected Item Banking System for Indonesian Ministry of Education

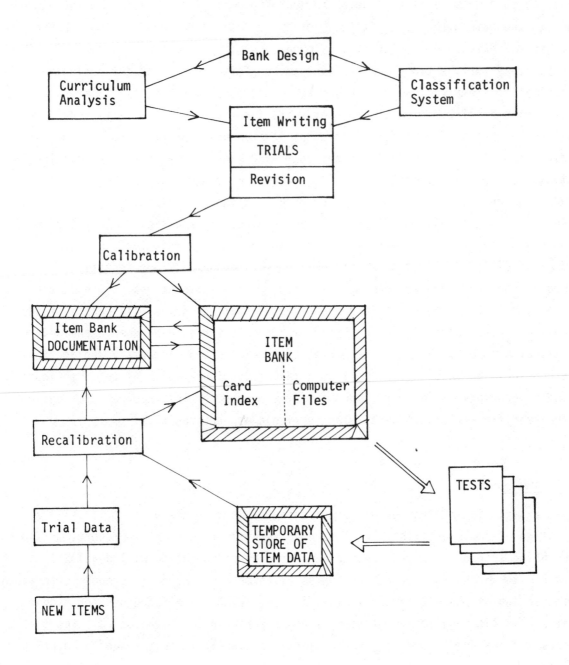

in later re-calibrations.   The third cycle concerns the creation of new items and their incorporation into the item bank.

Indonesia is a very large country, comparable in size and population with all of Western Europe, and in consequence there have been serious difficulties in operating a system of national examinations which it is hoped that the projected item bank will overcome.

The first of these difficulties is a language problem.   Although there is a national language, there are also about thirty 'local' languages of importance in different regions of the country.   In many of the nation's schools 'Bahasa Indonesia' is not yet used as the normal language of instruction, yet hitherto officials in Jakarta have seen no alternative to the conducting of 'national' examinations in the 'national' language.   The flexibility of the item banking system will permit different students to be given different examination questions. This opens the possibility of generating examinations in local languages as well as in the national language, so that students whose training in the national language is limited may be more fairly assessed.

Secondly, the difficulties in communicating with remote island provinces, and the extreme pressure for places within the small university sector, have led to certain abuses of the examination system at the local level.   The most frequent source of trouble has been the copying and distribution of examination papers prior to the date of the examination itself.   With an item banking system which can generate many versions of an examination (such that the pupils in a given classroom may all be responding to different questions) it is hoped that this cheating will be easier to control.

This is an ambitious project on a very large scale and which has still a number of difficulties to overcome before it will have proved its worth.   It is operating at the frontier of our psychometric experience and yet I hope that if successful it may be a model for future assessment schemes elsewhere in the world.

REFERENCES

COMBER, L.C. and KEEVES, J.P. (1973). Science Education in Nineteen Countries:
An Empirical Study. New York: Wiley.

GULLIKSEN, H. (1950). Theory of Mental Tests. New York: Wiley.

SCRIVEN, M. (1967). 'The Methodology of Evaluation' in Tyler R.W. et al
Perspectives in Curriculum Evaluation. AERA Monograph 1: Chicago, Rand McNally
(page 58).

WOOD, R. and SKURNIK, L.S. (1969). Item Banking. Slough: N.F.E.R.

AN INITIAL NATION-WIDE EDUCATIONAL EVALUATION EXPERIMENT IN FRANCE

C. Seibel & D. Bargas

Abstract - In April 1975 the French Ministry of Education carried out an experiment in psycho-educational evaluation with a sub-sample of the national cohort comprising some 1,000 pupils from three educational districts in their second year of secondary education, who sat tests in French or mathematics as well as general intelligence tests.

The pupils in branches (1) I and II achieved better and more even performances, although there was considerable overlapping with the performances of branch III pupils. The independent variables (sex, age, type of school) had less effect on branch III pupils.

These initial observations will be supplemented by the results of a study being carried out in 1976 on a broader group with a wider range of information.

---

(1) (="filieres"). French lower secondary education is divided into 3 branches. Branches I and II are for the more academically gifted pupils.

INTRODUCTION

a. Origin of the project

The Department of Evaluation Techniques and Studies was created within the Division of Statistical and Data-processing Studies in July 1973. Its task is to provide policy-makers in the Ministry of Education and the Secretariat of State for Universities with information, studies and methodological assistance in the field of educational evaluation. In the early months of its existence, the department tried to ascertain needs in this regard in the light of work being done in France and abroad.

In contrast to countries like Great Britain or Sweden, although many local surveys of small representative samples have been carried out by psycho-educational research teams in France, there have been few national surveys of pupils' achievements and abilities. The INED-INOP (1) survey of the intellectual level of children of school

---

1   INED: Institut National d'Etudes Démographiques-National Institute for Demographic Studies
INOP: Institut National d'Orientation Professionnelle-National Institute for Vocational Guidance.

age, based on a 'collective intellectual level scale' devised by INOP, is already more than ten years old (2).   Similarly, apart from Girard's and Bastide's study(3), there has hardly been any longitudinal survey showing the development of a cohort or enabling variations in academic performance over a certain period to be assessed. Thus the department's main field of study was considered to be the knowledge, skills and attitudes of pupils on a national scale.

After several experts had been consulted, a survey was proposed to the department's steering group, under the chairmanship of the Director General for Planning and Co-ordination, which agreed with its main lines.   After revision, the project was accepted by the Minister of Education in July 1974 and implemented between September 1974 and April 1975.   The first methodological decisions to be taken concerned the sample, the level of schooling and the test instruments to be used.

b. The reference population

The general reference population chosen for the project was a 'cohort' formed by the Central Statistics and Survey Office in the second term of the 1972-73 school year. This is a purely random sample of children born on the first day of an even month, whatever their age, in their first year of general or specialised secondary education in a State or private school in metropolitan France during the 1972-73 school year. It is roughly a 1/60 sample, comprising nearly 14,000 pupils in 1972-73, an average of three pupils per school.   In the same way two more cohorts were formed in 1973-74 and 1974-75.   The objective chosen was to observe and describe the academic progress of the pupils concerned, identify the various factors which may influence schooling and shed some light on problems which cannot be treated through annual general inquiries.

The questionnaire used for the survey was deliberately confined from the start to a minimum number of variables: pupils' identities, their present grades, some inform-ation about their pre-school and primary education, their parents' occupations, the number of children in the family and the pupils' rank among them.

No information was sought about achievements, except some indicators of school prog-ress, viz whether the pupil was behind-hand, whether he had repeated a year or vice-versa.   It is intended that each pupil in the cohort will be observed, if possible, at least till he leaves the educational system.

---

2   BENEDETTO: 'Enquête nationale sur le niveau intellectuel des enfants d'âge scolaire' - L'Orientation Scolaire et Professionnelle - 1972,4.

3   GIRARD et BASTIDE: 'De la fin des études élémentaires à l'entres dans la vie professionnelle ou à l"Université'. Population. Mai-Juin 1973 n⁰ 3.

It seemed useful to add to these statistical data some objective information concerning the academic knowledge and general intellectual ability of at least a part of the reference population.   Moreover, the selection of several cohorts makes it possible to compare school performances at the same grade over a certain period, provided that educational objectives and curricula remain relatively unchanged.

The comprehensiveness of this national sample led us to adopt it for our own purposes. The population covered by our study is in fact a sub-sample of the national sample. However, the choice of such a sample entailed some technical difficulties due to the dispersal of the pupils among a large number of schools (more than 500 for the three educational districts in which the experiment was carried out).   The difficulties were mainly concerned with the grouping together, transportation and accommodation of the pupils and of the teams responsible for administering and marking the tests.

c. Level of schooling and choice of instruments

The end of the school year of secondary education was chosen as the testing level for two reasons: first, it was at the time an initial orientation stage reached by almost a whole age-group; secondly, tests devised by INRDP (4) and INETOP could be used for the two basic subjects, French and Mathematics.   In 1978 the pupils are to be retested when they have reached the end of the fourth year of secondary education. Surveys of a similar type may be usefully carried out in primary education when the relevant instruments are available.

The following report describes the pilot project carried out in 1975 and sets out the main results.

DESCRIPTION OF THE PROJECT

Objectives

The pilot project carried out in April 1975 had four main objectives:

   1.   To make a survey of the pupils' knowledge, so as to establish a reference point regarding the acquisition of certain basic concepts.

The aim was not to take stock of all that the pupils were capable of doing by the end of the second year of secondary education but to see whether they had really assimilated certain basic concepts and important reasoning processes in French and mathematics.

---

   4   INRDP - Institut National de Recherches et Documentation Pédagogiques -
National Institute for Educational Research and Documentation.

2.   To make a longitudinal study of knowledge, abilities and skills.   If the pilot survey is deemed satisfactory, a further survey may be held in identical circumstances in 1979 or 1980 to show how achievements and certain psychological characteristics develop.   This would be particularly useful as, although between the two surveys various structural and educational changes will affect teaching in the second year of secondary schooling, enough items relating to the main parts of the curricula will probably remain valid.

3.   To identify certain relations between the pupils' achievements and characteristics.

By comparing the results of the tests with other information previously gathered about the individual pupils, it is possible to study the general influence of such variables as age, social background and type of previous education.   More detailed studies could then be made of the role of these variables.   As the members of the cohort are to be observed for several years, it will also be possible to verify forecasts made about them on the basis of the knowledge test results and to compare different instruments in this regard.   Later on, it will be possible to try to establish the characteristics of pupils who repeat a year or drop out, to determine their chances of success in different branches, and to produce 'profiles' of pupils in different sections.

4.   To make teachers more aware of evaluation problems by letting them take an active part in the experiment.

The fact that the reference population was scattered made it easier to convince teachers that the survey was not intended to assess their professional ability.   From the start it was hoped that teachers and guidance officers would co-operate with one another.   It was thought that such co-operation could encourage the teachers themselves to devise tests and incorporate them in their teaching.

5.   One final objective was to enable the new department to deploy on a limited, experimental scale the technical administrative and financial resources needed for a complex survey.

The reference population

Two populations took part in the project: a group of pupils and a group of teachers.

1.   The population of pupils came from two different sources:
a sub-sample of the cohort formed for national statistical purposes;

whole classes of the lower secondary schools in a town in the Creteil educational district.

(a)   The cohort sub-sample included all the cohort pupils in the second year of secondary schooling in the educational districts of Dijon and Montpellier and the Department of Pas de Calais in the Lille educational district.   The pupils came from two sections of the cohort: those repeating their second year belonged to section 1, those just entering their second year to section 2.   Altogether, 1,018 pupils took the intelligence test and one of the two knowledge tests (mathematics or French).

(b)   The sample from whole classes of five lower secondary schools in a town in the Creteil educational district consisted of 464 pupils who took the intelligence test and both knowledge tests (mathematics and French).

Table 1 shows the distribution of pupils in both samples according to test, sex, age, branch and school.

TABLE I   -   Pupil Population Taking Part in the 1975 Test Operation

		Intelligence	Maths	French	Intelligence	Maths	French
	TOTAL	1,018	517	501	464	447	449
SEX	Boys	495	251	244	232	225	224
	Girls	523	266	257	232	222	225
BRANCH	I + II	829	425	404	302	291	292
	III	189	92	97	162	156	157
TYPE OF SCHOOL	'Lycée'	167	97	70	-	-	-
	'CES'	635	318	317	464	447	449
	'CEG'	216	102	114	-	-	-
AGE AT 1.1.75.	14 or over	95	51	44	66	59	62
	13	448	210	238	191	186	182
	12	430	227	203	189	185	187
	11 or under	45	29	16	18	17	18
		COHORT SUB-SAMPLES Pupil group sizes			WHOLE CLASSES SAMPLES Pupil group sizes		

TABLE 2 - TEACHER POPULATION

NUMBER OF TEACHERS	MATHEMATICS	FRENCH
TOTAL	51	51
Branch I	24	24
Branch II	6	14
Branches I & II together	17	10
Branch III	4	3

2.   The population of teachers consisted of teachers who had volunteered to:-

help guidance officers to administer and mark the knowledge test in their own subjects (mathematics or French);

reply to a 'critical' questionnaire on the knowledge test concerned while the pupils were sitting the test.

51 teachers in each subject took part in the experiment, which involved their dealing with classes in different branches.   Table 2 (above) shows their distribution.

Instruments

1.   In French: A test in syntax and one in spelling (both ordinary and grammatical) devised by INRDP;   A silent reading test devised by INETOP, dealing with the comprehension of logical relations between the various parts of a text and the monitoring of thought processes involved in reading.

These tests were not intended to cover all the knowledge expected of the pupils concerned.   In particular, verbal ability was not investigated, and written ability was only partially evaluated.   However, the tests did provide an objective assessment of some basic knowledge.

2.   In Mathematics: A standard test in mathematical reasoning (ESRM 5/4) devised by INETOP with help from INRDP for a level corresponding to the end of the

second year and the beginning of the third.

This test too is designed not to give a full picture but an evaluation of ability to reason and to relate mathematical concepts.   It is suitable for pupils about to enter the third year, the subjects covered being more systematically dealt with in branch I/II (ordinary curriculum).

Arithmetic and problem-solving test (CP 5).   Devised by INETOP, at the request of the General Inspectorate, this test supplements ESRM 5/4 by verifying various concepts (quick calculation, proportionality, measuring of areas taught in primary education and the first year of secondary education.

     3.   <u>General intelligence tests:</u>   Two such tests from a series of eight devised by INOP, one of which applies to all pupils (GAA).

     4.   <u>Critical questionnaires on knowledge tests.</u>   These questionnaires were answered by the mathematics and French teachers marking the tests.   They were intended to:-

provide information on the teaching of the concepts covered by the test;

give success forecasts for each question in the tests;

enable the tests to be reviewed in the light of the remarks and criticisms made by the teachers.

Variables

Among the possible variables, only the following were accepted for the study:

Independent variables: branch, sex, age, type of school.

Dependent variables: partial and overall marks for each test.

Administration of the tests

The teams responsible for the administration of the tests consisted of a voluntary teacher and a guidance officer.   They provided as uniform conditions of administration and marking as possible.

INITIAL RESULTS [5]

Only the results of the knowledge tests (French and mathematics) are presented in this document. The intelligence tests, of which the GAA is one, were applied experimentally in 1975 to the pupils in the sample and are now being studied before being circulated by the authors to guidance services. All the analyses covered the whole sample; no analysis by educational district was made.

1. <u>Population as a whole</u>: The range of pupils' marks in the different tests was wide, extending from the lower end of the scale in mathematics, to the upper end in French.

2. <u>Pupils in branches I and II</u>: The range of marks was narrower. There were fewer low marks, resulting in a higher average mark and a lower dispersal index rating.

3. <u>Pupils in branch III</u>: On an average the marks were low, especially for the ESRM 5/4. The range of marks tended to be narrower, although only because there were fewer good marks. It was in the spelling test and the CP5 that the pupils performed best.

4. <u>Comparison between branch I and II pupils and branch III pupils</u>: Although all the pupils were in the second year of secondary schooling, the two types of branch produced different statistical results (probability threshold less than .0005) in all the knowledge tests. It is important to note that in the ESRM 5/4 all the pupils who obtained a mark higher than 35.5 (the average for the whole sample) came from branch I/II. Although the performance of pupils in branch III were distinctly inferior to those of pupils from branch I/II, there was considerable 'overlapping' in the mark ranges of the two branches. This was particularly significant in the CP5 and the spelling test: almost 50% of the pupils from branch III achieved the marks obtained by almost 50% of the pupils in branch I/II.

It would appear that pupils in branch III had a better grasp of what they had learned at primary school than of concepts relating to the more specific curriculum of the second year of secondary education.

Influence of independent variables in the case of branch I and II pupils

1. <u>Sex:</u> The girls performed better in syntax and spelling; the boys better in the CP5; differences were statistically insignificant so far as silent reading and the ESRM 5/4 were concerned.

---

5   See Table 3 and Figures 1 to 18 which conclude this paper.

2. <u>Year of birth</u>: The younger children scored well in all the tests; the marks show a distinct fall from one age group to the next. An analysis of each test seems to show that pupils whose ages are average or below average for the second year of secondary school perform much better than those who are behindhand.

3. <u>Type of school</u>: Differences between pupils from C.E.S.' and lycées (6) were statistically insignificant, except for the ESRM 5/4. On average, pupils from C.E.G.s (7) scored lower, but there was considerable overlapping with the other types of school.

<u>Influence of independent variables in the case of branch III pupils</u>

1. <u>Sex</u>: No statistically significant difference, except in spelling, for which girls scored higher.

2. <u>Year of birth</u>: In syntax and silent reading, the pupils born in 1961 scored higher than those born before 1961. For the other tests, no difference was noticeable.

3. <u>Type of school</u>: The differences between C.E.S. and C.E.G. pupils were slight except for the CP 5 where the latter scored definitely higher. It may be assumed that primary education skills and knowledge are more frequently used in C.E.G.s; that would explain why C.E.G. pupils feel more at home with arithmetic.

<u>Comparison of observations concerning branch I/II pupils and those concerning branch III pupils</u>

A study of the results suggests that the individual variables (sex, year of birth, school) have less effect on pupils from branch III than on those from branch I/II, for on the whole the results achieved by branch III pupils seem more homogeneous.

<u>CONCLUSION</u>

The pilot project implemented in 1975 by the Department of Evaluation Techniques and Studies achieved its objectives. However, it was only a first look at the situation from which it would be wrong to draw hasty conclusions either nationally or regionally, as the tests used did not cover

---

6   'Lycées': traditional type of secondary education school. The lower forms of lycées have been turned into independent CESs ('collèges d'enseignement secondaire').

7   CEG: 'Collège d'enseignement général' = College of general education, equivalent to a CES in a rural area.

the whole range of knowledge, the samples were not fully representative and the results of the analyses cannot be fitted together.   The analyses amount to a picture rather than an explanation.

It was decided to repeat the survey in 1976 on a wider scale: geographically wider, since about 3,000 pupils in five educational districts will be concerned; and wider in terms of information, since all the pupils are to sit both the French and the mathematics tests, and questionnaires are to be used to evaluate their position in their classes and ascertain their interests and their aptitudes for guidance purposes.

TABLE 3 -   RESULTS BY TEST

Subject	Test	Branch	Number N	Average M	Dispersal Index (S.D.)	Range of marks			
						Theoretical		Actual	
						Min	Max	Min	Max
MATHEMATICS	ESRM 5/4	Total	517	35.58	18.55	0	100	0	90
		I/II	425	40.45	16.44	0	100	5	90
		III	92	13.10	8.43	0	100	0	37
	CP 5	Total	517	12.80	6.28	0	35	0	31
		I/II	425	13.72	6.06	0	35	2	31
		III	92	8.55	5.57	0	35	0	29
FRENCH	SYNTAX	Total	501	28.26	9.62	0	49	1	48
		I/II	404	30.95	7.55	0	49	6	48
		III	97	17.09	9.33	0	49	1	42
	SPELLING	Total	501	47.15	12.03	0	66	3	66
		I/II	404	50.46	8.75	0	66	18	66
		III	97	33.39	13.99	0	66	3	62
	SILENT READING	Total	501	26.09	8.04	0	45	0	43
		I/II	404	28.38	6.44	0	45	11	43
		III	97	16.61	7.10	0	45	0	33

FIGURE 1 - SAMPLE AS A WHOLE : TEST ESRM 5/4

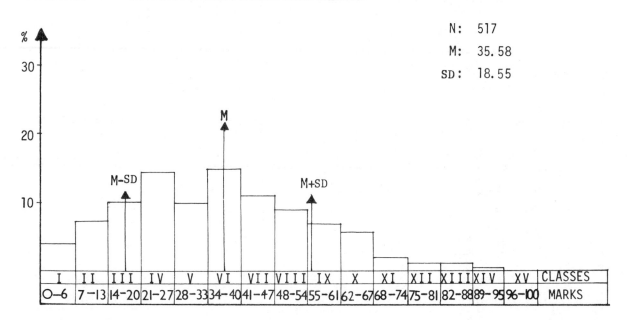

N: 517
M: 35.58
SD: 18.55

FIGURE 2 - BRANCH I AND/OR II : TEST ESRM 5/4

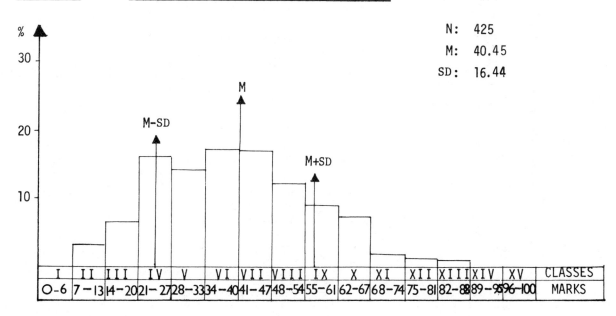

N: 425
M: 40.45
SD: 16.44

FIGURE 3 - BRANCH III : TEST ESRM 5/4

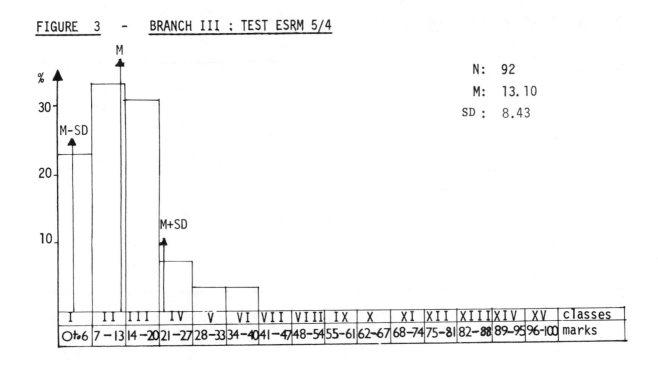

N: 92
M: 13.10
SD : 8.43

FIGURE 4 - SAMPLE AS A WHOLE : TEST CP5

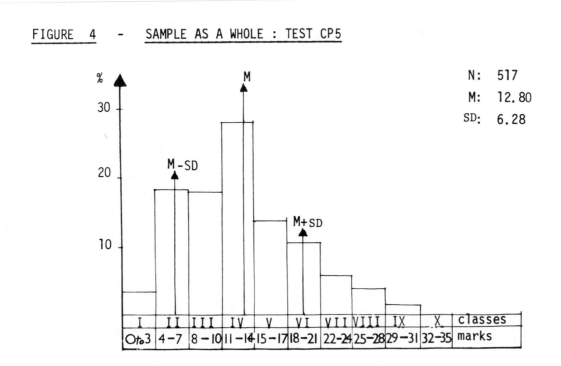

N: 517
M: 12.80
SD: 6.28

247

FIGURE 5 - I AND/OR II : TEST CP5

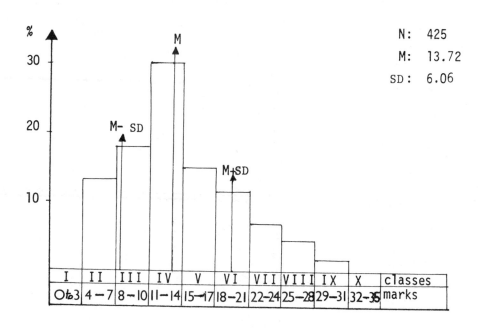

N: 425
M: 13.72
SD: 6.06

FIGURE 6 - BRANCH III : TEST CP 5

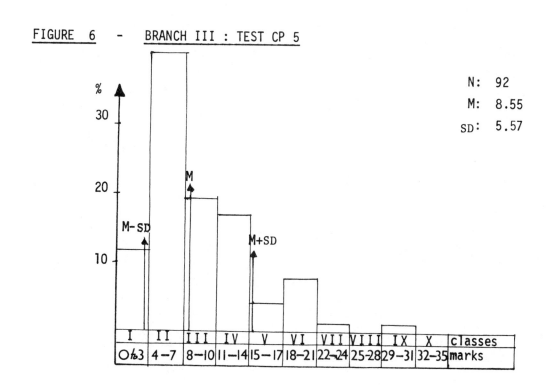

N: 92
M: 8.55
SD: 5.57

FIGURE 7 - SAMPLE AS A WHOLE : SYNTAX

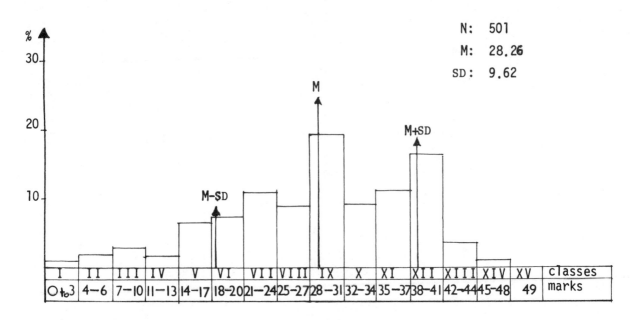

N: 501
M: 28.26
SD: 9.62

FIGURE 8 - BRANCH I AND/OR II : SYNTAX

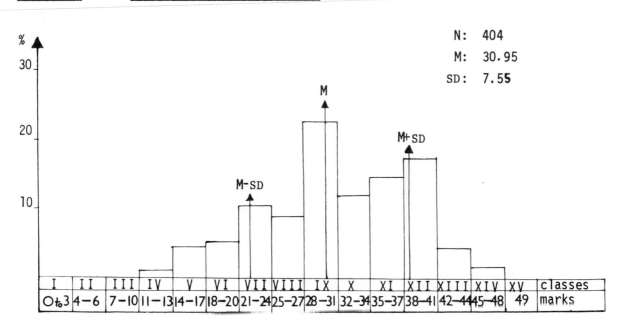

N: 404
M: 30.95
SD: 7.55

FIGURE 9 - BRANCH III : SYNTAX

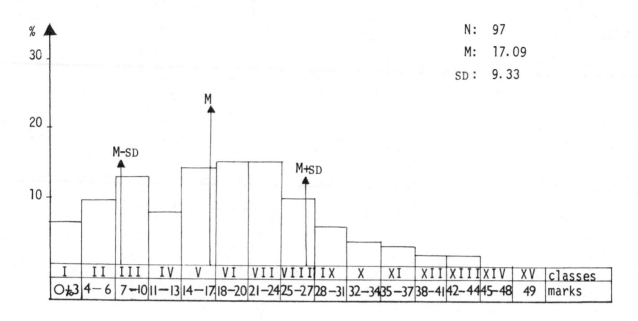

N: 97

M: 17.09

SD: 9.33

FIGURE 10 - SAMPLE AS A WHOLE : SPELLING TEST

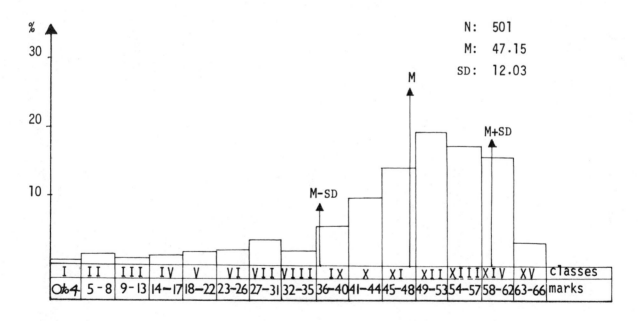

N: 501

M: 47.15

SD: 12.03

FIGURE 11 - BRANCH I AND/OR II : SPELLING

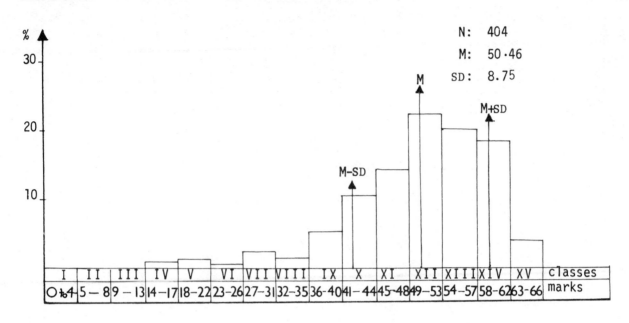

N: 404
M: 50·46
SD: 8.75

FIGURE 12 - BRANCH III : SPELLING

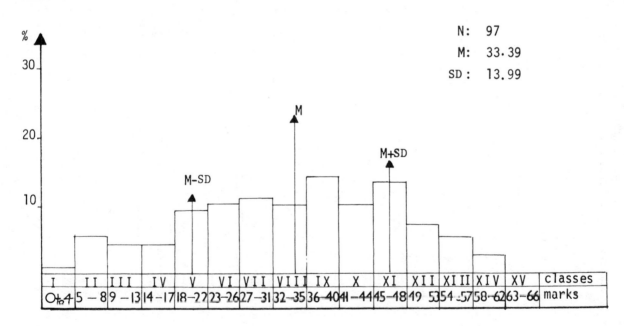

N: 97
M: 33·39
SD: 13.99

FIGURE 13 - SAMPLE AS A WHOLE : SILENT READING

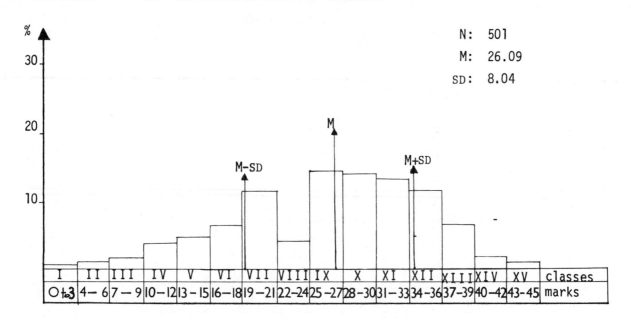

FIGURE 14 - BRANCH I AND/OR II : SILENT READING

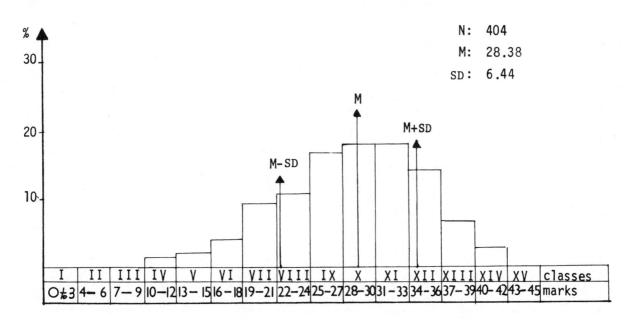

FIGURE 15 - BRANCH III : SILENT READING

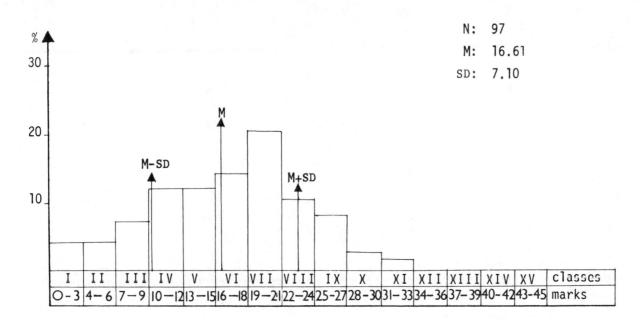

N: 97
M: 16.61
SD: 7.10

FIGURE 16 - SAMPLE AS A WHOLE : INTELLIGENCE

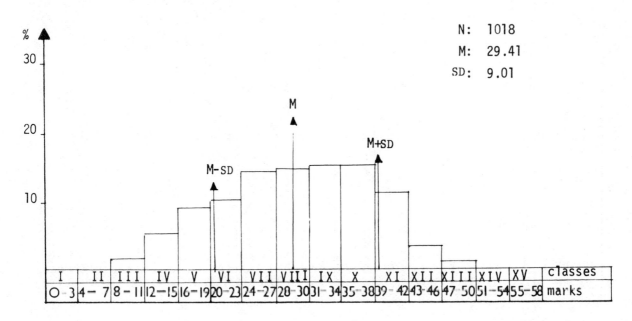

N: 1018
M: 29.41
SD: 9.01

FIGURE 17 - BRANCH I AND/OR II : INTELLIGENCE

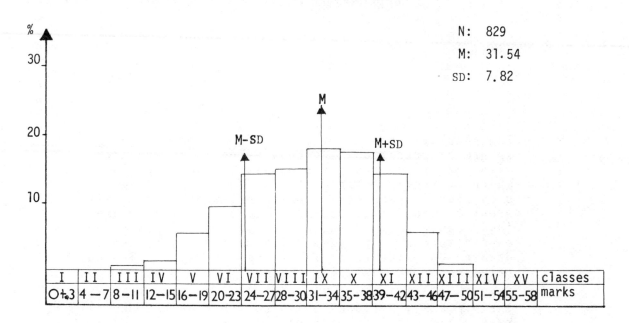

N: 829
M: 31.54
SD: 7.82

FIGURE 18 - BRANCH III : INTELLIGENCE

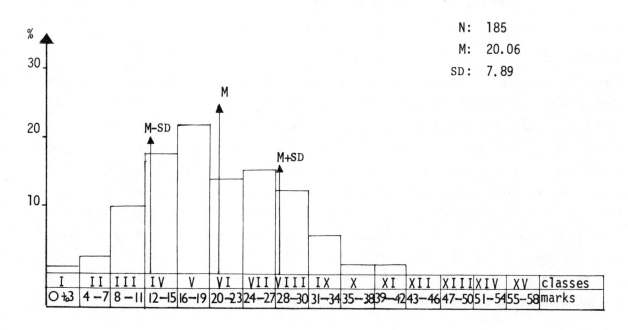

N: 185
M: 20.06
SD: 7.89

THE PROBABLE POLICY EFFECTS OF MONITORING EDUCATIONAL PERFORMANCE

B. RODMELL

abstract - The peculiar aspects of policy formation, in the sphere of education, are considered in conjunction with the frameworks for consultation and decision which currently affect national developments in the provision of resources and the balance between different types of institution. Constraints increasingly apply to funding, hence systems for planning expenditure are utilised which call for judgements drawing on evidence from various sources, including research of an evaluative kind.

The substantial enquiries organised, for example, by the N.F.E.R., National Children's Bureau and Medical Research Council are referred to as instances of surveys which have had some effects on policy formation, albeit by inference. The possible benefits of procedures for monitoring performance are anticipated, in terms of levels of application and the parts of the educational community likely to be most influenced by the results.

INTRODUCTION

I have to begin this paper with three disclaimers and an appeal for clemency. The first disclaimer is that, though I come from the D.E.S. and will be talking to some extent about activities within the Department, what I shall be presenting is essentially a personal view of the potential and limitations of performance monitoring, and is not a prediction of Departmental policy. The second disclaimer is that I am not an educationalist but an economist, and though I have participated in Departmental discussions about the development of performance indicators, I have no pretensions to the expertise in educational measurement that is possessed by many of my audience. The third disclaimer is that I am not a policy-maker either, for that is basically a task for Ministers, whereas my function is to contribute towards the improvement of the information on which they base their decisions.

The appeal for clemency comes because the conference organisers have set me an impossible task. Since there is not at present in Britain - nor in any other European country so far as I am aware - a complete system for monitoring educational performance, I cannot know what the findings of such a monitoring system would be, and so cannot even guess at the policy response to such findings. What I may be able to do, however, is to provide you with some assistance in reaching your own judgements about the possible effects of monitoring by sketching the nature of educational policy formation and the constraints within which it is undertaken, and to illustrate this by reference to certain past decisions which were influenced, though not determined, by partial measures of educational attainment.

EDUCATIONAL POLICY FORMATION

First, on the nature of educational policy formation.   Fundamentally this is the same as policy formation in any other Department of State - Balancing objectives given by the personal convictions and political commitments of Ministers, the general pressures of public opinion and the particular pressures of those directly concerned with the service as teachers, parents, students, and employers; taking account of new knowledge and new opportunities offered by research and technical development in educational organisations, methods and equipment; and finding the most acceptable combination of policies possible within existing institutional manpower and financial constraints.

Stated in such general terms, educational policy formation might appear as but one special case of the general problem of making best use of limited resources which is of interest to me as an economist.   As an economist, however, I am also conscious of a significant difference between decisions in education and in a number of other fields.   Normally economists would try to compare the costs and benefits of applying marginal increments of resources in different ways, but in education we find it very hard to say exactly what benefits will result from an additional item of expenditure; while we may be able to predict the cost of new policies fairly closely, we cannot provide correspondingly detailed information about probable benefits on which the policy-makers could base their decisions.   Inevitably the contribution of economists to educational policy formation tends to be rather limited, and more reliance is placed on the informed opinions of educationalists about the probable effects of change.

This would, I think, be true of educational policy making in all countries, though the extent to which quantitative considerations can be brought to bear will vary from one country to another.   First there is often a certain amount of evidence about the economic benefits of education - it may be shown that national incomes are rising faster than could be explained by growth in manpower and capital alone, and a guess made that part of the excess arises from better education, though it could also arise from other factors including technological progress (perhaps education at one remove), improved social organisation, etc.   Secondly it may also be shown that more educated people usually hold the better-paid jobs that are apparently in some cases contributing more to the well-being of society though it is arguable how much of their apparently greater contribution arises from their superior education and how much from their inherent personal qualities.   Third, it is also possible to distinguish certain key people in society, such as surgeons, whose essential skills are clearly attributable to the specialised training they have received, though these usually represent only a minority of all those who have passed through higher education.   Taken together, these three approaches may provide persuasive, though not conclusive, grounds for believing education to be of material benefit to society, but they are certainly not enough to answer the practical questions of how much benefit might be expected from an additional item of expenditure.

It is even more difficult with the non-pecuniary benefits of education, which many people would rank at least as highly as the economic ones.   There are scraps of evidence linking education with other things contributing to the quality of life. It seems, for instance, to have some association with health, since better educated people are generally healthier, though the causal relationship is obscure.   It may help in creating an ordered society, for delinquency is often found to have followed interruptions to schooling from truancy or other causes, though here again it is not clear whether the relationship is causal.   It seems to assist the enjoyment of leisure, for the well educated can be seen to participate more fully in reading, concerts, the theatre, etc., and the transmission of a cultural heritage is clearly dependent on grounding in the means of communication and on the services of trained actors, musicians, etc.   But when all this is said, the kind of evidence that can now be assembled by statisticians and sociologists does not add too much more than grounds for belief that education is 'a good thing', and does not give the policy-makers sufficient guidance on how much or what kind of education should be provided.

Such guidance seems unlikely to be forthcoming without considerable work on the measurement of educational performance - relating learning gain and attitudinal development to the type and extent of education   received - in the way that this conference has been discussing.   The educational system, however, is already in being within all advanced countries and by its very existence imposes a constant stream of policy decisions - whether to provide finance next year at this year's rate, whether to build a new college or close an existing one for the student number expected four years hence, etc., - even where there is not any conscious intent to re-design the system.   All these decisions must involve some judgements, implicit or explicit, about their probable consequences for educational attainment.   These judgements may be of various kinds - that a curriculum change will achieve the aims for which it was designed, that a cut in funding will be absorbed by more efficient operation rather than by lower standards, etc., - but judgements there must be.   They may be based on expert advice, on evidence of present shortcomings, on the findings of small-scale research and partial measures of output, or on the peculiar amalgam of all these that gradually permeates and modifies public opinion.   They may be more or less well-informed, and to the extent that actual measurement of educational performance improves judgements about the effects of policy decisions it may contribute towards improvement of the decisions taken.

INSTITUTIONAL FRAMEWORK

The ways in which it might contribute seem likely to vary according to the organisation of education and the distribution of responsibility for educational decisions. In a country such as France, which has a centralised system including central control of curriculum content as well as of resource availability, the development of performance measures might well bring greater efficacy of central decision making. In countries with an overtly federal organisation of education, such as Germany or the United States, performance monitoring would probably be more significant at state than at national level.   In Britain, where, as Brian Kay indicated in his opening paper, we have a diffused organisation of education, the effects of performance monitoring seem likely to appear in different ways according to the differing responsibilities of each element in the system and the varying roles now played in educational policy formation.

The British structure has been described as a "national system administered locally". Within it central government has some general responsibility, and more particularly a responsibility for the total resources available to education, which is exercised mainly through the D.E.S. (for universities throughout Britain, but for schools and Further Education (F.E.) only in England, there being separate arrangements for Scotland and Wales).   Apart from a few unusual categories however, D.E.S. is not a direct source of funding for educational institutions, which look instead to the University Grants Commission for the universities and to the local authorities for schools and F.E. colleges.   The Department also has certain regulatory functions, particularly a loan sanctions procedure for new building, a requirement for Ministerial agreement to changes in examinations and in the size and character of institutions, and a Ministerial power to review unreasonable local decisions; it also exercises, through Ministerial guidance to providers of training institutions, an overall control over teacher supply, and can influence, through its participation in the agreed projections of local authority expenditure and revenue needs, the general character of local spending.   There is, however, no central control of resource allocation to particular schools, this being a responsibility of the local authorities. The local authorities in turn, though deciding each school's location, buildings, major equipment and staff complement, do not exercise detailed control of internal organisation and curriculum, which are formally vested in school heads and governing bodies, while decisions on teaching methods, textbooks, etc., are in practice often made by heads of subject departments or individual class teachers.   Some central influence on the curriculum may be exerted through guidance publications, plus the advice of H.M. Inspectorate as Brian Kay indicated, and also through the research and development projects of the Schools Council (financed jointly by D.E.S. and local authorities but largely governed by teachers' association representatives), but this is still influence rather than control.   (I might observe here that each partner in the educational system could thus be interested in rather different kinds of inform- ation from monitoring - D.E.S. in measures of national progress and regional diff- erences, in general matters such as teacher supply and training, and in broad comparisons of those organisational arrangements and educational approaches having different resource implications; local authorities in guidance about resource allocation among different institutions; individual teachers and schools in the relative effectiveness of the different curricula and educational approaches they might adopt - and this has implications for the monitoring system to which I shall return later).

In such a diffuse organisational system educational policy formation normally pro- ceeds by formal and informal consultation among the various partners - D.E.S., local authority associations, teachers' associations, Schools Council and others - the extent of the consultation and the influence of each partner upon the final decision varying according to the topic concerned.   For certain topics there is specially designated consultative machinery, such as the Advisory Committee on the Supply and Training of Teachers.   There is also consultative machinery of a rather different kind extending beyond the educational field, notably the Consultative Council on Local Government Finance, in which D.E.S. participates alongside the Department of the Environment (D.O.E.) and other Ministries responsible for various aspects of local spending.   The task of the policy-makers thus appears as one of finding the combination of measures likely to secure widest acceptancy by the various interests that may be possible within overall resource constraints.   An understanding of these constraints may thus help towards indicating the scope for policy response to performance measurement.

RESOURCE CONSTRAINTS

It has been a fairly general European experience, in which Britian has shared, that educational spending, and public expenditure generally, have long tended to take a rising proportion of national incomes, and the longer this has continued the clearer

it has become that these faster growth rates could not be maintained indefinitely.
In the last couple of years the gradually hardening resistance to public expenditure
growth has been sharply stiffened by an upsurge in prices of oil and some other
imported commodities requiring resources to be switched from domestic use into
imports and by the onset of a depression reducing total resource availability. OECD
has for some time been studying the growth of educational expenditure within its
members and has found four causal factors occurring almost everywhere, though their
relative importance has varied from country to country.   These have been:-
rising proportions of children in the population; increasing participation in post-
compulsory education; the effect of higher earnings upon the relative cost of
labour-intensive activities; and a trend towards improving standards of educational
provision, as indicated by rising average costs per pupil.   While the first of
these factors may now have been removed by the fairly general downturn in birthrates,
the second seems likely to be perpetuated by rising aspirations and the growing
complexity of society, and the third would also continue if the pay of those employed
in teaching and the education service generally were to rise in line with that of
other workers.   This suggests that, if progress is to be made in checking the
growth of educational expenditure, attention has to be given to the fourth factor,
i.e. there has to be some challenge to the rising trend in resource requirements per
pupil.   This could mean a halt to improvement in standards of provision, or, more
hopefully, better provision without additional cost by means of improved efficiency,
and here performance monitoring could prove particularly significant.

In Britain we have long been conscious of the need to observe overall resource constraints when planning public expenditure, and over the years have developed fairly
sophisticated machinery for this purpose.   This has included regular production of
medium-term economic forecasts designed to show Ministers the likely growth of total
resources, and also the claims of investment and external payments, as a basis for
their decisions on the balance between public and private expenditure.   There is
also a regular review of public expenditure projecting the cost of existing programmes as a background for Ministerial decisions on new policies, the results of which
appear in the annual Public Expenditure White Papers.   A regular reader of these
documents would note a shift in emphasis during recent years, and particularly in the
last two years since the oil price crisis.   The former approach via projection of
the costs of maintaining existing services in the face of demographic and other
changes has given way to a new approach starting from expenditure ceilings and
adjusting service programmes to fit within these.   A parallel change has occured in
the procedures for determining Rate Support Grant, the rather complicated device we
have for transferring central government funds to the local authorities which are the
main providers of education and other local services but which are unable to raise

more than about a third of their revenue needs from the "rates", a local property tax.

POLICY MACHINERY

Thus far this paper has sketched out the ways in which educational policy-making in Britain has to take account of the limitations imposed everywhere by the institutional structure - in our case highly diffuse and consultation-oriented - and by resource constraints - in our case expressed through a well-developed system of public expenditure control. How are these influences brought to bear - what is the actual machinery of policy formations? The most important policy decisions, those on overall resource availability and others affecting more than one Department are made by Ministers collectively. Within D.E.S. the purely educational issues to be decided by our Ministers, and also guidance on the inter-Departmental issues, may come up as submissions from the heads of the policy branches concerned or through the Departmental Planning Organisation. This latter comprises a Policy Steering Group headed by the Permanent Secretary, together with two main Policy Groups, for higher education and general education, comprising the heads of the relevant policy branches, plus a number of other groups and sub-groups set up to consider more specific issues.

It is these Policy Groups which are largely responsible for assembling alternative policy packages which appear feasible in the light of the resource constraints and of the various formal and informal consultations with other partners in the educational system. The Policy Groups include appropriate members of H.M. Inspectorate to advise on the educational implications of proposed measures, and they are also supported by accountants, economists and statisticians estimating the cost of each option considered. Information on probable benefits, as well as costs, is considered as far as practicable, and where there is output data from small-scale research projects this may be taken into account, but generally this is less detailed and more subjective than that available on costs. To a considerable extent participation in education is taken as a proxy measure for benefit from education, particularly when policy options involving changed participation opportunities in non-compulsory education are under consideration.

At this stage it may be appropriate for me to deal with a misapprehension I have occasionally encountered about the extent to which the Department does take output measures into account in its planning. This misapprehension seems to have arisen from the title "output budgeting" adopted at one time for the Department's programme budget, or PPB system. I do not want to deal here in any detail with our programme budget, since this was covered in another conference paper three years ago, but only to recall the key point that it was introduced with an initial concentration on inputs, as an internal aid to expenditure planning, and that it did not set educational benefits on one side against expenditure figures on the other as its name might suggest.

SOME ILLUSTRATIONS

So far my paper may seem to have been a rather arid description of the institutional and resource constraints and the planning machinery within which performance indicators might influence policy.   It may help in putting a little flesh on these bare bones by giving a few illustrations of educational decisions in Britain which have been influenced to some extent by the partial measures already available.   There are a number of these partial measures - the formal examinations system, which has in the past tended to be of more relevance to post compulsory education and higher-ability pupils, though its applicability has widened since the raising of the school-leaving age; the periodic small-sample surveys of reading ability conducted for D.E.S. by N.F.E.R.; the international comparison of attainment in various subjects organised by I.E.A.; a number of research projects concerned with particular areas or aspects of educational provision, sometimes based on very small samples; cohort studies tracing children's development over a period of years, particularly the large cohorts organised by the Medical Research Council and the National Children's Bureau, plus the rather smaller exercise undertaken for the Plowden Report, all of which incorporated performance data.   Together these have provided a good deal of useful information that has entered into educational decisions, decisions which have had to be taken on the basis of whatever information was available at the time.

The first illustration comes from the sample surveys of reading ability, conducted at about 4-yearly intervals for over 20 years.   At first these showed a fairly steady improvement from the level recorded in the immediate post-war period, and this improvement was regarded within D.E.S. as some justification for the increasing resources going into education.   The 1970 survey, however, showed that the improvement had ceased and that some retrogression may even have occurred since the previous survey in 1964, giving rise to some public anxiety.   This helped to prompt action at the D.E.S. level in the form of the appointment of the Bullock Committee to review all available evidence on the teaching of reading and other communication skills.   The Committee's report which has since appeared recommends, amongst other things, increased attention to the subject in teacher training, greater awareness of responsibility for teaching communication skills across the school curriculum, and an enlarged monitoring programme, using annual samples, covering written and spoken

English as well as reading.   The example is of interest as showing diffusion of responsibility for action, the first two of the quoted recommendations being for action at institutional level, by education colleges and schools respectively, while the third is now being pursued by Brian Kay's Assessment of Performance Unit.   I do not want to make too much of this example, for the 1970 survey findings were certainly not the only factor prompting the appointment of the Bullock Committee, since there were already some other surveys being conducted by various local authorities and also some public controversy about the effects of new teaching methods and organisational forms upon reading attainment.   The 1970 survey did, however, give some quantitative precision to the debate about standards, making it clear that there was a problem calling for further investigation, and also stimulated the holding of local authorities' own surveys.

For my second example I have chosen the related topic of one of the new methods used for teaching reading - the Initial Teaching Alphabet, a phonetic script used to give beginners an easy introduction to reading before conversion to traditional spelling. The new method was launched in a number of infant schools, aided by persuasive publicity from the publisher of I.T.A. materials, and its spread was further encouraged by enthusiastic reports from the first users, who found that children did indeed start reading faster in I.T.A. than in normal English.   Subsequent measurement by several researchers of the net advantage remaining after conversion back to ordinary spelling gave rather conflicting results, however, and a Schools Council evaluation exercise reviewing these various studies concluded that on balance the losses during the conversion period offset the initial gain.   Further less favourable indications came from the 1970 reading survey, which carried some suggestion that the net effect might even be negative, though the number of I.T.A.-trained children covered was too small to be meaningful, and from the qualitative impressions of a number of teachers (not, unfortunately, recorded in any systematic manner) that spelling difficulties persisted for longer than the expected conversion period.   The best that can now be said for I.T.A. is that the case is not proved - the Bullock Report is studiously neutral in its conclusions.   Available evidence suggests that some schools which had adopted the new method have since abandoned it, but that the proportion using it remains around 9%, though precision here is limited by both adoption and abandonment being for individual schools' decision, with D.E.S. and local authorities being involved only indirectly through their advisory services.   The example is thus of interest as one where the measurement findings were principally for individual schools' application, and also as one where earlier impressionistic judgements were subsequently modified by more systematic performance measurements.

The third example also comes from the curricular field - this time the experimental scheme for beginning the teaching of French earlier than the normal starting time at entry to secondary school.   This was tried out in a number of junior schools in the hope of raising attainment and improving pupil attitudes to the subject, the experiment being carefully monitored by N.F.E.R.   It would be superfluous for me to try to say much about the findings - sufficient to recall that the report struck a somewhat negative tone, with the favourable points (performance gains in early years, no detriment to other junior school subjects) being rather outweighed by the unfavourable ones (no significant advantage remaining at the end of secondary schooling, and some hardening of attitude patterns, i.e. those poor at the subject disliking it even more). The immediate effects of this appraisal seem to be discouragement of any more junior schools from entering the experimental scheme, and possibly some suggestions about withdrawal to those schools where French teaching was less well conducted.   However, the question may still be asked whether this is the right conclusion to draw from the experiment, the results of which appear oddly at variance with the foreign language teaching experience of several other European countries which begin earlier than we do and seem to achieve much higher standards (as English participants at international conferences usually discover to their shame).   Perhaps the explanation is to be found in N.F.E.R.'s indication that one reason for the loss of the initial lead established by early-starting children was that secondary schools were often ill-equipped to handle mixed entries of pupils from different junior schools with and without French teaching and so unable to capitalise upon the experience of the former.   If so, this particular example could prove to be one where the main relevance of the findings was to the local authorities, which might need to arrange for all the junior schools in the catchment area of a certain secondary to teach French and for the secondary to be prepared to take the subject to a higher standard. The report may also have implications for teacher training, both to improve the quality of teaching in primaries, which was shown to be a significant variable, and to prepare secondary teachers for a different pupil intake; changes in textbook and equipment provision might also be indicated.

My fourth and fifth examples are concerned with aspects of educational disadvantage, stemming from findings of the cohort studies and various research projects showing that poor performers at school tended to be mainly children of ill-educated parents, often living in unfavourable conditions, and that these children were also more likely to be early leavers and to have little participation in continuing education. Considerable policy interest developed nationally in measures to break into this revealed circle of disadvantage, stimulated by the focussing effect of the Plowden report.   One of the means proposed for this pre-school education, on the basis of the high correlation found between children's attainment at earlier and later ages, and most of the variation in measured intelligence having occurred by ages 7 or 8, widely interpreted as meaning that much of a child's mental capacity was developed by experience in the first few years of life, and this eventually led to the introduction of the nursery education programme in 1972.   I do not want to make too much of this as a development from performance measures, for there had built up by that time a widespread popular demand for nursery education, partly owing to increased employment of women, which it had not been practicable to meet so long as any additional school building and teacher resources had been pre-empted by rising numbers of compulsory-school-age children; the actual timing of the nursery education programme, several years after Plowden, owed more to easing of these resource pressures after passing the primary child numbers peak then to any additional data on pupil performance. Nevertheless, the performance material had been an important contributory factor, and the announcement of the programme was accompanied by the wide-ranging plans for monitoring through observation in selected areas and through measurement of effects on linguistic and numerical attainment and social adaptation after the nursery child had passed into primary school.   Since then the scale of the nursery education programme has been reduced, partly because of the public expenditure pressures mentioned earlier, partly because a steepening decline in primary numbers has given the possibility of providing for a larger percentage of the age-group and of accommodating more pre-school children in existing buildings, thus reducing needs for new construction.

The other example of policy to break into the revealed cycle of educational disadvantage is the concept of positive discrimination, i.e. the channeling of additional resources into certain areas in an attempt to offset their existing disadvantages. This has taken several forms - additions to the school building programme to permit replacement of some sub-standard premises, also special allocations within the nursery education building programme, designation of social priority schools permitting payment of salary supplements to reduce staff turnover, (though the need for these has since been reduced by general improvement in salary scales and the changed employment situation) special weighting within resource allocation formulae enabling certain schools to receive additional staff and funds for extra equipment, and also a series of action-research projects under Dr. Halsey investigating particular applications in selected areas.   There has also been:-   the establishment of the Assessment of Performance Unit, with a remit including identification of under-achievement; the Educational Disadvantage Unit, as a focal point for consideration of problems within D.E.S.;   the Centre for Information and Advice on Educational Disadvantage, designed as a source of assistance for schools and local authorities; and the holding of a series of seminars intended to focus attention on the educationally disadvantaged and to share experiences in this area.   So far the main emphasis of this positive discrimination policy has been upon action at the local authority level to channel resources towards particular concentrations of disadvantage, as identified by the social characteristics of school catchment areas and the number of pupils from low-income families with free meal entitlements on the school rolls, and towards identifiably disadvantaged groups - perhaps an inevitable starting point in view of the lack of attainment measures to permit more precise identification of disadvantaged pupils.

The final illustration of policy response to performance measurement concerns class sizes and teacher supply, and is chosen as an illustration of findings applicable primarily at national level.   I do not wish to make too much of this, partly because the evidence is very controversial, partly because decisions on teacher supply are influenced by many other factors besides evidence on the effects of class sizes. Indeed, it is probably fair to say that the decision to halt the growth in the teaching force in the face of the expected decline in pupil numbers owed more to:- stiffening public expenditure pressures; evidence of local authority unwillingness to employ ever increasing numbers of teachers; the steady improvement in pupil-teacher ratios already achieved over the past 20 years; and the adequacy of the teacher stock already in prospect to give by the early 1980's staffing ratio's permitting schools to implement the declared objective of reducing maximum class sizes to 30.   Never-theless, the decision-makers might not have been uninfluenced by the fact that performance measures did not show any benefit from smaller classes over the range of variation experienced (except to a limited extent in remedial education).   This evidence contrasts with the widespread teacher preference for smaller classes, which are felt to make their task easier and to permit more freedom in teaching methods, and it has been criticised as relying too heavily on measured performance in reading and mathematics, without taking account of attitude changes that are argued to be favourably influenced by smaller classes.   The controversy is unlikely to be resolved unless attitude measures can be developed to the same degree of reliability as now expected when measuring attainment, but the use of attainment measures has certainly served to clarify the issues remaining for investigation.

IMPLICATIONS

Six illustrations of ways in which evidence of pupil performance, often of a frag-mentary kind, has influenced educational decisions - all put forward with the caution that in no case was this the sole determining factor and that there is room for disagreement both about the weight to be assigned to each cause or factor and about the interpretation to be placed upon the measurement findings.   What implications can be drawn from them about the ways in which regular monitoring of performance might influence future decisions?   First, it seems clear that where, as in England, there is a widely diffused responsibility for educational policy, decisions arising from monitoring data will have to be taken at many different levels. Where consultation and dialogue among the various partners are now the rule, further consultation will be needed about ways in which effect is to be given to monitoring lessons within each field of responsibility.   It will be a better-informed dialogue enabling each participant to specify more precisely the objectives, attainments, and shortcomings, and should thus promote the sense of accountability about which Brian Kay spoke.   A better, more effective dialogue should, at least in principle, promote a better, more efficient educational system.   By permitting precise comparison of benefits as well as costs of alternative educational approaches and organisational forms, performance measures could assist the more efficient use of educational resources that seems particularly important in a situation where growth of these resources may be severely limited.

The gain in precision may often be gradual, depending on the pace of development of monitoring techniques.   At first much may depend on subjective observation, and, as Brian Kay has indicated, there are always likely to be some aspects of educational performance which can only be assessed by such means.   As objective measures are developed, however, they should improve the effectiveness of the monitoring process, providing some validity check for the remaining subjective appraisals and helping to overcome the inherent limitations of the latter.   Among these are the difficulties in standardising observations by different observers at different places and points in time, even where, as among H.M. Inspectorate, some guidance is available from working together with colleagues and from the specific criteria adopted by those participating in particular surveys.   The compiler of subjective judgements may also be influenced by attitudes among those reporting on educational approaches, particularly the enthusiasm of the originator of a particular method, which may incline him to view it as working very well - as indeed it may do for the originator, because of his own enthusiasm, without being similarly effective elsewhere - and thus the development of more objective measures should permit more reliable assessment of effectiveness across the whole educational field.   In this way performance measurements should help create a more rational process of curriculum change - speeding the adoption of those innovations which were demonstrably successful, but preventing premature commitment of resources to those not adequately tested.

New policies may require development of new methods of assessment, as in the nursery education programme.   Conversely, new performance measures may enable policy aims and instruments to be specified more precisely, perhaps as in the positive discrimination programme, which is now unable to cover all the educational disadvantaged because of its concentration on areas and groups rather than on measured low performance, but which might need supplemental information on an individual performance basis should there be any widespread demand or a policy decision favouring a full test of the effectiveness of the programme.   Existing monitoring instruments may uncover problems requiring more fundamental enquiry, as with the Bullock Committee, but this is hardly suprising in view of the general tendency of knowledge to build upon itself as new discoveries create new unknowns (the jet engine might not have been invented if man had not previously learned to fly).

The differing levels of application of the monitoring findings have their own implications for the development of performance indicators.   Initially, as Brian Kay has indicated, the A.P.U. work in defining areas for assessment and starting to draw up criteria for performance has been carried out on the assumption that measures need to be constructed for application on a light sampling basis, as appropriate to the D.E.S. interest in indicators of national progress.   To satisfy the Department's other interests in knowing about the relative effectiveness of approaches with different resource requirements and about the effects of positive discrimination would require more intensive sampling in particular areas and types of school.   This might be accomplished by a co-operative arrangement for Departmental retrieval of results from more detailed investigations undertaken by local authorities and academic researchers, whereas it would be beyond D.E.S. capacity to mount such surveys unaided.   The local authorities in their turn would require this more intensive sampling as a guide to allocations within their own areas.   At a more detailed level of potential application, by individual schools and teachers, there might well be considerable interest among the more enterprising teachers in the possibility of using nationally-validated measures to gauge the effectiveness of their own teaching.   After all, the idea of performance monit-oring is not new - every good teacher seeks feedback from his class as a guide to possible modifications in his teaching, and devises his own questions accordingly. Such teachers might see attractions in using questions with known response norms that would enable them to check performance not only against their own experience and expectations but also against the results achieved by other teachers and with other approaches, and thus give rise to a demand for the test materials to be made available for classroom use.   While there are some technical difficulties conn-ected with the use of the same questions for both national testing and classroom diagnostic purposes, these can be fairly simply resolved by the device of a const-antly renewable question bank, in which all items are used first for national monitoring and a proportion subsequently for classroom purposes, with some new items coming in for each national application - a device which also has other attractions as a means of accomodating curriculum change.   This points to a potential partnership in performance monitoring, with D.E.S., to the extent that financial resources allow, sustaining research and development work on measures for subsequent wider use, which would be an appropriate counterpart to partnership in making and implementing the educational policy decisions likely to be prompted by the performance findings.

CONCLUDING REMARKS

As well as discussing the prepared papers, sessions were organised for the consideration of issues arising from the proceedings or of special concern to groups of workshop members.   Two major groupings of interest emerged; one focussed on the scientific and technical problems of monitoring, whilst the other centred on a range of educational and socio-political matters.[1]

Prior to these discussions, we had benefited from the lead given by Dr. Westphal, who presented some preliminary thoughts on the issue of 'pedagogical freedom versus accuracy of assessment'.   He perceived the danger that certain pressures within the educational system could lead towards a standardised curriculum, and he identified one of the forces at work as the restrictions imposed by the attempts to maintain academic rigour as the means of creating generalizable truth.   There are other distinctive signs, in the U.K., for instance, that interest in a 'common' or 'core' curriculum is growing; with activity ranging from Schools Council working papers (Numbers 53 and 55, philosophical argument (e.g., Lawton, 1976) and D.E.S. pronouncements on the curriculum showing the intention to become more involved in its determining (e.g., T.E.S. article by A. Stevens, September 1976, No.3198).
In such contexts the possibility was raised that the measurement expert might become a part to this kind of movement, albeit unwittingly: alternatively he might believe from the study of his results or from other evidence, that more agreement or prescription is desirable.   However, it was thought insufficient for those who work in assessment to be aware that these trends exist, but to give careful and informed consideration to the social and political consequences of adherence to any persuasion, whatever the educational implications.

A different ordering of papers in the workshop programme might have anticipated some of the points raised by the 'non-technical' group, but nevertheless, their list presents a forceful reminder to 'assessors' that their role in monitoring may not be inconsequential.   Under the banner of 'What for, and Who by?' they saw three major areas for debate: these were

      i   the implications of monitoring

     ii   the influence of monitoring on teacher/pupil relations

   iii   what information to gather and how it should be used?

---

1   I am grateful to Dr. Wilmott and Professor Skemp for their notes on the deliberations of these two groups.

Under (i) _Implications_, they saw the need to make explicit what the implications of monitoring standards might be. Allied questions were:- Who is responsible for good education and who takes decisions? Is monitoring concerned with the goals of education or the goals of educational systems? What are the relations between the structures of law and the structures of assessment? How should assessors react to the demands from the administration?

The key question affecting (ii) _teacher/pupil relations_, was, How do we take into account the teacher/pupil variables? Other questions were:- What are the pupils' goals and how do these relate to the goals of the researcher in the teaching-learning and test situations? Does the desire for rigour lead to the trivalisa-tion of teaching? How can research data be rendered to a useful form for teachers and 'the public'?. How might assessments of overt behaviours provide inferences about the 'deep structures' with which much of education is concerned?

The question subsumed by (iii) _the uses_ for monitoring information was:- What kinds of information 'other than about attainment' should a survey collect? Further questions were: Are there situations which would warrant the withholding of information from the public? Should we also be concerned with the whole range of input measures? Is there not excessive emphasis on the literacy, math-ematical and scientific areas for attainment in relation to the aesthetic, moral and physical, areas? The question was also asked as to whether human rights are violated by measurement - can the ends justify the means - who would decide?

The last workshop paper illuminated some of these questions and illustrated how a gradual accumulation of knowledge or specific enquiry can lead to enhanced efforts to improve educational standards. However, there appeared to be a strong feeling that monitoring activity may, in certain contexts, become allied with political movements; whilst those involved should, however, attempt to examine the ethical issues, they may be ill-equiped to do so as their training and experience lies in other spheres.

The 'technical group' seemed to agree on several points; principally that educat-ional considerations must always be borne in mind whenever statistical criteria are applied in test or item analysis. It was noted, too, that how pupils respond to questions or why they adopt particular approaches is not known. Whereas, ideally pupils' responses would totally define the dimensions (or styles or traits) which have been invoked by responding to questions, the reality is that the multiplicity of effects would induce an 'error of generalizability' into any survey result. The practicalities of assessment and its contrast with the 'ideal' were seen to be of central importance in interpreting results. All data obtained during the educational testing process were held to be multi-trait in nature, and this fact was thought to constitute the major reason for confusion over the meaning of experimental results derived from test data.   It was considered that clarity of objective has been an over-emphasised, but under-applied, concept.

The nature of the Rasch Model in the context of the Classical Test Model, Generalizability Theory, Multiple Matrix Sampling and the Analysis of Variance was discussed; the conclusion was reached that the differences in approach stemmed from the different ways in which the results were required to be interpreted (as well as the different assumptions which were able to be made) rather than from any fundamentally different measurements which were made.   Thus, the Rasch Model is a two parameter linear model, as is the two-way Analysis of Variance model although the interpretation of the results of using the two models will not, however, generally be the same.

On the use of item banks, the main problem was seen not as technical, but as one of informing teachers, who were, perhaps rightly suspicious of technical innovation carried out at a distance.   It was felt that an item bank could help teachers to look at the structure of their subject (or, actually, their teaching of their subject) in terms of objectives, thus leading to improvements in this teaching. If an item bank was to be used, then it was agreed that it must be used with insight. The discussion led on to the use of measurements for the purpose of evaluation; the need to decide before the start of any assessment exercise just what the objectives of the study really were was felt to be an element lacking from many studies.   The points arising from such considerations would then lead to the adoption of a certain type of data collection scheme and analytical design.   This point was highlighted in the case of national monitoring experiments by the need to establish a bank of questions for investigative purposes before executing an actual study.

The consideration of the use of Bayesian approaches brought out the feeling that 'all good statisticians are Bayesians' in any case, but that the facets of this theory dealing with aspects of Decision and Utility could be more widely used with some benefit.   This type of approach could give a certain direction to the construction of hypotheses when an investigation into achievement was being formulated.

The technical group also was agreed that many methods of analysis were applicable to problems where, at present, only a single approach was being followed.   It was felt that there was often little justification for using only a single analytical method, since there was unlikely to be a single way out of any problem; the use of alternative methodology was considered to be the most useful asset of those involved in the technical evaluation of educational data.

At the closing session, several suggestions for continuing the study of monitoring educational standards were made, along the following lines.

i.   That the diversion of interests apparent when the discussion groups were formed should be encouraged in the short-term.   This would entail a number of small working groups each tackling a specific, well defined problem area.

ii.   There should be a periodic combination of working groups to review the progress made, integrate new developments, and to set fresh enquiries in train.

iii.   Bi-lateral exchanges should be promoted, with the aim of encouraging technological transfer between institutions or countries whose current or projected lines of enquiry converged.   The exchange could involve materials as well as people, e.g. item banks, computer programmes, survey designs.

iv.   Apart from exchanges designed to facilitate a particular enquiry, secondment of research staff for training or teaching was proposed.   This might be initiated by setting up a register of research staff available for or desirous of exchange experience.

v.   Both formal and informal consultancies were envisaged, where exchanges of people would not be practical..

vi   A clearing house for information on research into the field of monitoring was suggested and an offer to produce and distribute an occasional newsletter with summaries or outlines of projects, methods, results or developments was made by Mr. G. Pollock, of the Scottish Council for Educational Research.

Perhaps four major conclusions can be drawn from the workshop proceedings, as a whole.   As set out below, these are a somewhat personal interpretation.   Firstly, there now is the capability for dealing effectively with a number of hitherto troublesome survey design and measurement problems.   Many of the questions to be answered are empirical, so that future developments are dependent on field work, initially conceived as feasibility studies rather than definitive surveys.   Much of this work will call for extensive re-analyses of assessment data and replication on cohort samples.   Data interpretation as well as techniques will tend to shift from the estimation of population parameters towards more conditional relative parameters, especially when examining the changes in achievement over time.

Secondly, the 'European Scene' at the present includes a range of educational systems, some quite centralised and prescriptive of curriculum content and others completely diffused and relatively uncontrolled.   The inherent interpretations of 'monitoring' must reflect these contexts, which themselves embody differing political and moral outlooks.   National monitoring in one ethos might necessarily imply 'enabling' in that individual schools are supplied with the know-how and materials to conduct their own evaluations on their own practices; in another ethos it might permit, but not approve of, a centralized survey scheme aimed at delivering appraisals of the national state of education in schools; in yet another ethos, localised enquiries might be appropriate and acceptable.   It is clear that a methodology for one country may not transfer to another without considerable adaptation.   The workshop theme assumed that 'national monitoring of achievement' would be relevant to any country: but only in discussion with colleagues from else-where did some of us learn that our concept of 'achievement' was markedly different from others, that their idea of political influences differed considerably from ours, and that their catalogues of educational objectives had different elements and emphases.   The conclusion here is that whilst methodology may be used eclectically its selection and application must be sensitive to the ethos within it must operate and towards which, to be justified in any terms, it must also make a contribution.

The third aspect, which researchers tend to overlook, is the larger impact of the findings from monitoring surveys; these will reach far beyond the journals or even the administrative boundaries of the educational system.   Interpretation and communication will thus become major aspects of professional competence especially in the rendering of intelligible findings to members of the bodies responsible for educational provision.

The fourth conclusion concerns an omission in the programme; one that went by de-fault in the workshop planning rather than by deliberate exclusion. The vast territory of assessment concerned with students' own original productions was not discussed in its own right.   Objective-type assessment, it would seem, has reached a level of sophistication whereby, in particular scaling terms, it is even possible to gauge the achievement of one age group of pupils against another age group when neither group attempts the same questions; but, in the main this capa-bility is confined to responses to set-piece items rather than challenges to the imagination.   No amount of ingenuity in devising questions with prescribed answers will provide for the individuality of an answer, whatever taxonomy is used as a basis.   And though it is conceivable that taxonomies can be used for the assessment of students' idiosyncratic, productive work there is virtually no

experimental activity in this respect to examine its appropriateness as a method or its acceptability to the teachers.   To be duly credible (it has been argued) monitoring must include work in which creativeness has been encouraged as well as work calling for more standard forms of learning; though the corollary is that the accepted tenets on the reliability of measurement may have to be relaxed.   Perhaps this argument must be accepted on the basis of present knowledge; but nothing like the effort invested in objective-type measurement has been put into investigating even the qualitative aspect of students' original productions.   The workshop sessions only touched on these issues but by the close, there was a substantial body of opinion that efforts should be made to come to grips with assessments of this kind and general assent that a workshop devoted to this theme should be high on the list of priorities.

A gathering of specialists discussing its own peculiar interests encourages an 'us and them' cast of thinking.   The national monitoring of pupils' performances, whether designed to appraise 'the system' or intended to relate achievement more closely to school and social circumstances, may run into a parallel but much more serious danger; that of setting the assessors apart from the teachers and organisers whose work they will examine and comment on.   The papers and discussions at the workshop, implicitly or otherwise, underlined this problem.   And it would seem to go deeper than the issue of 'dissemination', important as the styles of reporting may be.   It means, surely, that the 'monitors' should be part of the educational system, not merely adjuncts to it; sharing the values of those promoting and providing education in the schools; developing a mutual dependence in the drive towards enhancing the quality of childrens' experiences in learning.   To do so will entail looking from within rather than from without.

REFERENCES

LAWTON, D. (1975).   Class, Culture and the Curriculum. London: Routledge and
  Kegan Paul.

SCHOOLS COUNCIL (1975).   Working Paper No.53.   The Whole Curriculum.   London:
  Evans Methuen.

SCHOOLS COUNCIL (1976).   Working Paper No.55.   The Curriculum in the Middle Years.
  London: Evans Methuen.

STEVENS, A. (1976) HMI: Secretive Gloom or Prophets in the Gloom,
  Times Educational Supplement, No.3198.